Praise for Michael Gurian

"Filled with stories and practical advi[...] adolescent boys. Michael Gurian takes a thoughtful look at nature and nurture and at the role of culture and testosterone in the lives of boys. I recommend it to those who want to raise fine young men."

—Mary Pipher, Ph.D., author of *Reviving Ophelia*

"Michael Gurian is a leader in the rediscovered field of helping young males to become successful men. His new book, *A Fine Young Man*, picks up where *The Wonder of Boys* left off. Gurian astutely provides advice and direction for today's parents, educators, and caregivers about how to understand and deal with problems facing today's 'fine young men.' "

—W. Brewster Ely IV, president,
International Boys School Coalition

"In *A Fine Young Man*, Michael Gurian brings new understanding and insight into the lives of adolescent boys. This is a book that our families and culture urgently need if we are going to shape our young males into the men we need them to be."

—Geoffrey T. Boisi, co-chairman and president,
The National Mentoring Partnership

Praise for Michael Gurian's *The Wonder of Boys*

"A provocative book that may electrify the debate over how this nations raises its sons."

—*USA Today*

"Full of good insights and advice."

—*Los Angeles Times*

"*The Wonder of Boys* will help future generations open the lines of communication between men and women by giving us what we need to raise strong, responsible, and sensitive men."

—John Gray, Ph.D., author of *Men Are from Mars,*
Women Are from Venus

"What Mary Pipher has done to raise our national consciousness in *Reviving Ophelia*, Michael Gurian has done in *The Wonder of Boys* for the care and rearing of our young men. Important, needed, timely, and crucial."

—Bettie B. Youngs, Ph.D., Ed.D., author of *How to Develop Self-Esteem in Your Child*

"This book gives us incredible insight into the minds, hearts, and souls of male children. I strongly recommend it to every parent of a male child and every young man old enough to read and comprehend its wisdom. I also recommend it to any woman who feels baffled and angry with the behavior of men."

—Beverly Engel, author of *Raising a Sexually Healthy Child in a Sexually Unhealthy World*

Also by Michael Gurian

Books

The Wonder of Boys
Love's Journey
Mothers, Sons and Lovers
The Prince and the King

Videotapes

The Role of the Mentor
Understanding the Mother/Son Relationship
Are You Tough Enough?

Audiotapes

The Wonder of Boys
Mothers and Sons
The Prince and the King

Michael Gurian

A Fine

JEREMY P. TARCHER/PUTNAM

a member of Penguin Putnam Inc., New York

What Parents,

Mentors, and

Educators Can

Do to Shape

Young Man

Adolescent

Boys into

Exceptional

Men

Most Tarcher/Putnam books are available at special quantity discounts for bulk purchase for sales promotions, premiums, fund-raising, and educational needs. Special books or book excerpts also can be created to fit specific needs. For details, write Putnam Special Markets, 375 Hudson Street, New York, NY 10014.

Jeremy P. Tarcher/Putnam
A member of
Penguin Putnam Inc.
375 Hudson Street
New York, NY 10014
www.penguinputnam.com

First trade paperback edition 1999

Library of Congress Cataloging-in-Publication Data

Gurian, Michael.
    A fine young man : what parents, mentors, and educators can do to
    shape adolescent boys into exceptional men / by Michael Gurian.
        p.   cm.
    Includes bibliographical references (p. 279) and index.
    ISBN 0-87477-969-3 (alk. paper)
    1. Boys.   2. Boys—Psychology.   3. Teenage boys.   4. Teenage boys—
Psychology.   5. Teenage boys—United States—Social conditions.
6. Masculinity.   7. Men—Socialization.   8. Child rearing.
9. Parental influences.   10. Mentoring.   I. Title.
HQ775.G86   1998   98-16775 CIP
305.23—dc21

Printed in the United States of America
10   9   8   7   6   5

This book is printed on acid-free paper. ∞

BOOK DESIGN BY RALPH FOWLER

Acknowledgments

In the web of insights, stories, theory, and practical strategies you'll find in this book, I am beholden to many voices, agencies, and community organizations, as well as families and individuals with whom I've worked.

My thanks to Big Brothers and Big Sisters of America, Boy Scouts of America, The International Boys School Coalition, and numerous schools and agencies for information, data, and their care of boys.

My thanks to Jeremy Tarcher for being an essential mentor in my publishing life, Joel Fotinos for his genuine love of publishing, Mitch Horowitz for his generosity and acumen as an editor, Ken Siman for his savvy and support, and all those at Tarcher/Putnam for nurturing this project and so many other fine books that help shape the lives of our communities.

My thanks to Susan Schulman and her agency for guiding my projects with perceptiveness and care.

My thanks to my parents, Jay P. and Julia M. Gurian, for raising me with high standards, even through the difficult adolescent years.

My thanks to many people for research and other technical help, among them: Sue Amende-Plep and Gary Plep, Dr. Phon Hudkins, Jesse Trueman and Terry Trueman, Annie Reid, and Clancy Aresvik.

My thanks to the cultures other than my own that have welcomed my researching eye and heart—Turkey, India, Israel, Germany, and the Southern Ute Reservation—and the many people whom I've observed and interacted with in these worlds. My perspective is what it is because of the world's generosity.

My thanks to all the boys and young men, mothers and fathers, educators and other professionals who have given me their stories, wisdom, and energy.

My thanks to all the local and regional voices, whether liberal or conservative or in between, that are now being raised in care of our sons.

And as always, my deep thanks to Gail, my constant companion.

For Gail, Gabrielle, and Davita

Contents

A Fine Young Man

Introduction

I turned fifteen in the early 1970s, in Durango, Colorado, a small, beautiful town in the Rockies. My best friend was a boy my age, Stan, with whom I shared some secrets and a lot of time. Behind our block of houses lay vacant land and a web of bike trails he and I knew well. The land, the trails, the spots of trees, and the ditches of debris were havens during those confusing years of adolescence.

Stan and I were neither popular nor unpopular. We knew little about girls, though we pretended our fair share. On my fifteenth birthday, as we rested on our bikes at the top of a trail, I looked out over the vacant land and said, "I'm fifteen years old. I'm not a grown-up; I'm not a kid. What am I?" Stan had no answer. I did not know anyone who had an answer.

At the time, I didn't understand my parents very well, nor they me. We didn't have much information about each other, or didn't have the right information, and we had little interaction about the really deep things in our lives. With its new urges and daily changes, my own body kept betraying me. Girls were able to manipulate me like those malleable Gumby dolls that pervaded the '70s. Girls seemed smarter and less fragile. They seemed to want something from me. It became my and every boy's mission to supply it, even though we didn't know what "it" was.

Few close elders were available to talk with me. My parents often feuded with my grandparents, who lived across the country. And I grew up in a time when what elders had to say smelled of rot. My elders, including my parents, sent me a message they didn't fully intend. It went something like this: "By the time they become adolescents, boys just want to be left to their own devices. A parent's job is pretty much done."

My peers became my life-teachers. With them, I drove fast, felt pain, and sought relief in things like drug experimentation and alcohol, which gave me a sense of importance and an escape; I pretended prowess and nursed insecurity; and I looked for a few solid ways to prove my manhood, no matter the consequences.

Introduction

I was, I think, a relatively typical adolescent boy. While it seemed to me at fifteen that I didn't need my parents and elders, I needed them desperately. While I rebelled against them, elders and society, I did not want the kingdom I rebelled against to so easily toss me out.

While I did not know how to speak about my feelings very well, I felt life at my heart's core. While I liked to appear self-sufficient, I was worried most of my waking time about how to be good enough at nearly anything of substance I attempted.

While I wanted love constantly, I made sure to convince the world I'd be fine without it. While I became easily angered and, at my tall height, scared my parents, I was not saying, "I hate you." I was really saying, "My own demons scare me more than I can express."

While I pretended to be a man, I was still a child.

It was not until well into my adulthood and professional life that I realized there is something wrong with the adolescence I lived as a male in a modern society; it was not until the beginning of my own middle age that I noticed something very wrong with the adolescence our boys live today. This "something" became clear to me as I taught and did research in other cultures, then returned to the United States to work with boys, young men, and men as an educator, therapist, and consultant.

It is best put this way: *We do not understand adolescent-male development, and therefore are unable to give our adolescent males the kind of love they need to become fully responsible, loving, and wise men.* This circumstance is not improving over the decades, and in many ways is growing worse.

Boys on Fire

In terms of character formation, physical development, brain and bio-chemical activity, and social acumen, a boy's adolescent years are second only to his first few in their power over his identity and ability to live life. Had I the words as an adolescent, I would have said to Stan on my fifteenth birthday, "I am on fire. Where are the refiners of this fire?" I would have challenged my parents and teachers: "Don't leave me to my own devices. Give me the devices of manhood!"

I did not have the words, nor do most of the adolescent boys you and I know and love. Thus we who care for our boys come together to help form the words for them, and find paths we can give them. We come together to help them refine their fires. It is in that spirit that I offer *A Fine Young Man* to you.

I have devoted much of my personal life and professional life to studying and nurturing boys and men. I have come to understand that unless the natural fire inside a boy is carefully refined by parents, mentors, and educators, the physical, emotional, moral, spiritual, and social lives of all our young males will be consumed by flames. Some of these flames we'll see quite clearly in adolescent drug abuse, alcohol abuse, criminal behavior, juvenile death, steroid use, media addiction, learning disabilities, brain disorders, and obsession with girls; others will be more difficult to see and need more in-depth attention. These flames will show up during a man's midlife, when he is more harshly consumed by flames long hidden.

Though they are crucial, the adolescent years are, presently, the years we caregiving adults spend the *least* time on. We monitor those years in our boys' lives less than any others. We write fewer books about them, fewer articles. We do fewer exposés about them, fewer television shows. We know more about male infancy, Generation X, male midlife, and male old age than we do about male adolescence.

As I will point out in the first chapter of this book, the result of this inattention is that *these adolescent boys are now, arguably, our most undernurtured population.* Their challenges and confusions are in many ways worse than when you and I were adolescents. Thus the adolescent male's situation is even more urgent.

Our adolescent boys today are harming themselves and others in their communities more than we did a generation ago. There are fewer caregivers and less caregiver time provided to today's adolescent boy than there were a generation ago. The cultural temptations have increased, and the methods of being honorable have decreased. Though there are more role models available to our adolescent boys than there were when we were kids, they are characterized by only a few, limited stereotypes and have become far more merchandized. The culture of sex and sexuality is in the faces of our adolescent boys as never before, but the boys are provided too little commensurate sexual guidance. Social structures that over the ages have honored boys are getting dismantled, and there is no increase in the number of equally strong structural elements for teaching duty, meaning, and purpose. Family and community systems that once guided boys have been replaced by vague cultural signals from media characters with whom the boys will never be personally intimate. Our adolescent boys bring their yearning to their society, but often they are not rewarded with careful and forceful human love.

The Next Level

There are many reasons for our culture's present handling of its adolescent males and their development. Not the least of these was symbolized compellingly on the cover of a fall 1997 *Newsweek* magazine. A beautiful blond girl, about six or seven, with pigtails and soulful eyes, gazes at a red-and-white block that she holds delicately in her right hand. The headline reads: KIDS WHO DON'T LEARN. In smaller letters: *What Causes Learning Disabilities and How to Help Your Child.* It is a powerful front cover, one specifically created to elicit sympathy from millions of potential readers. The little girl looks very fragile, and our hearts go out to her in her disability. I confess that when I saw the cover, I felt a visceral concern for my own daughters, deftly inspired by the magazine's photo and cover art. When I look at the cover even now I feel pulled in.

And yet there is something very odd about that cover: the presence of the girl. Boys make up the vast majority of our learning-disabled children; conservative estimates put males at two-thirds of our special-ed kids. When an educator walks into a classroom of learning-disabled students, he or she sees mainly a room of boys. Yet the magazine cover shows a delicate girl, for that is the image that will better inspire sympathy and thus attention. How much more difficult it is to recognize the fragility of a boy—much less an *adolescent* boy—and even in an area where it is just that boy who is in the most distress and needs the most help.

That *Newsweek* cover may not symbolize very well the boy/girl statistical reality of learning disabilities, but it does symbolize perfectly something we will explore in this book: that our civilization does not understand and fully acknowledge the *fragility* of its male children. That fragility in me was not recognized and attended to by my communities during my adolescence. It is that fragility that our adolescent boys now beg us, in their various behaviors, to notice. We will explore and understand that fragile male development in this book and, in that understanding, realize with passion and wonder the many rewarding roles each of us can play in the lives of our adolescent boys.

Nature *and* Nurture:
Adolescent Male Biology and Culture

Understanding adolescent male development in the deepest way possible depends to a great extent on understanding adolescent male biology. Adolescence is a very "biological" time. The brain, hormonal, and physiological developments during a boy's second decade of life are, in a word, phenomenal. We will look carefully in this book at the developing "nature" of the adolescent in your home, school, or on your street. Some of what you read will surprise you. It will explain as never before so much about that boy's behavior.

My methodology for researching biological and neurological material is cross-disciplinary. When I discover a piece of the biological puzzle, I don't present it as fact until I check the study that produced it, its applicability not just in America (or in the country or culture where the study was done) but elsewhere in the world, and its rightness to me through my own professional and personal experiences with male adolescents. Using this approach, I attempt to combine medical science, psychology, anthropology, and personal observation.

As vigorously as we explore biological material in this book, we'll talk about the cultures and subcultures individual boys live in, from video games to hip-hop pants, movies to peer groups, Boy Scouts to girly magazines. We'll not avoid any part of adolescent male culture.

Using our knowledge of adolescent male nature and nurture, we'll try to answer practical questions like these:

How does a mom set limits with adolescent boys?

When can we consider adolescent boys to have become "men"?

How do we teach them to be responsible adults?

What if my adolescent boy doesn't like sports?

What is happening to my adolescent boy's self-esteem?

How are video games, TV, and the Internet affecting my sons?

Why does he hardly talk to me anymore (or, conversely, will he ever stop!)?

What's going on between him and his dad?

Introduction

We'll focus on how an adolescent male's emotional structure develops; the ways he adapts to his social groupings; how to teach him compassion; the ways in which his sense of emotional safety in the family changes; the rites of passage he needs; and the important role he must be given in his culture if he is to become the loving, wise, and responsible man we want him to be. Some of the best wisdom I've learned about raising our adolescent boys has come from individual families and their innovations. We'll meet many of these people in this book. We'll also meet families and traditions from other cultures in which I've lived, worked, or studied. I have experienced male development in India, Turkey, Germany, Israel, and on the Southern Ute Reservation. To these personal experiences I've added the scholarly study of nearly twenty other cultures. Without romanticizing any one particular culture, we can learn from all a great deal about raising our sons amid everyday adolescent challenges.

A Unique Opportunity

One of the biggest lessons my private practice, my consulting, and my life experiences have taught me is that as parents, mentors, and educators of young men, we exist in our homes and schools not only as individual caregivers but as representatives of a truly unique time in human history. Not fifty nor five hundred years ago did our children have the opportunity they have now.

Over the last one hundred years, and especially in the last thirty, we've realized the need to reevaluate adolescent girls' lives and roles. I hope as you read this book you'll join me in an historic reevaluation of the lives and roles of adolescent boys. I hope also that no matter where you fit on the political spectrum, you'll agree that we lower our standards and expectations when we base our children's futures on pitting males and females against each other. Whatever we do, let's not pit boys against girls, or women against men.

As we reevaluate the lives of adolescent males, as we reshape, one family and school at a time, our care of our young men, we can provide the adolescent boy or boys in our lives the gift of love: the permission to find a spiritual, emotional, and moral center from which to contribute to life's cycle. I offer you this in the hope that the boy you know will not have to sit on a bicycle, or in a classroom, or at his computer, or in front of a TV, or at the dinner table wondering whether he will ever understand how to be a fine young man.

"Nothing measures the quality
of a society better than how it
raises its children."

PETER BREGGIN

PART ONE

The Emotional

Lives of

Adolescent Males

CHAPTER ONE

Jason and His Brothers

What It's *Really* Like for
Adolescent Boys in America

*"We cannot rescue America's families unless
we make up our minds to save the boys."*

WILLIAM RASPBERRY

I met Jason when he was twelve years old. His grades had been falling since he was nine. He had a problem with anger, as his mother put it. In fact, he had broken his wrist once from smashing it into the wall. He had been diagnosed with attention deficit disorder at ten by his teacher, and was on Ritalin. There was some improvement but now also a kind of blankness in him—his father's words. He had difficulty in athletics, mainly because he was a discipline problem, yet he wanted to play soccer.

He was a hard shell of a boy already at twelve. Though he and I lived in a middle-sized American city in the Pacific Northwest, he reminded me of urban youth who feel they have nothing going for them at all, trapped in inner cities, dangerous schools, and more dangerous streets. Jason dressed in the hip-hop style, and he had a buzz cut, his baseball cap on backwards, baggy jeans, and a flapping belt. He liked to talk about music, rap music, of course. He liked to show off.

Jason, his family, and I met a few times, with little progress. But one day Jason came in enraged. His mother apologized as she dropped him off and scooted out of my office, leaving him to me. I worked with him for a few minutes, until he started to cry. I listened, and pieces of a story came out. I found out he had been sexually abused by the father of a friend when he was ten, for a period of three months. He confessed, as his tears dried, that he couldn't get along with anyone, and he hated himself for it. He couldn't stay focused. He thought he should kill himself.

He had been enraged today, he said, because he'd just found out his parents were divorcing. He hated them, he hated himself, he hated life. Jason opened up to me, a man whom he barely knew, because he had no one else.

The activity that gave him the most solace, I knew, was playing violent video games. When our time was up, I knew he would return to them, soothe himself with them and whatever other distraction he could muster.

Jason's Brothers

Jason represents a "difficult" case. He is among those in our adolescent male population who are considered high risk. They are the adolescent males who are hurting most obviously and will hurt others most obviously. In my experience, no adolescent boy is immune to the pressures that can, over his decade of adolescence, put him at risk. Jason and his brothers are not so different from any mother's son.

Brian was seventeen when he killed himself. He was a high achiever, an A student, a lacrosse player. His father was a physician, and Brian planned on going to law school. Brian's girlfriend left him. He became depressed. "He wore his Walkman all the time," his mother said, "listening to bands I'd never heard of." He hanged himself, leaving a note: "I'm not worth loving and it's not worth living."

Kellen had very little fathering, no real relationship with grandparents; he was a quiet, inactive thirteen-year-old. His mother worried about his love of video games and TV in general. His grades were in the Cs, though he was naturally bright. His mother felt he was constantly unhappy. He smoked marijuana and cigarettes; what else, she didn't know and he wouldn't say.

"There's nothing wrong with me," he told me. His intelligence was wonderfully expressed in his ability to analyze games and media. He knew the computer games Myst and Riven very well. He loved the TV series "Men Behaving Badly." He confessed once that he felt he would never amount to much, so he had stopped trying. He was on Ritalin and Prozac both, a kind of typical media-linked and medicated youngster whose mom just prayed he would get through adolescence with a high school degree or G.E.D.

Max, fourteen, reminded me of a bird—he was six feet tall, with a pointed nose and chin, and filmy blue eyes. He had already tried cocaine. He too was on Ritalin. He had been kicked off the football team. He got in fights. He had been to three junior high schools. One day he said, "I'm gonna live hard, die young, and leave a pretty corpse," a strange statement of self-esteem he had learned from an old movie he couldn't name. "I'm gonna freak everyone out!" he said proudly.

He meant something else, too, in the end. After a number of weeks, he finally really opened up, cried, and said, "I'm like a top; I try to keep spinning and spinning so no one will notice how fucked up I am."

None of these weeping or stoically hard boys wanted me to hold him in the kind of physical embrace he truly needed, but what heart cannot go out to him?

The State of Male Adolescence Today

Statistics and stories about our homicidal adolescent males are dramatic enough to garner most of the headlines: the fourteen-year-old in Mississippi who killed two children and wounded seven; the fourteen-year-old in Kentucky who shot three dead; the thirteen-year-old in Washington who opened fire in his school and killed three; the eleven- and thirteen-year-olds who killed five in Jonesboro, Arkansas. But they don't describe the whole picture. It seems impossible for us to fully comprehend the state of male adolescence in our culture, yet it is essential we do so. There is hardly any social or personal health indicator in which adolescent boys do not show the lion's share of risk today. Decades ago, our females suffered more in more high-risk areas, and now our adolescent males are suffering privation we have not fully understood. I will take a moment here to lay out statistics for you, statistics that present just some of the areas of distress experienced by our adolescent males as a group. If you do not find your son fitting into one of these, you can be nearly assured that he knows boys who do. You yourself will know such boys. Your family life, your business, your neighborhood, your school has met them and been affected by them for years.

The Declining Safety of Our Adolescent Boys

- Adolescent boys are significantly more likely than adolescent girls to die before the age of eighteen, not just from violent causes but also from accidental death and disease.

- Adolescent boys are significantly more likely than adolescent girls to die at the hands of their caregivers. Two out of three juveniles killed at the hands of their parents or stepparents are male.

- Adolescent boys are fifteen times as likely as peer females to be victims of violent crime.

- One-third of adolescent male students nationwide carry a gun or other weapon to school.

- Gunshot wounds are now the second leading cause of accidental death among ten- to fourteen-year-old males.

The Mental Health of Adolescent Boys

- Adolescent boys are four times more likely than adolescent girls to be diagnosed as emotionally disturbed.

- The majority of juvenile mental patients nationwide are male. Depending on the state, most often between two-thirds and three-fourths of patients at juvenile mental facilities are male.

- Most of the deadliest and longest lasting mental problems experienced by children are experienced by adolescent males. For example, there are six male adolescent schizophrenics for every one female. Adolescent autistic males outnumber females two to one.

- Adolescent males significantly outnumber females in diagnoses of most conduct disorders, thought disorders, and brain disorders.

Drugs, Alcohol, and the Depression Link

The majority of adolescent alcoholics and drug addicts are male.

Terrence Real, a Cambridge, Massachusetts, psychotherapist, uses this statistic, among others, to point out the obvious: Although females are popularly considered to suffer more depression than males, in fact it is "overt depression" that our adolescent females experience two to four times more often than males. "Covert depression"—evidenced in drug and alcohol use, criminal activity, avoidance of intimacy, and isolation from others, especially family—brings the male/female depression ratio at least to par.

Terrence Real makes another important observation about male depression. Depression in males often has been overlooked because we don't recognize the male's way of being depressed. We measure depression by the female's model of overt depression: She talks about suicide, expresses feelings of worthlessness, shows her fatigue. Unaware of the male's less expressive, more stoic way of being, we miss the young depressed man who, in a town in Washington, walked into his high school and opened fire on his classroom, killing his classmates.

Suicide

- Adolescent males are four times more likely than adolescent females to commit suicide. Suicide success statistics (i.e., death actually occurs) for adolescent males are rising; suicide success statistics for adolescent females are not.

   This suicide statistic is one of the most startling to health professionals not just because lives are lost but because it indicates dramatically how much trouble adolescent males are in and the degree to which male psychiatric illness is increasing.

- One of the most important findings of youth suicide studies is that adolescent males seem to have so much more trouble than their female peers in reaching out for help when they are in deep trouble, except through violence against others, society, or self.

Body Image

Steroid use among adolescent boys is now on par with their use of crack cocaine. Consequences of steroid use range from increased rage to early death.

Attention Deficit Hyperactive Disorder (ADHD)

This brain disorder, like so many others, is almost exclusively a male malady. Only one out of six adolescents diagnosed with ADHD is female.

   ADHD is one of the reasons for the high rate of adolescent male vehicle accidents and fatalities. Adolescents with a history of ADHD (or, in fact, any conduct disorder) are significantly more likely to commit traffic offenses and be in accidents.

   While many adolescent males do need Ritalin, many are misdiagnosed and do not. Misdiagnosis is dangerous. The social labeling of an ADHD kid in the school stretches into national interests—children who are diagnosed with ADHD at twelve or older will not be allowed in the military. Ironically, many of the kids who have ADHD or are active enough to be misdiagnosed with ADHD would find the military one of the *best* environments for their particular way of being—well structured, well led, well focused.

Sexual Abuse

One out of five males has been sexually abused by the age of eighteen. Most of our sexual offenders are heterosexual males who have been physically and/or sexually abused as boys themselves. In this area, adolescent females suffer at a higher rate: at least one in four. However, male sexual abuse has only recently been studied and some researchers have found that as many as two out of five male children are sexually abused—comparable to the rate of female sexual abuse.

These numbers should frighten us terribly. A sexually abused adolescent male is more likely than his female counterpart to act out against someone else, generally someone younger and weaker than himself, through rape, physical violence, and sexual molestation.

Adolescent Males in the Educational System

Although well-publicized studies by the American Association of University Women, David and Myra Sadker, and the Wellesley Report on Women have done much to pave the way for a better educational atmosphere for my own daughters and millions of other girls, unfortunately, we have neglected the problems of our boys. Our boys are not in better shape than our girls in schools. Not only are they the primary victims of violence in schools, and not only do they comprise the majority of dead, injured, mentally ill, and substance-abusing adolescents in the schools, but they exhibit the majority of *academic problems* as well. Statistically, there is only one area of healthy activity where males outnumber females: sports.

Adolescent boys are twice as likely as adolescent girls to be diagnosed as learning disabled. Two-thirds of high school special-education and handicapped students are male. One colleague of mine, a teacher of speech pathology and a consultant on student-disability curricula, put the situation this way: "When I walk into a classroom of learning-disabled students, I know I'll face a sea of boys." She has further pointed out to me that adolescent male adaptability is a problem as well. Adolescent male learning disabilities are more intractable, on average, than those of adolescent females. When teachers and consultants face a roomful of learning-disabled adolescents, they know that they'll have greater impact on females than on males.

Adolescent males drop out of high school at four times the rate of adolescent females (this includes females who drop out to have babies).

Ninety percent of adolescent discipline problems in schools are male, as are most expulsions and suspensions.

Adolescent males are significantly more likely than adolescent females to be left back a grade.

Adolescent males on average get worse grades than adolescent females. The majority of salutatorians and valedictorians now are female.

Adolescent females now dominate school clubs, yearbooks, and student government.

Often we will hear in the media that before middle school, girls and boys are on par academically, but then by the end of high school, boys end up academically ahead. While this statement may be true for some girls, most of the time it is in fact the boy who ends up behind. The boys finish their education less frequently, they finish high school with lower average grades, and fewer go to college.

More college students are female (55 percent) than male (45 percent). More graduate students are female (59 percent) than male (41 percent). The discrepancies that did exist thirty years ago—the gender gap that put female school attendance lower than male—have more than reversed. This reversal began more than sixteen years ago. Since 1981, more women than men have been enrolling in college. The problem regarding low male college attendance prompted an article devoted to that subject in a recent issue of *Chronicle of Higher Education*: "Where Have All the Men Gone?"

Only our public consciousness has not caught up to the changes that have occurred in the many gender gaps, including the educational ones that statistically favor the adolescent female rather than the adolescent male. The area where males still are favored is in SAT scores. Females are slightly behind males in their college-application test scores. The Educational Testing Service has offered to change the SAT test, most likely to include a more developed essay format—girls generally test better than boys in essay writing—in order to make the test more fair.

According to the National Center for Education Statistics of the U.S. Department of Education, *fewer* boys than girls now study advanced algebra and geometry, about the same number study trigonometry and calculus, and *more* girls than boys study chemistry. What was true about gender gaps in these math/science areas twenty years ago is not true now.

Even more dramatic is the gender gap in reading/writing. Adolescent males are outscored by adolescent females by twelve points in reading and seventeen points in writing. The U.S. Department of Education recently pointed out that this gender gap in reading/writing is equivalent to about one and a half years of school! That is how far behind our adolescent males have fallen. While some boys read far better than some girls, the average high school freshman girl is reading as well as the average high school junior boy.

According to the U.S. Department of Education, eighth-grade girls are twice as likely as eighth-grade boys to aspire to a professional, business, or managerial career. When twelfth-graders are surveyed, the results are nearly similar. Twelfth-grade females are more likely to aspire to a college or graduate degree, on top of their professional aspirations.

The Fragile Self

As you read the statistics on everything from physical to mental to educational health, you may have noticed a common theme: that the adolescent boys are not as tough as we may think. Let's go even further and say they are far more fragile than we like to think. When boys lumber around the room at six-feet-two and push their little sisters, their fragility is perhaps farthest from our minds. When we watch them on the football fields or tossing baseballs or riding waves on their skateboards, we see risk takers, we see tough guys. When our adolescent males experience failures in social life or school and won't talk about it, it's difficult for us to see that they are not hard, that they might be falling apart.

What the statistics and study show us is that these boys, to a great extent, have us all fooled. That is certainly what my experience tells me. As an adolescent, I was good at fooling everyone most of the time. I've seen the "I'm fine" mask on the faces of the adolescent boys of this generation. We all have.

Fortunately, we now can join together as parents, mentors, and educators to see through the masks and notice the fragility of the adolescent male self. Science can help us a great deal.

One of the clearest ways for us to see the fragility is to look at the very fragility of the male brain, first by noticing trends in psychiatric illness of adolescent males. According to Dr. Judith Rapoport, chief of the child psychiatry branch at the National Institute of Mental Health, results of MRIs (magnetic resonance imaging) show the male brain to be "more vulnerable" than the female and prone to psychiatric diseases more often than girls'. Inherent within the male brain structure (which we'll study in depth in later chapters) is a vulnerability we have tended not to notice. That vulnerability, according to other studies, like a recent one out of Australia, has become more pronounced over the last decades rather than less, revealing itself most clearly in a dramatic increase in adolescent male psychiatric illness (a higher percentage of adolescent male psychopaths, emotionally disturbed males, males with brain disorders and thought disorders than ever before).

This recent increase in adolescent male mental illness—a higher statistical increase than in female—seems widespread throughout the industrial world. One theory about what's behind it combines the new brain research with environmental research and concludes that the world adolescent boys live in, a world of constant neural stimulation and undernurturance of emotional needs, is in fact dangerous to their brains. Their brains are less flexible and able than the female brain to handle both overstimulation and undernurturance.

Another way of measuring the hidden fragility of the adolescent male is to notice the inherent intellectual fragility in the male brain system, a fragility that begins in a boy's childhood, that contributes to the problems boys have in schools—problems that have now, as we noticed earlier, reached very painful proportions, especially in academic areas like reading and writing—and that continues to manifest itself well into his old age. Thus, the child most likely to suffer a learning disability is the male child; the first-grader most likely to have academic trouble is the male, as is the sixth-grader, eighth-grader, tenth-grader, and so on.

According to Nancy Bayley at UC Berkeley, who has studied the effect of parenting styles on the intelligence of boys and girls, when children are raised by withdrawn and hostile mothers, the girls' intelligence scores are the same as the scores of girls raised by loving and attentive mothers. Yet the boys' intelligence scores are steadily *below* the scores of boys raised by loving and attentive mothers. Brain system fragility shows up even when we look at elderly males and females. Female stroke victims recover intellectual powers with far greater frequency than men after strokes. Brain researchers have found that the male brain compartmentalizes its intellectual functions more than the female. When a female stroke victim suffers a left-side stroke, she often still retains right-side language functioning. Much more often, the male does not.

The researcher's lens into the hidden fragility of the adolescent boy reveals that adolescent males on average seem to have more difficulty rebuilding the self after a divorce than do adolescent females. The fragile, developing male self—what psychologists often call "the fragile male ego"—seems to suffer more trauma than the female during the transition into a divorce-based family life. Often because his father is away, or because he feels a pressure to be the man of the family and yet is too young to fulfill this function, or because he is less able than his sister to process his feelings, a boy experiences his fragility and may not know how to manage it. The more likely adolescent child to commit suicide or engage in at-risk behavior after a divorce is the male.

Adolescent males seem to handle the trauma of failure in social situations, school environments, and relationships more overtly than their sisters. For instance, the adolescent child most likely to commit suicide after a girlfriend/boyfriend breakup is the male adolescent. When psychologists (and parents or family members) talk about male adolescents "having less emotional resources" with which to manage family or personal problems in appropriate or healthy ways, they are referring to this inherent male fragility.

Another way to measure the fragile self in the adolescent male is to watch criminal behavior. Crime statistics show us that the adolescent child who is most vulnerable to moral disturbance is the adolescent male. Far more than his adolescent sister, it is the adolescent male whose concept of right and wrong is tenuous. There are many arguments from many quarters as to why this occurs, from those specialists who look at the way biochemistry—testosterone—affects the way the male brain develops to those who study the female/docile, male/aggressive cultural stereotypes. Wherever we look for causes, the result is clear: The adolescent male's moral development is more fragile than the adolescent female's.

Studies of male responses to their sex roles in modern life also show immense male fragility, a fragility that has been clarifying itself more and more in the last few years as male role conflict increases in the ever-changing masculine landscape. Greater numbers of adolescent boys are having trouble measuring up to the high and very contradictory standards cultures teach them to inculcate—on the one hand, superrationality, high competitiveness, repression of emotion and vulnerability, and high sexual prowess, *and on the other,* high levels of complex emotional expression, withdrawal of competitiveness so that females can excel, expression of feeling to please others, and decrease of sex drive so that females can take more control of sexuality.

In addition, families tend to push male children, in both early childhood and early adolescence, toward increased independence. In a surprising and comprehensive National Institute of Child and Human Development study, it was discovered that little boys seem to suffer more negative consequences, stemming mainly from insecure attachment, when separated for long periods of time from mothers. Pennsylvania State University researcher Jay Belsky, along with numerous other brain researchers around the world, has reviewed data from similar brain scans and research. These researchers have noticed that despite boys' needing a great deal of attention and guidance (and perhaps in some areas needing *more* than the average girl because of a more fragile brain system), boys often receive *less* than girls as they are pushed more quickly toward independence, both in early childhood and in early adolescence.

Jay Belsky put the situation for males quite clearly: "Over the whole life span, males have a more vulnerable biology." Given the psychiatric, mental, intellectual, moral, and social distresses our adolescent males experience, and given the recent and somewhat startling increases in these distresses, can we afford any longer to neglect the basic fragility and vulnerability of the male self? So many parents have said to me, "My son was going along just fine, and then it seemed like just a couple little things happened and he got derailed." These sons could not articulate the vulnerability within themselves. A lost girlfriend, a failure at competition, a problem with parents, an ostracism in peer groups, and usually more than one compounded, can cause a boy to withdraw or become inappropriately aggressive, obsessing, or immensely docile.

Students of adolescent self-esteem are beginning to notice low self-esteem for adolescent males that is more than comparable to the low self-esteem we've been focusing on lately in relation to our adolescent females. Educators Diane Ravitch and Valerie Lee, researchers at the U.S. Department of Education and at Harvard, are beginning to throw light on adolescent male self-esteem and cause-effect relationships with the media, the schools, the families, and the peer groups.

Adolescent Male Self-Esteem

My understanding of adolescent male self-esteem has been something of a journey. I hope it will reflect in some ways the journey that you may have had to make toward seeing adolescent male self-esteem issues in your own family.

While I knew, as a professional, that much of what our adolescents face is rooted in general in the transitional disturbance in self-esteem that they experience during the second decade of their lives, and while I knew that by most psychological measures not only our females but also our males encounter the adolescent drop in self-esteem, I couldn't see how it worked in males as well as in females. In this I was like most people—parents or professionals or in between—who find it hard to reach behind the toughness and isolationism of so many adolescent males to the emotional life hidden inside. But as a parent in the 1990s, I had another problem. Seeing males clearly meant noticing how most of our self-esteem research concerns only adolescent girls and grown women. We haven't spent much time as a culture focusing on self-esteem issues in our adolescent boys. Unfortunately too, much of our research into female self-esteem has pitted females against males, or shown males to be tough and females to be the only fragile ones.

When the Ms. Foundation for Women launched the Take Our Daughters to Work® Day, it provided as rationale the "fact" that "adolescence takes a greater toll on the self-esteem and school performance of girls than boys." This kind of blanket statement was echoed by reports such as that of the American Association of University Women (AAUW) in 1991, the Wellesley Report on Women, and the David and Myra Sadker research. These studies came out in the early to mid-1990s. Some of them mentioned boys, mainly as problems. If the boys could be taught to calm down, be less aggressive, and "have less of a sense of entitlement" in the classroom, the playground, and the home, then girls' self-esteem would not be destroyed.

During this time, a study came out showing that black adolescent males have the highest self-esteem of any demographic group, far higher than white females. I knew from experience that this was absolutely false, and I noticed that the press and some researchers as well had mistaken bravado and compensatory grandiosity for self-esteem. For them, self-esteem was measured by the aggressive show, the mask, of self-esteem. Boys, of course, would show higher self-esteem, especially the boys who had perfected the business of posturing. Press and researchers thought posturing showed a healthy core self. When I realized that this kind of study was being used to bolster the cause of adolescent girls, I became disappointed. Self-esteem research obviously needed to move to the next level.

Fortunately, that next level is available to us.

Just after the AAUW study came out, *Science News* asked leading scholars and researchers to evaluate the AAUW report. Their conclusion was that *both* adolescent males and females experience significant drops in self-esteem during adolescence. Researchers Tim Blankenhorn, Michael

Reichert, and Joseph Healey, in their study of Philadelphia boys, concluded that all boys, even privileged ones, go through male versions of what Mary Pipher describes in *Reviving Ophelia:* a drop in self-esteem during middle-school years and soon after. Says Blankenhorn, "Boys lose themselves at just about exactly the same time."

Even more startling, since 1991, further research has suggested that in many circumstances, adolescent males experience a *worse* self-esteem drop than females. Under pressure to check their findings, the AAUW commissioned an independent study, conducted by Valerie E. Lee of the University of Michigan. Her study of 9,000 eighth-grade males and females showed no significant difference in self-esteem drops between males and females, but concluded that in many academic categories where self-esteem might be measurable—for instance, study habits, grades, engagement in school activities—the females were, quite simply, doing better than the males. The Michigan study is consistent with similar research on eighth-graders and twelfth-graders by the U.S. Department of Education.

Researcher Diane Ravitch, in *Forbes* magazine in 1996, summed up the self-esteem research this way:

> *If there is a crisis in self-esteem, it is not among young women. Girls are doing very well indeed. Boys, in the meantime, are killing themselves and each other at alarming rates. If either sex is in trouble in our society, it is the males.*

If we could view every statistic and anecdote, we would find that there is no reason to argue about who "has it worse." Both our adolescent females and males need our help. We would also find, however, that paying attention to adolescent male fragility is absolutely essential, and we must reeducate ourselves in order to learn how to do it. Research into self-esteem has developed along the standards of how *females* show self-esteem drops—talking less often in class, letting others talk for them, becoming more passive, become overtly depressed, becoming body-image obsessed to the point of anorexia.

Boys often will show their fragility in different ways.

Bravado and Beyond

Many times, boys will show their fragility not through increased passivity but through increased bravado. When compared to adolescent girls, adolescent boys experiencing an average drop in self-esteem will pretend more self-confidence, will admit less weakness, will posture more, will pursue more overt attention, and will appear more aggressive. A teacher at a workshop once said something very powerful about who she calls on in class.

> *When I went to a gender-fairness workshop I was shocked to notice that I, like so many teachers, called on my eighth-grade boys more than my girls. I've worked hard to be more fair. But at the same time what the trainers don't tell you is that a lot of the quiet girls just need a lot less attention in school than the loud boys. Truthfully, I don't worry as much about them as some of these boys who seem to live on the edge of failure so much.*

The bravado, the aggression among the males, in her experience, was hardly a show of high self-esteem. I have heard her words echoed all over the country.

Another high school teacher told me, "In my classroom, all the kids do a certain amount of posturing, but it's mainly the boys who lose their focus to the posturing. Their self-concept is so easily shaken. The girls seem more able to 'be cool,' but still keep their minds on what they have to do."

About her fourteen-year-old son, a mother, who was also a teacher, said:

> *He was doing great in elementary school, but by the time he finished junior high I felt like we lost him. No matter what we do, he just seems to think he's never okay, never good enough, never cool enough. He won't talk about it. He just tries to walk around now like he's tough enough to handle anything.*

In the next century, as we expand our self-esteem research, both personal and cultural, we will be better able to decipher fully the self-esteem picture our boys and girls are painting. Researchers will have to see beyond bravado and posturing—something the AAUW study, based on a questionnaire given to students about self-image, was not able to do. Questionnaires that require self-reflection by children are answered by boys and girls in some very different ways. Generally, boys will posture higher self-esteem than girls, will practice more bravado, will have access to their innermost feelings less instantaneously than girls, and will, on average, have weaker verbal skills in answering questions involving emotive data. When the 1991 AAUW report found slightly higher self-esteem results for the males than the females, it did not inform the media or anyone else of the vast limitations of a questionnaire format as a measurement of self-esteem among boys and girls.

Now we are challenged to look beyond bravado in our assessments of how fragile boys really are. Recall how you may have watched your three-year-old boy so aggressively playing with sticks or forming guns or tearing heads off dolls with his hands and yet you knew that behind that aggression lay a fragile self that could lose control in an instant and lie weeping in a puddle. An adolescent male will probably not weep in a puddle, but he is fragile indeed, and his mask of bravado is sometimes a greater clue to his fragility than a lesser one. His increased aggression or stoic bravado often is a sign of armoring against fragility.

From Posturing to Trauma Responses

Because we have paid little attention to male fragility, we certainly have not connected that fragility with the social dangers males create. Let us make that connection in earnest now. Much adolescent male posturing may not lead to any significant danger. Much male armoring is necessary and healthy for the male at a given time in his life. Much of it can transpire with emotional development taking place as well. Much of it can soothe a self-esteem drop—for instance, in that difficult year, the high school freshman year, when male self-esteem is very much at risk.

Simultaneously, much of the posturing and armoring can move from the safe to the dangerous. It does so when adolescent male self-esteem drops so low and the fragile self's resources are so minimal that the adolescent male feels *traumatized*. The majority of adolescent male suicides, violent deaths, and violent activity grow from what we call *endangering trauma responses*—triggered responses to threats within the fragile male self that create behavior and physical action that endanger the self, others, or property. Interestingly, not just among human adolescent males, but among the other primates, *when an adolescent male is most fragile we often can expect him to cause others and himself the most, not the least, crisis and distress.*

An adolescent male's despair at the loss of his father or mother through divorce, the loss of a girlfriend, lack of age-appropriate social and economic opportunity, a failure of small or large proportion, an inability to compete— each and all may translate into emotional and social withdrawal or increased bravado and posturing until the point at which an action is taken that is more physically and socially violent than the female peer, in equal distress, would entertain. In addition, an adolescent male may respond to his stress either immediately or a year or two after the situation has passed. For example, in a Southern state recently, two adolescent males, both fifteen, committed suicide. Just before killing themselves, they held up a gas station and traveled by car illegally for three days. The boys' intention to take their own lives was precipitated by a girl's not choosing one of them as a boyfriend, at a time when the boys' self-esteem was very low. Specialists called in on the case have noted that the boys did not respond to their long-term stress—stored-up trauma—until *much later*, when a new stress factor—the girl's rejection—was introduced. Similarly, a thirteen-year-old boy in Washington state who walked into his school and shot three classmates dead was responding not only to his present psychiatric illness but to a history of family traumas and stresses, including his parents' fights.

The basic fragility of the male self becomes increasingly clear when we see beyond the terrible and reprehensible acts and the internal histories that led up to them. We are dealing with adolescent males who broke down internally and had no resources to repair internal damage to fragile psychological structures.

Adolescent Male Posttraumatic Stress

We are dealing with adolescent males experiencing posttraumatic stress. Millions of our adolescent boys have experienced a trauma of some kind, from broken families to lack of male role models and extended family support, from failures in school or society to relationship failures. They are unable to internally and adequately process the traumas because of poor personal emotional development and/or inadequate time and energy spent with them by caregivers and community. Like soldiers traumatized in wartime, these males act out, experience heightened levels of psychiatric illness and disability, use drugs and alcohol, and/or become violent. While our female children experience immense stresses of their own from family breakups, lack of role models, and personal failures, they differ from our male children in some significant ways—they are better able to process the posttraumatic stress verbally and in caregiving communities; their brain systems may very well be inherently less fragile than their brothers'; and, as we will explore in the next chapter, their internal hormonal systems actually *help* them process stress internally, making it easier for them to resolve more emotional stress and to prevent direct damage to self and others.

Just how many of our adolescent males suffer posttraumatic stress? Crime figures give us perhaps the clearest indicator. While in any generation males constitute the majority of criminals (in our era, around 85 percent of nonviolent criminals and 90 percent of violent criminals), the number of *adolescent* males who are now criminals, especially violent ones, is incredible. When all violent crime is combined, adolescent males comprise about 20 percent of the arrestees nationally. American arrests for juvenile violent crime have increased by 600 percent over the last thirty years, the highest increase of any industrialized country (year by year we hear of fluctuations, juvenile crime activity up one year and down the next, but the *overall* picture is one of huge increase). This increase has taken place during a time when the actual juvenile population has remained stable. The rate of increase in juvenile criminality has now outpaced the rate of criminality in adults. What this means: *Juvenile males are now committing crime at a higher rate than adult males.* During my three years as a contract counselor in a prison, I formed the opinion that most of the young men there experienced posttraumatic stress. They exhibited the armoring, emotional confusion, denial, episodes of rage, and painful nightmares of PTSD (posttraumatic stress disorder) victims.

That the number of these PTSD criminal men is increasing is especially frightening because of the increase in the juvenile male population over the next decade. Louis J. Freeh, director of the FBI, recently warned: "The ominous increase in juvenile crime, coupled with population trends, portends future crime and violence at nearly unprecedented levels." John J. DiIulio, Jr., a professor of public affairs at Princeton who has studied the rise in juvenile crime, warned in 1997 that with 40 million kids ten years and younger who are about to become teenagers, we'll have, as the century turns, the largest group of adolescents in a generation. A growing number of them will be posttraumatic males who turn to crime and violent behavior.

Trauma-causing adolescent males are everywhere, and yet our culture has not been able to do much more than ask "Why? How could this happen? What has gone wrong?" Let us go beyond these natural but incomplete utterances. These boys who "go bad" are provocative, sometimes violent teachers not only of larger social issues but also of hidden realms in every boy's inner life, realms even our "normal" boys don't express.

Adolescent Males in Shock

For years now I have watched young boys who are full of pride and spark become adolescent males who are angry, alienated, and desperate. I have counseled "normal" families with steroid-using, drug-abusing, alcohol-addicted, media-mechanized, and underachieving adolescent boys. I have looked into eyes once passionate, now deadened; bodies once innocent, now poised and posturing. I have known what's normal for an adolescent boy to experience, and seen too much that's not normal. Two million learning-disabled boys, millions on Ritalin, millions in juvenile court, hundreds of thousands diagnosed as emotionally disturbed, increasing numbers of thirteen- and fourteen-year-old boy murderers tried as adults, high adolescent male suicide and dropout rates, more than a million adolescent males addicted to drugs, the most violent nonwar adolescent male population in the world—this is no longer "normal." These are adolescent boys in trauma shock.

I hope the material I've presented in this chapter will inspire you to notice adolescent male fragility wherever it occurs in your life, call it to the attention of people you know, and minister to it in the lives of the boys you know. We must not only attend to our own sons' developmental needs—"My son's doing fine, he's just a normal adolescent"—but also stand with his hurting, confused, traumatized friends in this adolescent male crucible—an increasingly painful place that calls everyone, all of us, to form a true culture of care.

In this chapter we have focused mainly on high-risk adolescent males whose problems are somewhat obvious once we know where to look. In the next chapter, let's delve into more subtle areas of adolescent male emotional development.

CHAPTER TWO

Protecting the Emotional Lives of Adolescent Boys

"Do you know who I am?"

"You are my mother."

"Do you know who I am?"

"You are my father."

"Do you know who we are?"

"You are my aunts and uncles."

"Yes. So you can see how we are all about you.
*   But you look sad. Why is that?"*

"Because you do not love me."

"How can you say that! Of course we love you!"

"Well, if you love me, tell me why I do not grow."

"THE LAMENT OF THE ETERNAL BOY,"
FROM NORSE POETRY

Tim was our friend Jean's fifteen-year-old son. I had known him since he was eleven. Initially, my wife, Gail, and Jean had become friends. Then I got to know her son better after his parents divorced. One summer day we sat out on our lawn, watching her son walk off with another his age, and watching my younger kids and other kids at play. Jean said, "Something's been happening to him, or inside him, I don't know what it is. It's been coming on for about a year, I guess." She described his growing attention to television and video games. He had wanted a television in his room, so she gave him one. His interest in his computer, television, and games had become, in her words, "almost an obsession."

"He loves this new comic book, *Spawn*. Will someone please explain that to me!"

Jean was worried about her son and asked me to talk to him. A week or so later, I asked him to help me run some errands and move some firewood. He readily agreed. He had always been a good, helpful guy. Like most of his peers, he closed down more and more as the adolescent years went along. He developed armor, which is not in itself a bad thing, but I did know what Jean meant—he was getting that hardness that comes into adolescent males, a hardness that can defeat itself because it doesn't get talked about, understood, or opened up, sometimes, ever again.

Tim had never been easy to talk to, so I didn't try directly. But while we were moving wood, I asked if he wanted to go to a movie, and I suggested *Spawn*, which was still in theaters. That lit his eyes up. There's hardly a thing a young man wants more than to turn an older man he respects on to a vision he loves. I remembered myself at eighteen, sitting my father down and making him listen to a Pink Floyd album. He was patient with me, and we engaged afterward in a pretty intense conversation. I wanted to be patient with Tim now, though *Spawn* wasn't tops on my viewing list, and see what we could talk about.

We did go to the movie, and afterward we went for ice cream, a sweet-tooth habit he still loved even into his middle teens. He said, "I know you must have thought the movie was weird, right?" I admitted the truth—it wasn't my favorite movie and briefly explained why (one minute or less), then I refocused us on what I *did* like and asked him to explain the story to me, what he knew about Spawn subculture, what he got out of it. He enjoyed being asked, being attended to, being admired for his knowledge.

We talked a long time, walking, driving, hanging out. I could tell how starved he was for love by how intensely we related to each other. Toward the end of our time together, following on the direction of his mother's worries, I asked him about the armor that the hero of *Spawn* is able to produce around himself just by thinking about it. He said he liked the armor. "I wish I could have armor like that," he said. "It closes Spawn in and makes him safe."

It would have been ludicrous to ask him at the moment the obvious question—"Don't you feel safe in life right now?" ("Of course not" would be his most honest response, though I wouldn't get it.) Doing so would elicit a pained look at the abstract, out-of-placeness of my question and would insult the sacredness of the moment. Teen boys aren't stupid. They know when someone's trying to put his hand inside a boy's heart and pull out a "heartfelt" response.

"I'm writing a book about boys your age," I said instead, "and I have a challenge for you. Would you take your computer out tonight and write me as much as you want about why you like that movie, that character, that armor, all of it, but write it not like a movie critic but like a fifteen-year-old who's about to start driving and has started to become a hell of a flirt and sometimes gets sad and sometimes gets happy and just is who he is? Can you write something like that?"

"Something *real*, you mean?" he said wisely.

I smiled. "Yeah, something real. I want to know what's going on inside you, inside your friends. *Spawn* was made for you guys, not for a middle-aged guy like me. So educate me, but do it from your heart and soul."

He agreed to do it and wrote me a kind of personal essay too long to reprint here. One of the most telling paragraphs follows:

> *The assassin (the agent of the good) says, "The war between heaven and hell depends on the choices we make. That's why we're here." I agree with that. I think there's a war going on all around me. It's inside everyone, even people who love each other, or say they do. When I was younger I wanted it to end, but now I see it can't end, so I have to become strong and make choices in that war. Lots of the choices I make now are choices some people who love me won't like. But one day they'll understand, because I'll survive. I'll make it through. I'll cut the head off the clown. Then they'll see I'm someone worth loving.*

The Emotional Neglect of Our Adolescent Boys

T hen they'll see I'm worth loving.

It is a powerful and telling line. It is a rare adolescent boy I meet who feels, on a moment-by-moment basis, that he is worth loving. Recently I watched an emotionally moving episode of the television show "Touched by an Angel" in which a fifteen-year-old black male has nothing to live for except his anger. When one of the angels asks him if he understands that God loves him, he responds, "I don't want God to love me, I don't want anyone to love me." As the boy sits in tears, the angel asks him why he does not want love, and he responds, "Because I'm not . . ." dropping off the last part, which you can fill in: "worth anything," "worthwhile," "worth loving," "lovable."

With all the talk these days of "boys having it made," or "this world is male dominated," or "this culture is run by and made for males," reality comes as a surprise to us: So many "normal" adolescent males reach college age with holes inside themselves, deep holes they will fill later, in their twenties, with money, status, or some other real or illusory power.

In the previous chapter, we explored the instances in which boys who are traumatized involve themselves in high-risk behaviors as a cover for the fragile, undernurtured self. In this chapter, as we define the biological and cultural components of an adolescent boy's emotional structure, we will notice also that while the majority of our adolescent boys have enough support systems to get by in adolescence and do not develop mental illnesses or violent lifestyles, nonetheless the same majority of adolescent boys—mainly because our social and family systems do not understand fully what an adolescent boy needs in order to flourish—grow into adulthood having experienced a sad and unnecessary degree of *emotional neglect*. In my experience, it is a rare adolescent boy these days who does not experience some clear emotional neglect, which, while not maliciously bestowed is also avoidable if we just knew more than we know now.

This chapter will take you deep into the emotions of adolescent males, showing you the biologically hardwired *emotional disadvantage* they bring to adolescence and the ways, in the face of both hard and soft wiring, we have not fully attended to male emotional development in our culture. As we explore this painful terrain together, please know that we will end up at the other end with hope.

Male biology is an essential part of the emotional picture. Let's begin there.

Male Biology and the Adolescent Boy's Emotional Disadvantage

A mother once said to me: "My boys just don't get as deep into their feelings as my girls. In some ways, this is great. There's something so direct about them—less of the ups and downs of emotions. But in other ways it is so sad, because I can tell my boys don't really get all there can be in life either."

As we probe male emotionality in these pages, let us agree that every male and female is an individual, and thus, some of what we say won't apply to your boy. In fact, in some cases you'll know an adolescent female who seems far more emotionally disadvantaged than her brother. Furthermore, brain systems develop not as polarized male or female brains but on a spectrum, so when we talk about "the male brain" we are not talking about a single entity but a spectrum of possibilities. Also, individual personality, your child's birth order, and other factors can "form" your child as much as or more than his brain structure and biochemistry.

Nonetheless, there are certain features of what I call "the male emotional system" that seem uniquely male.

The Male Emotional System

The development of the male emotional system follows the path of the development of male testosterone and brain development, and adaptations in male sexual biology. Over a period of millennia, human beings have been adapting all systems, including emotional systems, to changing conditions.

We have been adapting from hunting/gathering groups, when our main enemies were creatures of the savannah and when males didn't even know who their offspring were, to agricultural extended families, when monogamy became normative and family relationships were considered of paramount importance, to industrial child-raising units, called families, but wherein only one caregiver—generally the mom—concentrates on children.

Our bodies and brains have adapted so that they can take in more stimulation and use creative and inventive functions far more readily.

Our testosterone levels, body size, and genital size all have increased because of both increased population demands and increased aggression demands. For instance, as the need to fight wars developed over the last ten thousand years, our males needed to increase their testosterone levels in order to help humans survive. Our present testosterone levels are continually increasing as the population increases because high population creates more competition for resources.

Over the last few thousand years, our sexual biology has adapted to include romance, a kind of human intercourse that was not needed tens of thousands of years ago when a male just mated with an estrous female and moved on. Now we try to mate for life with the help of romance strategies.

All these human adaptations comprise your adolescent boy's history. Simultaneously, his brain and biology still resemble what his male ancestors' were millennia ago. In some ways, our brains have changed; in other ways, our sexual biology, brain activity, and hormonal flow are still what they were in hunter/gatherer times. This is not surprising, since we have lived 98 percent of our human history as hunter/gatherers.

As we explore the biological aspects of our adolescent boys' emotional systems, we'll divide this material into two sections, first studying testosterone then the male brain. We'll explore how each of these crucial components of our adolescent males' lives affect their abilities to be or not be emotionally vital and expressive.

Testosterone and the Emotional Disadvantage

So much of how an adolescent boy lives depends on his hormones, especially his testosterone, the human sex and aggression hormone that makes him into an adult male. Adolescent males (pubescent, postpubescent, and then continuing on into adulthood) secrete between five and seven surges of this hormone through their bodies each day. By late adolescence, their testosterone levels can be as much as twenty times that of their female peers.

This is the hormone that, combined with a male's sexual biology, compels him to seek sex as a physical act with more statistical frequency than females do. A female is fertile (ovulates) approximately three hundred times in her life. When she is ovulating, her sex hormones increase so that she will seek a mate. This is one reason why most women recognize an increase in "horniness" during their monthly cycle. If women could imagine the adolescent male receiving in his body seven of these "horniness increases" per *day*, she can begin to imagine how his body is wired for sexual intercourse.

Testosterone is also a hormone that stimulates physical aggression. Since the beginning of time, males have needed high amounts of physical aggression in order for our species to survive. That aggression has, of course, been modulated by other biological and sociological factors, but that that aggression exists like an ocean in the male is evidenced every time we turn on a television or go down to the park and watch males at sport and play. It is an essential part of human life. Simultaneously, this hormone sets a male up for immense emotional disadvantage, as we'll explore now.

GETTING IT DONE.   Testosterone propels the male to be, in general, more directed toward the sex *act* itself than the female might be—therefore, less directed toward the emotional conversation, contact, and connection that surrounds that act. Once the male body ejaculates, it is often done. The hugging, cuddling, and talking that might follow the sex act is far more often initiated by the female than the male, often to her great frustration; similarly, the male's focus previous to the sex act is on emotional connection often for the sake of negotiating the sex act rather than the deep opening of the human heart.

The male's attitude toward the sex act is of course more complex than this short rendering, but this rendering provides an appropriate metaphor for not only the sex act but the male's attitude toward many other actions in which the male prefers action to ongoing intimate connection. Males want to get the intimate connection accomplished, not spend a lot of time talking about it! How many times have you heard this cry from a male? It is a cry that rises from deep within his biology.

It is a biology that also has built a male's internal system to deny lots of emotional opportunities. "Getting it done" means less time to "do it," make emotional connections in order to do it, and feel what it was like to have done it. One of the reasons why testosterone-driven social systems, like war and sports systems, teach teamwork as one of the primary principles is that they know the male must, more often than the female, be *trained* to act while relating emotionally to others.

QUICK TENSION RELEASE.   Testosterone propels the male toward quick tension release. Not only the sex act, but even a male's way of responding to physical pain show us this tendency. A ten-year-old girl and a ten-year-old boy smash a knee against the jutting edge of a table. The ten-year-old girl is more likely to cry real tears and ask to be embraced. A ten-year-old boy is more likely to kick the table, curse it, and otherwise release his stress quickly, without the long immersion of tears and the emotional contact that surround them. He wants to release stress fast (and, more often, independently—i.e., without a hug from a caregiver). She tends to want to get help in releasing her stress, and to use the stress as a way of creating emotional opportunity.

Recently, some adult women have begun experimenting with testosterone. There are lots of side effects to testosterone injection, so it's an experiment that's monitored closely. One of the interesting results of the experiments is the increase among the women in "independence behavior," the very kind of "I don't need any help" behavior often associated with males.

The emotional disadvantage here is clear. A male whose body tends him toward more independent, quick release of tension is less likely to use pain as a bonding agent.

CRYING.   You will probably notice that especially by the time males reach puberty—testosterone now a daily surging phenomenon in the male body—they cry a great deal less than they did before puberty. While acculturation—"Real men don't cry!"—is the cause of some of this change, biology is a larger factor.

Prolactin levels in pubescent and postpubescent males are 60 percent lower than in similarly aged females. Prolactin is the growth hormone that influences breast development, tear glands, and breast milk production. By age fifteen, females cry four times more often than males.

Testosterone-driven systems are also directed toward releasing tension quickly rather than engaging in an activity like crying which not only elongates the release of tension (as compared to a quick curse or physical act) but prolongs community involvement. If I start to cry, people come around to talk and help, and the emotional process is elongated. While this scenario may benefit me emotionally, it is not as hardwired into my system as it is, usually, into a female's.

DOMINANCE PATTERNS.   Testosterone also propels the male toward dominance patterns, which disadvantage him in emotional connections. His kicking and cursing at the table is a dominance pattern. Like thousands of other dominance patterns it scares people around him rather than encouraging them to embrace him. Spitting, a very male behavior, is an example of territorial dominance behavior, like urinating in the wild used to be. Spitting hardly causes people to want to reach out and embrace the male. (Saliva, by the way, is a bodily secretion in which testosterone levels are quite measurable.) Male conversation, even with the female, relies very much on one-upping and dominance patterns, a fact which Deborah Tannen, in *You Just Don't Understand*, has made so brilliantly clear, and is a pattern that pushes more people away than it brings close. From conversation, to spitting, to pain resolution, so it goes throughout male life—the search for quick action, quick tension release, and dominance, all of which don't inspire people to nurture a male's emotional system.

LESS TIME TO PROCESS CONSEQUENCES.   Testosterone propels the male to display physical and social aggression without as much thought of consequence and/or expression of empathy as a female counterpart might possess. Studies show this operating as early as six months old. The boy is more likely to push stubbornly and quickly forward, seeing an opportunity to brandish and hone his skills, focus, and power. This behavior creates less internal opportunity for emotional processing, and also scares people near him, diminishing the opportunities for emotional substance in his life.

DELAYED REACTIONS. Testosterone creates such a push for action, it causes delayed reactions to events that might otherwise bring emotional opportunity. A soldier, for instance, whose best buddy has just fallen to a bullet beside him cannot stop to feel empathy. If he did, he would not survive. So he must delay his reaction. So it goes with male emotionality. It is often a delayed-reaction emotionality and thus is a source of difficulty when males and females try to relate to each other. Females tend to process the emotional content of a situation—an argument, a moving film, a social interchange— long before the male does.

MECHANISTIC BEHAVIOR. Testosterone directs the male toward mechanistic behavior. As an aggression hormone, it links with brain systems (which we'll discuss in a moment) to create the most "efficient" (i.e., least emotionally stimulating) methods for goal reaching. The long continuation of an emotionally complex situation often feels dangerous to the male. Male problem solving—the quick solution—that females so frequently (and often rightfully) complain about is part of this mechanical male. For the male, emotionality is very often synonymous with danger, and danger is the very thing testosterone exists to contend with—by causing him either to persevere over it or to quickly solve issues and therefore deflect it. Once again, testosterone cuts off emotional opportunity.

MALE-SPECIFIC WAYS OF BUILDING EMOTIONAL DEPTH. The effects of testosterone on male emotionality have been known since the beginning of time, even though our ancestors a million years ago didn't have our words for them. Yet they knew the emotional structure of their males (of course, with variety and a spectrum in mind) and thus made sure males had male-specific ways of building emotional depth and substance, ways that allowed males to find *structures* for emotional development: hunting structures, work structures, mentorship structures, game structures, spirituality structures, religious structures, war structures. Testosterone wires its host body to need lots of *personnel* to teach that body how to manage the hormone, and lots of sanctioned social *structures*, in which rules and objectives are clear, to provide the arena for its management.

Structures of this kind, however, can limit emotional opportunity. They often require males to follow complex protocols before they can even begin to experience emotion, and they are so rule-oriented as to disallow many varieties of emotional content. In a sport structure, like basketball, for instance, males are inundated with a thousand emotional impulses that never get explored—basketball exists as a structure that generates a team effort toward a specific objective. Reaching that objective would not be aided but instead *stymied* by complexity of emotional life.

The Deal

Testosterone, then, is a major factor in naturally cutting males off from emotional development. Our ancestors were aware of that fact and so allowed time in work, play, relationship, hunt, and spirituality training for adolescent males to relate to other males in spiritual and emotional content, as well as to other females and their children. Our ancestors also did not have the high and deep emotional expectations of their males that we have of ours.

The deal that males and females struck over the millennia was one in which males would protect and provide for females, and females would carry the males' children, support their search for social status, and allow them to "do their thing." Adolescent males were brought up to continue the tradition of that "deal." It worked well for millions of years—the standard of success being that the human species survived.

That deal has been fading since the beginning of our century. Now, the economic protections against males' abandonment of females and families, and the social protections against females' emotional and sexual abandonment of males, barely exist—a male can be divorced whenever the female wants to divorce him, and vice versa.

From a biological standpoint, the Industrial Revolution was a milestone in human development. It represented the peak of mechanistic masculinity; it appeared to offer males and females the security both had been evolving toward; and it provided jobs that gave us the potential to increase standards of living, to overcome the dominance of nature over the human, and to create adequate nests for females and work structures for males. On the other hand, we know that the Industrial Revolution, and the concomitant social movement called the Enlightenment, caused huge emotional and spiritual gaps in our lives, increasing male mechanization and abandoning many of the ancient ways males bonded and developed emotionally. Now, in the late-twentieth century, we must understand that our males *still* are wired to operate mechanistically and need "The Deal" just to survive, but current marriage, spiritual, and social systems do not even protect that way of being.

We want to say, "Thank God for that!" Yet, what we're thanking God for is the abandonment of our males. Many of these males, especially adolescents, are, as it were, thrown to the wolves.

"Yeah," we may want to say, "but, as a gender, males brought this on themselves! They overdominated females. They spent immense amounts of energy investing in testosterone activities like war and sport. They limited male brain use from emotional development. So let them suffer a little."

The problem with this ideology is the biological truth males have faced: They were and are propelled by biology, and especially the circumstance of exponentially increasing population, toward dominance and mechanism—a world with billions of people in it competing for resources is one that requires dominance strategies by which to manage huge groups of people without much attention to emotional detail. The males took on and still take on most of this dangerous work, and have done so with cultural scaffoldings in place that make this dangerous work possible. Now, many of those scaffoldings have collapsed, and the confusion falls on our adolescent males.

If you review the list of testosterone-related factors, you'll see that in our present day, we've stripped away most of what little opportunity did exist for emotional development among our males.

- Our males used to have much more spiritual development, and therefore much more emotional contact with themselves and others through the conversation with God. They have little of that now.

- Our males used to have time in their work structures to form intimate relationships with other men and in which to mentor the young. They have little time for that now.

- Our males used to have clear guidelines concerning how to nurture their families and mates, and how to find some emotional sustenance through marital stability. They have far less of that stability and those guidelines now.

- Our males used to seek a depth of relationship with nature, in which they learned not only to hunt the fruits of nature but to transform, like alchemists, the relationships between man and nature into emotional and physical nurturance for whole communities. They have little time for this direct contact with nature's divinity now.

- Our males used to have extended families in which to develop their muted emotional beings. They have little extension of family now. In fact, many American men report having no other people except their wives with whom to discover life's most important matters. If a divorce occurs, a man's access to mirrors for his own emotional development diminishes dramatically.

Testosterone driven, emotionally disadvantaged, males have always had structures to help them compensate for that disadvantage. For good reasons, some of the "macho" structures of "patriarchy" need dismantling. But unfortunately for our boys, not only the dangerous but also the developmentally crucial structures are in vast decay. Between the Industrial Revolution and then the social revolutions of this century, we have thrown the baby out with the bathwater when it comes to helping a testosterone-driven male develop emotionally. We have done the same when it comes to helping the male brain compensate for its emotional disadvantages.

The Male Brain, Sexual Biology, and the Emotional Disadvantage

Simultaneous with the millions of years of testosterone development are the millions of years of brain development. Just as male and female hormonal systems have developed to include significant differences over the millennia, so have their brain systems. We know of seven structural differences between the male brain and the female brain. We will surely discover more as the years go on and we get to know the brain better. As we explore this material now, let's remember that brains exist on a developmental spectrum. Males can possess well-developed qualities of what we call a "female" brain, and vice versa. Not every adolescent male will fit every point we make here. Some will be more spatially or verbally oriented, and some just the reverse.

What are some of the effects of male brain development on male emotional life? How do some of these structural brain differences affect sexual biology and therefore emotional life?

THE SPATIAL BRAIN.   The male brain is hardwired to be better at spatial relationships than emotional ones. There are many examples of this wiring, including the smaller corpus callosum in the male brain than in the female brain.

The corpus callosum is the bundle of nerves that connects the right and left hemispheres of the brain. Since the female's is larger, she is better able to process "hard emotive data"—emotional information that needs to cross between hemispheres to be processed and, ultimately, communicated. In the 1980s, researcher Laurie Allen discovered not only the corpus callosum difference but also that two other brain sections, both of which perform functions similar to the corpus callosum, are larger in women. The frontal lobes of the male brain, which handle many social and cognitive functions related to emotional relationships, develop more slowly in the male brain than in the female brain.

The male brain has been needed mainly for hunting—a spatial activity—and for building/designing—again, spatial activities. Whether we like it or not, that's how the brain still is formed. *This does not mean males can't learn emotive skills.* The male brain is not empty of neurons for processing emotions! It is structured like any human brain to process emotive data.

However, the male brain is structurally disadvantaged in this area compared to the female. For millions of years, the female brain has been better equipped for emotive skills, in large part to take care of children.

Cultures have done everything they could (as we'll see in the next chapter very specifically) to teach young and adolescent males emotional development with depth and care in order to make up for their disadvantage.

This is not something most of us, spending too little time with our boys, do now.

THE OBJECTIFYING BRAIN.   The male brain is tuned to relate to non-emotional objects with less tension than to emotional objects. In other words, part of the male brain's relational strategy, part of how it projects meaning onto entities in the world, is by objectifying them.

Here's what we mean, and here's how this happens. The male brain, as an outgrowth of its spatiality, loves to experience *objects moving through space.* It is primed to hunt, which is a process of following an object that's moving through space and then striking the target object with a projectile object of some kind—an arrow, a rock, even a bullet. Nowadays, most boys don't hunt animals, they hunt balls—basketballs, footballs, soccer balls, baseballs—and all kinds of primitive, primal human objects on video games—dark warriors, ghouls, monsters, etc.

The hunter brain is an object-oriented brain. It is often most interested in the object's place in the scheme of activity the brain is focused on. In the male brain, the deer fits in the object-scheme as prey to be killed and brought back to the tribe for food. The basketball fits in the object-scheme as a means toward a living, if the boy dreams of being a professional, and also as a safe object for self-esteem development, physical skills development, teamwork development, and so on. For the soldier, the enemy on a battle-field fits in the scheme as an object to protect family and nation from.

The male brain does not spend as much time processing the emotional core of deer, ball, or enemy soldier as we might like. If it did spend a lot of time wondering about the emotions of the object, it would not be as effi-cient at fulfilling its function, which is, in hunting, to gain dominance over and, through dominance, to transform the object into something useful to self and community.

The female brain, on the other hand, evolved *toward*, not *away from*, processing the emotional core of the object. Constant and intensive child care (as well as hands-on care of sick, elderly, and disadvantaged) propels a brain structure to evolve toward in-depth emotive processing. The child is not an "object" to be transformed into food for a tribe. The child is the emo-tive center of life. So the female brain humanizes the object and makes it an object of care, while the male brain dehumanizes objects, making them ob-jects of useful, even abstract, design.

The disadvantage of the male brain in emotional development is pro-found and gets especially exacerbated in a heavily relationship-oriented cul-ture like ours. Here's what we mean.

A BRAIN UNDER PRESSURE.   When female culture directs more of the intimate relationship energy of a society, as it is doing now, the male brain appears less and less adaptive, and thus more pressure is put on a brain that often simply cannot conform to that culture's demands.

In our long-term development, we have been moving toward more and more emotional closeness between the sexes. Remember, millions of years ago, males mated but didn't even know who their own kids were—so little was male/female closeness a necessity then. But beginning early in this mille-nium, and evidenced in romance traditions like courtly love, then in our Renaissance art, then in the complexity of marriage ceremonies not just for royalty but for all socioeconomic classes, then in the extreme marital codes of conduct in Victorian times, then in the intensity of emotional focus in the nuclear-family experiment, then in the feminist insistence that males emote like females, we've seen an intensified mutation in human develop-ment toward emotionality as a highly valued trait.

The male brain is still far behind in the development of these traits and is under increased pressure to catch up. With most of the old processes for this catching up—big extended families, intense mentoring, in-depth spiritual life—unavailable in contemporary male adolescence, and new processes (coeducation, sexually focused media) still nascent and/or rife with stereotypes, our adolescent males are abandoned to being, and knowing themselves to be, emotionally immature. Their self-esteem plummets when emotional manipulation by females begins.

CORTICAL ACTIVITY.   The female brain has more gray matter, the active brain cells that perform thinking, than the male brain does. Furthermore, according to Ruben Gur of the University of Pennsylvania, whose MRI brain scans are revolutionary, the rate of blood flow in the female brain is faster, and electrical activity quicker, than in the male brain. The female brain activates both sides of the brain more often, while the male brain "lateralizes" more often—i.e., restricts activity to one side of the brain (hence males may look at computer or television screens and not hear what spouses or parents are saying). Gur says about brain activity, "Women run hotter and are more revved up."

With their increased blood flow, higher gray matter content, increased electrical activity, and more dual-functioning brain, adolescent and adult females on average score higher on communication- and social-skills tests than males, and higher on emotional-recognition tests.

The male brain, over the millennia, has adapted to its natural cortical deficiency in a number of ways. Dominance behavior patterns are one way: behavior strategies in which the male forces others to behave as he behaves. The male brain, wired for single-task focus and testosterone driven, lives in an inherent insecurity. But hierarchy and dominance patterning seem to help the male manage. Often he feels secure when he can control conversation, emotional flow and therefore brain activity, molding his environments to fit his brain systems. The problem, of course, is that emotionality is inherent in environments, as well as in the male brain, and to use dominance patterns is to create a modicum of personal neural safety but also relational disadvantage: conflict both in others whose emotions are shut down by the male dominance and may rebel, and conflict in the male self, whose emotions are shut down but want to breathe.

It is essential that we understand the depth to which basic emotional insecurity is a given in male life—insecurity as to whether the hunt will result in the acquisition of prey or failure to feed his people; insecurity as to whether the competitive game system will result in success or failure; insecurity as to whether he will survive the war at all. In each case, emotional risk is high and frightening, especially the risk of failure. The male brain system is emotionally fragile and often chooses to avoid emotional stimulation; meanwhile, his testosterone compels him to take huge physical risks and the social/professional risks of climbing corporate ladders and dominating fields of play. *There is, thus, a deep conflict in the male between innate fragility and outward aggression.* The heart of an adolescent male pumps with this conflict.

DOMINANCE PATTERNS WITH LOVED ONES.   Parent after parent, especially moms, has told me stories of a son's getting calls from females who, in one mother's words, "know how to walk all over him." Because an adolescent male is not generally apt to discuss in depth (or even know) his feelings about emotional manipulation by females, he stores resentment and confusion, which he will act out over the next one to two decades, mainly against females. He will probably, at some point, fall back on a dominance strategy with the very person he loves and respects the most in the world.

One of the most wonderful things going on these days is that sons and mothers are able to psychologically separate themselves enough for the adolescent son to come to trust his mother (or stepmother) as a female confidante on issues relating to girls and to feelings about how girls relate to him. One stepmother told me about her relationship with her sixteen-year-old.

> *At some point he started cussing when he talked to me, saying, "I don't give a fuck what that guy thinks of me." It took me by surprise but I realized he trusted me more, like an adult friend. So now I tell him I don't like the language, but I don't shut him up. He opens up to me now, especially about girls. He finds me easier to talk to than his mother. One day he told me he wouldn't know what to do if he didn't have me to talk to. I almost cried.*

A mother of a seventeen-year-old told me a similar story.

> *I could tell he had decided to let me back into his life when he tested me with the word "shit." He wanted to see if I could take it. I kept a good sense of humor, and a few days later he apologized for saying it so much. He decided on his own he respected me too much to say it in front of me. Since that day, he's been opening up to me more, especially about the thing that confuses him the most: girls.*

This same mother said something I've heard from so many parents: "Why do people—people who don't have sons—think teenage girls have such low self-esteem? The girls are so powerful, and come after Layne so hard, he just feels overwhelmed."

When we look closely at how adolescent males and females relate, we must look more deeply than the bravado of a male's dominance pattern. The adolescent males I know are, pure and simple, very insecure with females. It comes as a surprise to most of them and most of their caregivers that females are "the weaker sex." When we look at the adolescent male-female relationship from the standpoint of emotive power, the male generally faces a disadvantage of epic proportion.

THE QUICK-RESOLUTION BRAIN.   Especially when relaxed, the male brain tends to seek ways to avoid processing emotive data intensely. Even the way the male handles the TV remote control shows us his brain formation. He is more likely than the female to want to move quickly through channels rather than settle on a particular show. He is also more likely to channel surf toward *action* and *objects moving in space*—i.e., explosions, moving cars or trucks, sports shows—rather than people sitting and talking about social/emotional life.

The use of the remote control is metaphorical of other ways the male carries out this internal imperative. At a party, when conversation about depth of emotion occurs at a table, he is more likely than his female companion to scan out into the backyard for a volleyball game, or for conversation with others, often "the guys," about sports, hunting, work, etc. He does not linger as long as females on one topic of emotional or relational depth.

If he does linger in an emotional-topic area during a group discussion, he is more likely than his female counterpart to seek a quick solution—a quick tension release. The emotional topic creates internal stress, and a solution alleviates stress quickly. The solution, also a function of a problem-solving brain, is often delivered in a style of relating—"Why the heck didn't Sue just walk out!"—that pushes conversation companions away rather than that brings them closer to the male.

This brain wiring (assisted by acculturation) gives the male a distinct emotional disadvantage. Whether it's a TV program or a topic of discussion, he tends toward quickness of action rather than the kind of slowness that allows emotionality to develop. He asserts his style with aggression that can turn others off. He often avoids entering into the emotional conversation at all, preferring more physical action and activity in which resolution is not as confusing.

SEXUAL OBJECTIFICATION OF THE FEMALE.   Males tend to sexually objectify females, by nature of sexual biology (and magnified by our present media and culture), which further retards emotional development in relationships with the female.

In order to become sexually aroused, males must often use internal fantasy. Very often a male is not attracted, at a given moment, to a female; very often he does not have the energy for intercourse when a female does; but his biological imperative to reproduce, and emotional need for sexual and sexually stimulated emotional companionship, is very strong. The human brain has developed wiring to make it possible for him to be sexually active as needed. Fantasy, in which the female is objectified, often as nubile (young and pretty), is commonplace among males and has been, as far as we can tell, since the beginning of human development.

The female reproductive system does not require arousal for intercourse (she does not need to become erect), so her brain system has not needed to develop as much sexual fantasy. Her brain system has developed more of what we call "romantic fantasy" (e.g., romance novels, in which males are objectified as success and power objects).

A huge amount of male emotional development and connection is lost because of the male's hardwired (and culturally amplified) reliance on fantasy-objectification. First, objectification distances him from emotionality within himself, magnifying the sexuality of his object and decreasing the emotionality. Second, it can distance him from the person he loves. An adolescent male whose eye strays to a nubile, scantily clad female risks, often, the anger of his girlfriend. He is considered emotionally immature because his eye has watched the attractive female object move through space. His partner or girlfriend pulls away from intimacy, offended and hurt. Our culture argues over whether he "should" or "shouldn't" look. Much of his "looking" is a quick, nonemotional, sexual-objectification reflex, a reflex that cuts him off from emotional life and bonds.

One college student of mine said something very revealing about this. "I was telling my girlfriend that it doesn't mean anything when I look at someone else, it's just me enjoying a pretty girl. Telling her that is like telling her you've slept with someone else. She hates you for a week. I told her I didn't want to be controlled, I'll look where I want. She called me a kid who can't grow up."

In helping young people understand sexual objectification, I teach them to understand how the brain works before condemning a "look" as immature. I also teach the males to learn to override their "looks" when with mates, and learn that the line between a "look" and a "catcall" is a line never to cross. A quick neural reflex rooted in sexual biology is not the same thing as a sexist dominance strategy. If an adolescent male looks at a nubile female then starts to verbally humiliate her, he has crossed a moral line.

Simultaneously, we are challenged by brain research to see our males more clearly than we do; to notice that the quick synaptic pleasure they get from looking at women is not necessarily a defect. It makes it possible for that same male to perform sexually for a female when she needs or wants him to, even if at that time he is exhausted or unattracted to her. Male fantasy, if managed well, can be as much her ally as his. When something is wired into the brain, making it an ally is better than fighting it. If we don't make adaptations of this kind with our males, his sexual fantasy and sexual objectification are seen only as defects, which cuts him off even more from the love and emotional contact he needs from those with whom he bonds.

WORDS.   A last brain system item we must discuss is the use and production of words in the male and female brains, especially words concerning emotional content. Males suffer a profound emotional disadvantage here.

Two great mistakes our culture has made over the last three decades—mistakes made though our hearts were in the right place—were to define emotional development from a mainly female standard and then to hold adolescent and adult males to that standard. We've said things like:

> "My little boy's as emotional as his sister, but when he starts growing up the culture crushes his emotions." The implication here is that he's, by nature, like his sister, and the culprit in crushing him is a male-dominated culture.

> "Why can't my boys talk to me more?" Talking is seen as inherently proper.

> "Men don't know how to relate." Relating is something women know about and men don't.

These sorts of comments are tips of a bigger iceberg that crushes the developing humanity of both males and females. They indicate an ideology in which (1) it is mainly culture that causes males to talk about feelings less than females, and (2) if males are to be "okay" they must talk more about their feelings. Not to do so is to be profoundly flawed, and is the primary causal factor in relationship distress.

Certainly, an essential part of emotional development for both males and females is the "talking" component. Boys and girls both need more and more stimulation to talk of and about feelings, to express emotions, and to care for emotions of others.

Also a reality, however, is that the female brain is generally superior at basic verbal ability from very early on—girls gain complexity of their verbal skills earlier than boys, sometimes one year earlier. Women use on average five times the number of words in a week that men do. From early on and all the way through life, female verbal abilities, *especially about emotive content*, are on average superior to male.

Among the structural differences between the male and female brains are a number of impediments to male verbalization of emotion, especially in comparison to female. With Ruben Gur's neural imaging scans, we can now see on video what we've intuited for millions of years concerning words and emotions. There's just not as much going on inside the male brain as in the female during the emotional process—the brain is less active in fewer brain centers, there is less cross talk between hemispheres, and so on, creating less verbal expression.

In other external tests, late-adolescent males and females have been asked to identify the emotions of people whose faces have been photographed. Not only do the males on average have less to say about the emotions, they very often do not see subtlety of emotion and therefore do not use words to describe it.

Many married couples will recognize this in "real life." Judith and Jim come home from a party. Judith says, "Did you notice that Millie looked kind of sad tonight?" Jim says, "Really?" Quite often, males will register, process, and discuss in words less emotional activity in a social situation than females. As one young woman, sitting beside her boyfriend, said at a Healthy Youth conference: "Getting him to talk about how he feels is like taking a kid to the dentist." Often we'll notice that a male's production is mainly about thinking and doing, and if you listen closely you'll notice that when males talk on and on it is mainly about projects related to thinking and doing in which they as males were challenged to show performance prowess.

While certainly some adolescent males do access their feelings with lots of words, and while your son may be one of them, his emotive skills are somewhat unusual. Countless moms have told me how they've raised their boys "to talk about feelings" and have ended up with "a great guy, who just doesn't talk much about feelings after all."

In this we are seeing not only brain differences but the effect of testosterone, too. Some boys will be very facile at accessing feelings in words at age nine, and then, by age sixteen, after puberty, will be less so. Testosterone's wash through the body and brain throughout adolescence causes adaptations in the boy's emotional system that cut down the emphasis on feelings and enhance emphasis on projects and activities in his word production.

Throughout time, cultures have known that adolescent males don't access or verbally express their feelings as well as adolescent females, and thus have provided different emotional development paths for males than they have for females. We've known that generally it takes more to stimulate complex emotional responses in males than in females, and so we've used complex social systems quite often to *train* our males rather than talk *to* them.

Now, as we reach into the next millenium, we are seeing a great deal of emphasis on the "talk strategy" and a denigration of other strategies. We've convinced ourselves that the supreme standard for emotional contact is not action but conversation.

In all of our strategic changes there is reason and there will be some growth. But I hope our understanding of brain and biological factors in male emotional development will inspire us to resuscitate—with modifications appropriate to democratic, female-equal, talk-sensitive civilization—the structures of male development—clan life, spiritual life, nature adventure, care-giving roles—on which, quite frankly, our adolescent boys depend. I hope too that we'll see that for many of these boys, talk is more an oppression than a liberation.

Philip

I will never forget the fourteen-year-old Philip, a very "sensitive," quiet, artistic boy who, after his mother left my office, said, "You know, she doesn't realize how much I just tell her what she wants to hear." His mother was a talker and wanted him to be one, too. He tried to respond to her through words but admitted that he "zoned out" after a few minutes of her conversation style—she tended to repeat things and add on tangential details rather than "get to the point." Out of love and respect for her, he would listen, zone out, give verbal and nonverbal feedback that indicated his listening, then tell her, in the end, what she wanted to hear.

When I talked to Philip's mom about this, she said, "But I have a right to talk just as I want to. Why should I change just because my son is bored by me?" Her position makes sense. Yet, if care of the child is most important, efficient communication with sons is often best. When talkative, tangential parents are dealing with adolescent boys, it is essential they realize that should they "go on and on," they may end up being "lied to" by the male. Sitting and listening to detail upon detail feels to him like being in a cage or trap.

We are challenged to look at what is actually going on during the conversation and notice that adolescent males bring their emotions out to us in many ways that often don't need words—a quick embrace; a single sentence or question that wants a simple answer; silent time with us, sitting on the hood of the car, looking up at the stars; going hunting or fishing together; playing a game passionately; experiencing awe and reverence in the face of a summer storm; standing by us, even if at a distance, when we are hurting, sad, or proud of ourselves.

Many adolescent males live the edict "Talk Is Cheap." If your adolescent male is one of those, know that his heart is full of passion but that he may need lots of relationships and activities in which to stimulate that heart, and words may do more, in many instances, to hide it than to bring it out. "Ten minutes of quality time," which for a while was considered the panacea for overstressed families, generally means ten minutes of talk. For an adolescent boy, ten minutes of quality time is probably not enough because he may not emphasize the words in his brain system the way we do. Three hours fishing at a nearby lake will often succeed better.

The Key to Offsetting an Adolescent Boy's Emotional Disadvantage

Having said this about talk, we are not saying that we should stop talking to our boys. We must keep challenging them verbally—through specific, concrete emotional questions and activities (for more practical details on strategy, see parts 2, 3, and 4 of this book). At the same time, let us now reinvent our parenting, mentoring, and educating to realize that perhaps the most profound way we emotionally neglect our sons in our culture is in the lack of *personnel, the lack of people,* we provide for the boy to relate, experience life, and talk with. Especially because boys are so much less emotionally verbal than girls, they need time spent with *more people* with whom to get the chance to stimulate verbal and felt emotion. What do we mean?

Because females have the emotional advantage of being able to talk so much more thoroughly than males, they can get more out of fewer bonds. Males don't get as much emotional stimulation from two or three relationships as females do; they need lots of relationships, surrounding lots of activities, among lots of elders and peers, to get the same quantity and quality of emotional stimulation.

One of the most intriguing and painful facts in divorce literature is the now common knowledge that males seem to recover from divorce trauma less quickly than females. Different theories have been presented, all valid, in my mind: that the removal of the father-male model traumatizes the boy's self-development more than his sister's; that the male child has more difficulty processing his emotions than the female; that his psyche is inherently more fragile than the female's.

In all these theories, the common element is the removal of personnel to help the male. First the father, then the father's elder male contacts go too. The adolescent son won't trust, perhaps for years, if ever, his mother's new mates.

Also, because divorce often happens in a boy's late childhood and early adolescence, when he is beginning his separation-individuation process (the process by which he separates psychologically from his mother's emotional dominance and discovers his own masculine identity), the adolescent male is psychologically traumatized vis-à-vis the mother. He wants to bond even more powerfully with her because of the father's absence, but is equally compelled to pull away from her.

The son of divorce is, thus, emotionally distanced from nearly every person in his roster—father, mother, mentors, father's extended family, and so on.

I bring up this example of divorce trauma because divorce is a crucible in which we can see so many issues rising for young males. One of the reasons why more than three-fourths of the crime, and even more of the violent crime in this country is committed by males brought up by single mothers and divorced women is that males have decreased personnel, and therefore decreased structures and relationships in which appropriate masculine emotional development can occur.

If we were to target in our legislatures and courts any single common denominator in nearly every social problem, we would find that the increase of emotionally bonding personnel in a male's life will solve most of those social problems. Getting an adolescent male to talk with one person more will help, but it will generally not have the profound effect that giving him a plethora of substantial, nurturing relationships will have.

David Blankenhorn, in his important book *Fatherless America*, has made a similar statement about fatherhood, saying that most of our problems would be solved if fathers were valued as they must be. He presents painful teen pregnancy, crime, drug abuse, and sexual abuse statistics and correlates them to the lost father. He calls the lack of father our predominant social problem. His point seems accurate to me, yet with some modification.

Ours is not the first era when fathers have been absent. Since the beginning of human development, fathers have been absent in boys' lives. They have been gone on the hunt, away or dead at war, away at work. Until relatively recently in human history—only ten to twenty thousand years ago— kids weren't clear about who their fathers were anyway.

When the father was gone, other personnel or tribe members stepped in. When the father wasn't known, other males protected and provided so the females and children were taken care of and then, when the young males as a group became "of age," mentored them through the social and emotional challenges of mature masculine life. The edict in the Old Testament that if a man is killed his brother must marry his wife, while hardly palatable in our day, was nonetheless a nurturing strategy required by a society that knew the risks of the lost father—kids running rampant, single mothers overwhelmed and unprotected, future problems for females who marry the males brought up without fathers.

Resistance to Biological Teaching

I hope you will now agree with me that in order for the profound requirements of our adolescent males to be met, and in order therefore for our daughters and our whole society to be better cared for, we will have to reinvigorate our understanding of the biology that affects our males so deeply. I hope this chapter so far has helped facilitate that understanding. In my ten years of teaching male development, I have found everywhere I go that when people resist biological material, our adolescent males don't receive the care they need.

Many feminists, for whom socialization and environment contribute 90 percent to the ways males and females are, present solutions in frameworks that show male structures to be deficient and archaic and female structures to be our salvation. If a person believes that 90 percent of a boy's development depends on socialization, s/he will not accept the essentiality of male forms of nurturance that are not controlled by female imperatives. S/he will not have the incentive to reinvigorate healthy masculine life. His or her idea will be: "Let's just wait it out, make the changes we need to make, modify boys' acculturation so that they won't be so aggressive anymore, they'll talk as much as women need them to about their feelings; and we'll reach our goal of the reinvented male." This type of thinking, while well intended, is immensely dangerous and neglects millions of years of human development.

By the same token I have also met many people from the other end of the political spectrum, who, while agreeing that biology is an essential factor, blame feminism for the plight of our adolescent boys and disallow the obvious emotional deficiencies in male biology, deficiencies that acculturation should exist to alleviate, deficiencies that feminism has helped us delineate and tend to. These people's motto is: "All we have to do is get rid of the feminists who are trying to turn males into females. Once we return males to their rightful place, we'll be okay." This notion, born out of some valid grievances against male-bashing, is immensely dangerous and ignores the reality of our human development over the last few hundred years, in which female and male roles have been changing and thus our biological seeds have been sown in ways we could not have imagined when the Bible was penned.

While being honored for what it is, male biology must be aided in its adaptation to modern life. Throughout time, long before the modern feminist movement in our society, male biology was known for having flaws in emotional development, which spiritual and emotional acculturation have striven to fix.

The reality we face, when we put aside our political ideologies and look into the eyes of our adolescent males, is one in which both male and female cultures have shirked their biologically driven duties to nurture young males. Male culture, especially in the Industrial Revolution, overemphasized the male's biological proclivity for physical labor and economic aggression and neglected the male's biological disadvantage in emotional life, and thus gradually broke down many of the existing structures for male development and emotional relationships that could help the male to develop emotionally. Simultaneously, the culture denigrated female self-esteem so that mothers would be lesser emotional parents to boys, and cut boys off from fathers and mentors by removing the father's work from the farm and the backyard and putting it in factories.

Female culture, more recently, has overlooked male biology in order to serve three primary female goals: reentering the workplace at par; revisioning housewifery, and restructuring males to be easier romantic partners for females. Female culture has encouraged the abandonment (without replacement) of the ancient structures for male emotional development in hopes that males could cleave to female culture and in that embrace become the boys and men females envision in the ideal. As we enter the next millennium, polls are showing greater female dissatisfaction with male-female emotional relationships than existed thirty years ago. Women make more money now and have more freedom, but they too feel emotionally forsaken. Perhaps from that base they can imagine how neglected their emotionally disadvantaged adolescent sons feel in the wake of female culture's disinterest in male biology and thus its forgetfulness of the subtleties of the male soul.

The Male Mode of Friendship

Vince was a man in his forties. He came to see me about a number of personal issues, and at one point we got to talking about his friendships. He described many different sorts of friends, then he described a camping trip he went on earlier in the summer. "I hadn't enjoyed myself with guys like this since my early teen years when Bill, who was my best friend, and I hung out together." His eyes teared up with nostalgic yearning.

Together, Vince and I reviewed his history since middle adolescence. He now had many kinds of buddies—motorcycle buddies, work friends, basketball teammates—but no "friends." He had no one he could talk to in the way he could talk to me, his therapist, about the loops of fear he got into, about the troubles he had at work or with his wife, about his mortality.

"Women are lucky," he said. "They form these intense intimate friendships and get down to the nitty-gritty with them. We men don't do it so well."

Paolo is a Shavante tribesman in Eastern Brazil. During his adolescent initiation process, he formed a "best friendship" with Jose. Jose went to the big city with him, where both of them did not fit in at all and, in fact, feared for their lives. Upon their return to their village, he and Paolo remained comrades. Paolo, at twenty-nine, while telling his story to anthropologist David Maybury-Lewis, stressed how his friendship with Jose had deepened over the nearly two decades, how dependent he was on Jose for his camaraderie, indeed how difficult his life would be without it.

Paolo lives in a culture in which the emotional bonds of adolescence are relatively clear and life relatively uncomplicated. Those bonds hold because boys share the journey to manhood and of manhood together. Vince lives in a culture in which the bonds of adolescence are unclear and very complicated. He moves away from where his friend lives, and the bond of friendship dissolves.

When I ask men like Vince who their best friends are, they invariably answer, "My wife." If they are not married, it is "My girlfriend." If they are divorced and single, it is often "When my wife and I were good together, we were best friends, at least for a while."

While having one's spouse as one's best friend is a wonderful thing, it is also immensely risky for males. Males overrely on females (and females on males), and the overreliance becomes burdensome to both. This overreliance is one of the most damaging aspects of marriage as we practice it these days—our tendency to insist our mates meet the majority of our emotional needs.

Much has been written about women who "love too much." Female overreliance rips autonomy out of the female psyche. Less has been written about male overreliance. If we are to help our adolescent boys make up for emotional deficiencies, we will have to study the dynamic more closely.

Male friendship is fragile in ways female friendship is not because male friendship is often not talk-dependent. It is proximity- and activity-dependent. By this we mean that it relies more on "being together" and "doing things together" than on "talking together." As a result, it is harder to sustain than female friendship. When the war, task, work, or life-period of friendship is over, the friendship is generally over. Conversation is not necessarily a glue.

Furthermore, in our mobile culture, males don't stay in proximity to their best friends, and because they aren't apt to call these best friends on the phone and chat on the weekends, they lose the friendships. Not only is the male friendship process inherently disadvantaged from the female, but our society exacerbates the disadvantage with its mobility.

Adolescent males, especially in middle and late adolescence, develop most of their self-perception and self-esteem through their peer contacts and nonfamily bonds. The most powerful peer contact, in a well-run masculine system, is friendship contact. The most powerful nonfamily bonds are intergenerational mentors who care deeply about the boys or young men.

As our adolescent boys bond more and more with media figures they don't meet and with peer groups in which individual friendships don't get established or, if established, dissolve because a family moves or life distracts the friendship with its various stimulants and activities, they lose yet another source of emotional nurturance, and their lack of intimate male friendships adds to hormonal, brain, and other cultural factors in creating emotional disadvantage for them, emotional neglect.

If adolescent boys invest in peer groups and take on their standards, but don't foment singular relationships through which to criticize the groups, engage in the groups, feel safe in the groups, and develop emotional depth in the groups, their emotional disadvantage continues. The extent to which their parents, mentors, and educators don't protect circumstances of friendship is the extent to which we caregivers neglect our sons' emotional needs.

Often we don't see a problem because the adolescent son forms relationships with girls and young women, a healthy developmental step but one which becomes problematic if various and in-depth male-male intimacies have not gone on: The girl becomes the mirror for the boy, a confusing mirror, one he will overrelate to and/or exploit, unchallenged by his best friends. Often mothers and fathers will tell me stories like this one: "My son met Tracie and the rest of his life was over. She was everything. He hardly saw his friends anymore." Their son is maneuvering through the stresses of adolescent friendship by bonding with a female who will guide his way. Again, that bond is not inherently dangerous, but when we discover that the boy never really found deep friendships without her, we must expect that later, if not sooner, his lack of masculine bonding will haunt him in work or other addictions or in other subtle ways of constantly proving he's okay as a man.

Large parts of the adolescent friendship puzzle are the roles of the elder, teacher, and mentor. The intergenerational "best friend"—Coach Fox, or Mr. Sims, or Dr. Quackenbush—serves not only as a direct mirror for the adolescent male's development, but also as the kind of emotional umbrella under which the adolescent male forms peer friendships. Coaches, teachers, other kinds of leaders are the keystones of relationship development among males in that young males form friendships because the males are brought together through a task set out by the coach (a sport), the teacher (a class project), the leader (a church or other service group). In doing the task under the tutelage of a teacher or mentor, the boys bond with one another, form camaraderies around a single, important task, and the potential for the creation of "best friendships" increases.

Research shows that adolescent males who participate in extracurricular sports are significantly less likely to participate in gangs, drug involvement, and crime. Among the reasons for this finding: Boys and young men bonded together in one task will not need, as much, the bonds of other communities, the altered states that fill in for inadequate self-esteem, and other aggressive activities to prove prowess.

When we do not provide our adolescent boys with elders to become friends with, when we don't protect consistent friendship opportunities with peers, when we allow adolescent boys the massive distractions from the bonding process that overreliance on the media constitutes, and when we push them quickly (or allow them to gravitate too quickly) toward female bonding before they are emotionally ready (e.g., letting them date before they are sixteen or so), we make their emotional disadvantage into nearly an assurance of lifelong emotional immaturity.

Emotional Trauma, Emotional Neglect, and *Your* Adolescent Boy

We have worked hard in this chapter to understand the emotional disadvantage that is both hard- and soft-wired into our adolescent boys. Recalling chapter 1, we noted that while millions of our adolescent boys are suffering actual *posttraumatic stress* as adolescent males, trauma to which they respond with criminal activity, addiction, psychiatric illness, and other disabilities, statistically far more adolescent boys proceed through adolescence experiencing varying degrees of emotional *neglect*. We have argued that the emotional neglect has become an institutionalized part of our social system.

Let us now be specific about exact ways in which emotional neglect and even trauma may occur in *your* boy's immediate family and social system, and about the signs of the neglect *you* may see in your adolescent boy.

The emotional hole in an adolescent boy you know will most likely grow from one of these:

1. Lack of an emotionally nurturing father (he may be abusive or simply unavailable), and/or lack of male mentors who compensate emotionally for the lost father

2. Lack of emotionally nurturing male mentors and role models with whom the adolescent boy is bonded and who augment the emotionally nurturing father

3. Lack of adequate female nurturing in one or more of these areas:
    i. Lack of emotional nurturance from the mother during adolescence and/or insecure attachment early in the boy's life (i.e., infancy)

    ii. Immersion in female subcultures that denigrate the male styles of emotionality

    iii. Immersion in relationships with females that abuse, physically or mentally, male emotional development

    iv. Immersion in relationships with females who simply don't understand males well enough to care for them fully and adequately, especially in adolescence, when the males become physically bigger than and often very different from their caregivers

4. Lack of spiritual development and intimate connection with nature and God (please, substitute your spiritual language), which has been, until recent times, the heart and soul of emotional life to adolescent males

5. Immersion in cultural systems that limit the emotional life of masculinity to mechanical models of self (e.g., immersion in video games and other media that teach very limited stereotypes of masculinity, usually types or models that require the boy to become unemotional)

An adolescent boy who experiences just one of these five may get good grades and try to please, yet is, nonetheless, growing up emotionally neglected. His self-esteem, or "core-self," is a hole he will discover during adolescence and learn, most probably, to conceal until well into his adult life, most likely midlife, until the concealment will no longer be possible.

If your boy experiences two of the five, his hole may very well show itself in acting-out behavior during adolescence itself. We can consider him at least somewhat traumatized by his culture and immediate emotional situation. We will probably want to seek solutions as soon as possible.

If he experiences three, he is probably suffering posttraumatic stress—being emotionally neglected, abandoned, and abused by his culture. We can expect his acting-out to be of danger to himself or society by the time he's twenty-one, though he may wait till later to abandon others or cause substantial damage.

We will most probably see signs of emotional neglect or trauma in one of these five areas:

1. Significantly weakened school performance, accompanied sometimes by significantly weakened athletic performance

2. Withdrawal from close friends

3. Significant drop in communication with parents, teachers, and/or mentors

4. Avoidance of activities that develop the self (family activities, hobbies, clubs, extracurriculars)

5. Significant increase in immoral behavior (behavior the boy knows to be wrong)

We may want to watch also for these accompanying signals:

• In his peer group, your boy tries to be cool and adjusts to his peer group until he is emotionally distant from you. (Sometimes people think it is normal and okay for a thirteen- or fourteen- or fifteen-year-old to be emotionally removed from his parents, but it is not. Perhaps his main emotion is anger toward parents, but at least he is being emotional. When all emotion toward and with parents and extended family break off, we must worry.)

• Your boy tries to perform well in his world and find a "crew," but often, for reasons no one can quite help him see, he fits no crew—he becomes alienated, hiding in his room or in a singular activity, and he may become desperate for attention.

• He uses drugs and/or alcohol and/or tobacco and/or another dangerous substance to a degree beyond normal adolescent experimentation.

• He is watching television and playing video games more than he's doing most anything else.

• He is on his computer more than he involves himself in any relationships.

• He cannot articulate what purpose his life might have, or discuss this issue.

• He practices bravado and posturing to such an extent that he can't carry on most conversations without it.

• He is sexually inappropriate for his age, perhaps to the point of being sexually obsessed.

- He has little sense of self beyond the shoes, clothes, and other modeled objects provided by the media.

- His basic moral character is changing from the way he was brought up.

- He is obsessed with the love of a particular girl (or boy) in a way inappropriate for his age.

As this book continues, we will explore specific strategies by which to care for our adolescent boys. Some of what we'll suggest as solution involves increasing the presence of men and decreasing the presence of women. This is, for many women, including single mothers, a disturbing call to action, and also unrealistic. In many mothers' lives, men aren't available.

I hope if you are such a woman, you will find in the later parts of this book a great deal of practical wisdom that you can directly apply to your relationship with your son. I hope too that the male communities around you will become inspired by your friendship with them, and by the changes that are building in our culture, to reinvest themselves in the lives of your boys.

The Next Step

Part 2 of this book lays out a practical plan for classifying male adolescence into three phases, and provides information, wisdom, and strategies by which to guide your adolescent boy (nine to twenty-one) to become an emotionally vital, socially adjusted man. As we work together to care for our adolescent males, we will end up deepening and enlivening our sense of what adolescence is for males. We will come to know this period of life better, perhaps, than we currently do, and even come to trust and love it more.

Chapter 3 begins that process.

"There is an inherent spirit within all living things to grow and to change."

C. L. PERRY

PART TWO

The Journey to Manhood: The Three Stages of Male Adolescence

CHAPTER THREE

The Crucial Passage

Nurturing the Second Decade of a Boy's Life

*"The information necessary to create a male is encoded
in our DNA, but it takes all the institutions of a culture
to produce a man."*

SANDOR McNAB

The day is hot and dry in eastern Brazil. A group of boys, their bodies
burnished in the sun, move into an open dirt meadow, where they are
greeted by men. Two ten-year-old boys stand together, bonded by
love, anticipation, and fear, for they both have been picked to move into the
next age-set and they know that for the next five years their lives will glow
with growth. They will learn to wrestle with their anger. They will learn the
true meaning of friendship. They will become proficient in hunting and
other earth arts by which to transform the world of flora and fauna into food
for their people.

They will learn the codes and rules of conduct for relationships with females. They will intensify their knowledge of how to act with elders. They will
be taken from their mothers and, for a time, from any females. They will
learn their responsibilities, their roles, and the room they have for independent action. They will become indoctrinated into an interpersonal
method of dealing with others in which to feel safe and challenged the rest
of their lives.

They will also be provided with directions for their destiny. One of them,
Paolo, will be told by his grandfather that he must make the seven-day jour-

ney to the big city. Paolo will make it a part of his adulthood training, accompanied by his friend Jose. He will nearly lose himself in the big city, and return frightened and more committed to his humble and empowered place in the village than he was as a boy.

The story of Paolo and the Shavante is captured beautifully by the PBS series "Millennium," in which anthropologist David Maybury-Lewis committed to film six hours of interaction between tribal and modern culture, roaming all over the world and finding an immensely diverse cross section of stories of girls and boys, men and women, finding their way through life's passages. In his story of the Shavante is the life of a boy, then a man, Paolo, who must be taught, through whatever means, even loneliness in a huge city, who he is, what he's here for, and how he can be of service as a man to both his loved ones and his humanity.

This circumstance of adulthood-training or "initiation" could take place, with minor variations, in Native American, African, Central Asian, South American, European, or any other culture.

Throughout the last few thousand years of our Western and Middle Eastern history, a small group of people, the Jews, have served as a kind of template, or magnet, for many of our greatest fears and our greatest accomplishments. This group held some clear political power for a small time, then became nomadic. Among them, the raising of sons was a richly complex maneuver of time and energy. The residue of that maneuver exists in synagogues today.

A boy is taught to read a sacred book, a book written by the tribe's one God. He is taught this skill in a concerted way by one primary male elder and a secondary set of male elders, including his own father, over a period of one to two years. At the finish of this teaching, a public trial is set for him in which, in front of the community, he must prove his intellectual prowess by reading from the sacred book and singing its song. Once this public occasion is successfully complete, he receives gifts, one of which is the mantle of "man." Despite receiving this mantle, he is tested on the material in this sacred book over a period of the next few years, often by his father, often by his teachers, and often by his peers. He fully becomes a man once he has children, proves himself in a trade, and/or occupies an important office of leadership in some other way. But he is confirmed as "manhood material" by his bar mitzvah.

Performance, testing, self-esteem building, role-training, self-worth development, social skills, camaraderie, self-sacrifice, honor codes, trade skills, quests, pilgrimages, confirmations, presentations to the world—these are just a few of the goals elders set for youth as they lead them through fields, dusty plains, rituals, secrets, public events, and personal challenges during the second decade of life.

Imagine now a culture in which machines and one or maybe two overwhelmed caregivers do most of the work of parenting. In this culture, the youth feels as if a great Mother and great Father are in argument over the lives of the very soul of manhood. The Father seems to call for performance testings, role-trainings, honor codes, and trade skills—but that Father is strangely absent in body, so his voice sounds disembodied. The Mother calls for a diminishment of what the Father calls for, appearing to be frightened of the Father. Her voice is not disembodied like the Father's, for she is around the boy much more than the Father, but like the Father's voice, the Mother's does not ring completely true: She claims to have little power, but to the boy there is no one more powerful.

In this culture the boy comes to rely more and more on his peers, both male and female, for direction. He knows that he and they are pretending to be adults long before they are, and this pretense at first troubles him. Soon, however, it becomes natural, and not until he is more than halfway toward old age does he awaken to the fact that he is not a man.

Which scenario is the most effective way to move boys through adolescence? The Jewish model is still practiced among a small group of people around the world but, like the Shavante and other existing tribal models, it is not one that will become universal for contemporary adolescent boys. While each tribal model has much to teach the monolithic mainstream culture we all live in, they generally have the most success within their own tribe. It comes as no surprise to anyone if we say that the contemporary American model serves some kids well but is also both incomplete and often dangerous for most of our adolescent boys. Chapters 1 and 2 have shown the "facts," and we each have experienced our adolescent males' emotional and social confusions.

When I talk to both adult and adolescent males about becoming men in the contemporary American model, comments like these generally prevail:

"I became a man through sports, though I still don't know what being a man is supposed to mean."

A Fine Young Man

"I became a man by deciding I was one in my late twenties."

"I'm becoming a man. I guess."

When I ask for specific examples of how the adolescent is now becoming a man, I often hear:

"I don't know."

"I'm working hard at school. I'm not partying now as much as in high school."

"When I had my kid, I guess I became a man."

"I became a man when I got my driver's license."

What is a crucial passage in the lives of the Shavante, or among many Jewish peoples, or indeed for all of our own ancestral cultures, has become a vague passage in our time. We are a monolithic culture with fragments of useful details by which to train our boys to become men, but few fully developed models.

Anthropologists have for some time now noticed our de-emphasis on complete and effective nurturing of adolescent males. Psychologist Erik Erikson, in the 1950s, compared numerous cultures, showing that each society trains its kids into adulthood in some very similar ways—by providing incremental rewards for each step of adulthood attained—and found our culture's attention to specifics of adolescent development already in flux. During the 1960s, that flux became a flood. Adolescence became a time to rebel, to find one's freedom from restraints. While in all cultures it has included time for experimentation and "sowing wild oats," there has never been a culture in which male adolescence has been given as much liberty from moral restraint, social expectation, and spiritual direction as in late-twentieth-century America.

In his book *Manhood in the Making*, anthropologist David Gilmore studied numerous cultures worldwide and came to define adolescence as "step-by-step sequences of growth which, when traversed, confer upon the individual simultaneously a sense of self and a cultural identity appropriate to his or her time and place." Adolescence, in Gilmore's view, exists as a time for the community to unite in order to build the individual *self* of the boy, and also the boy's *contributory path* in his society. In our contemporary culture, however, adolescence has become a time in which it is believed that the self of the young man will develop *on its own*, without much specific tribal direction from elders, and the young man's contributory path in the culture will manifest itself to the boy *if tribal directors would just get out of the way*.

For two generations now, this hands-off approach to male adolescence has prevailed. We stand now in realization of both the nobility of our experiment and its dangerous flaws. As gangs of adolescent youth tribalize themselves in search of adolescent development they are not receiving from the culture at large, we notice our own youth teaching us our mistake. As we continually deepen our understanding of male testosterone, brain systems, and culture, we notice how crucial it is for adolescent boys to receive a lot of attention, structure, discipline, goal-focusing, moral direction, and spiritual growth—all of which require effective community models for male adolescent development. The need for adolescent direction is hardwired in our boys.

Ironically, we now see that our culture is the very kind of culture in which effective adolescent-development models are *more* necessary rather than less. Technological, social, cultural, and economic diversity *increase* the necessity to attend, in effective structural ways, to a child's adolescent development, because the more diverse and complex the culture faced by the child, the more help he needs in order to learn its ways.

The anthropologist David Maybury-Lewis paints a revealing and haunting picture of the life of a contemporary adolescent male. He asks us to picture a wide-open field and lots of people in it. If we look at the field from a cliff above, it looks like all the people are free—they move about as they wish, they talk to whomever they wish, they seem to think whatever they wish. But if you're one of those people down in the field, you feel freedom for only a little while, then you realize you have no real direction, you are aimless, you have no in-depth experiences to share with the people around you nor a deep language in which to share them. Your life is busy, but purposeless. From far above, your movements feel like freedom. From within your life, you feel lost.

Redefining the Purpose of Male Adolescence

When I talk to parents and educators about our understanding of male adolescence, one question almost always arises: "I already have so much on my plate, how am I supposed to now focus on male adolescence the way I know I want to?"

Each of us is overwhelmed by our culture. We are overwhelmed by our lives, our children, all the changes we're living with, our responsibilities, our own hopes for personal development, the sacrifices we have to make just to survive. How are we also to take on the task of redefining male adolescence?

The rest of this book provides a number of strategies for taking on the task and making it a rich, rewarding adventure. This adventure begins with our joining together to become very specific about the *purpose* of the years nine to twenty-one in our boys' lives: *The purpose of male adolescence is to activate in the male the ideals of manhood, ideals to which he will commit, by the end of adolescence, to follow the rest of his life.* A boy who learns a set of manhood ideals becomes a man. A boy who does not, wastes his adolescent years, and he will, in some way over the next decades, lay that waste at everyone's feet—in violent behavior; in an inability to fully commit to loved ones; in early death, suicide, or avoidable physical and mental disease; in ongoing self-esteem difficulties; in addictions.

To become immediately practical about accomplishing the purpose of male adolescence, let's list ten specific goals. Let's keep them in mind throughout our effort, in this chapter, to redefine male adolescence in depth. They are not the only goals of male adolescence, but they are ten foundational goals. Strategies for meeting the goals will be presented throughout this book.

Specifically, the years nine to twenty-one exist for the adolescent male to learn:

1. Social codes of commitment, for instance to his family

2. Emotional intelligence necessary for adult life

3. Personal independence

4. Exploration and adventure

5. A spiritual role

6. Vocations and avocations

7. Personal attractiveness

8. Moral character

9. Toughness and tenacity

10. Adaptability and flexibility

In the ideal, a male in our culture will have gained the ability to accomplish these goals by the time he is in his late teens or early twenties. In other cultures, for instance, in India, where I spent some of my boyhood, he needed to accomplish most of the goals by the time he was in his middle teens.

I have gleaned these ten goals from studying our own and many cultures, and also the history of male adolescence, which is a fascinating account of males adapting to their world. As our culture takes the next step in redefining male adolescence, we are, literally, "making history."

A Brief History of Male Adolescence

For millions of years, males were led to accomplish the ten goals through various forms of a quick adolescence in which they learned rules and skills— training, unrefined and uncomplex by our standards. They learned spiritual appeasements of gods; they learned rules for dealing with the other sex; they learned social-communication rules; and they learned their trade, mainly hunting. Most of them knew how to hunt before they hit puberty.

As human culture grew, their learning process became more complex. They learned to kill not only animals but other humans, and they refine that skill to this day, not only in their play with swords and guns but in their constant attention to media that overfocuses on training killers. They learned more complex reproductive rules as polygamy and monogamy became the rage between about 100,000 and 10,000 years ago. They learned different spiritual visions, moving from worship of animal spirits to more abstract entities.

By the time agricultural civilization had taken over, moral codes became the basis of male upbringing. These were presented by or ascribed to a monolithic god, one who encompassed all other powers—Yahweh, Jehovah, the Infinite, Spirit, Brahman, Allah. Creation myths, behavior codes, and cosmological predictions got immortalized in sacred texts that laid out the rules of masculinity. These rules were never written before in the way the Bible, the Bhagavad Gita, and other primary religious texts recorded them. Male adolescence (as well as female) became institutionalized around these sacred code-texts between about 3,000 and 2,000 years ago.

Refinement and modification of these codes and institutions continued for hundreds of years, through many religious conquests and reformations. Religions held most of the moral coding of the culture, and so males were initiated, at least in large part, in a religious context. After the Middle Ages, other social systems began to take control of male life—universities and schools not affiliated with religion, for instance. Most males were initiated in the context of job and work, and most jobs and work were agrarian and of individual mercantile varieties. Unless they went to war or away to explore, males lived near, and were initiated into male codes by, close family members—in adolescence, by male family members, whether dad and/or extended-family males. Male roles, like female, were relatively limited in comparison to our contemporary, idealistic standards.

Industrialization, a science-based/technology-driven way of life, gradually revealed how limited masculine and feminine roles were to such a great extent that early in this century, cultural revolution began. We began adapting away from strict, encoded gender rules, using the workplace as our primary target of adaptation. Women wanted to work in industries, and now, in the Information Age, are performing many of the kinds of jobs a preindustrial society might have reserved mainly for men.

As human adaptivity has continued into this century, the rigidity of the old rule-making texts for adolescents came into question. We are in the center of that questioning now. Our males, born with the same brain structure and biochemical system as their hunter/gatherer and agricultural ancestors, needing the same profound sense of self-discipline, social importance, and spiritual security, nonetheless have no clear masculine code by which to live. The "masculinization" of the male (the development of adult male "masculature," the development in psychological terms of a masculine core-self) does not now occur universally by the time males reach adulthood. Many of our boys—certainly a majority, in statistical terms—do not develop enough of an adult core-self during the adolescent years to be truly called an adult by age twenty-one. Many cannot truly be called adults until they are in their forties.

The Core Self

When we talk about a male's "core self," we are referring to his in-depth understanding and acceptance of his own character, personality, adaptability, and social place. A boy develops a strong core self by being well taken care of by his parents and other caregivers. He comes to feel good about himself and feel secure in his place in the world. An adolescent develops a strong core self by being well taken care of by parents, mentors, and educators, who show him how to take care of himself. That adolescent develops an adult core self by testing what he's learning as an adolescent (and learned as a boy) in the larger world and being rewarded during each test with new elements of identity, autonomy, moral clarity, and intimacy.

Because there is nothing within an adolescent that makes clear when adulthood begins and adolescence ends, he relies on his culture (family, tribe, and clan especially) to tell him that he has become a man. If these parents, mentors, and educators falter in providing secure love and intense training, the core self of the adolescent, then adult, does not fully emerge. The adolescent will not fully become a man, and that lack of maturity will haunt him unconsciously until it affects him consciously. He is someone who will enter adulthood dominating and being dominated by, running toward and running from, lacking confidence in himself and hoping for others to save him from his sense that he is an imposter in life.

Workaholism, alcoholism, marital difficulties, the abandonment of children—these often affect men with undernurtured and thus underdeveloped core selves. When we think about "the ten goals of male adolescence," we are focusing on templates by which to help emerge in the adolescent male an adult male emotional and social body (his *masculature*) capable of uniting fruitfully with his natural physical body's development of an adult *musculature*.

The Second Birth

Since the beginning of history, male adolescence has existed as the time of natural brain, hormonal, and physical transformation (hardwiring) that is to be nurtured by emotional, intellectual, social, physical, and spiritual direction (soft-wiring). When, historically, our ancestral cultures and the world's tribal cultures have focused their energy on the purposes and goals of adolescence, they have called that adolescence a male's "second birth." The first birth, from the womb, was united with intensive years of brain and body development. So too the second birth, during adolescence, is united with intensive years of brain, body, and now hormonal development. Just as a fetus is transformed into a living boy, so the living boy is transformed into a man.

Richard Louv takes this tribal metaphor of second birth right into our own homes, writing in *The Web of Life*:

> *Childbirth is only the first of the miracles. Each growth spurt, each burst of consciousness in my sons, is a miracle. Even my older son's early adolescence, his tentative pulling away, is a miracle of one more birth. Something fully formed is emerging from the cocoon, with unfolding antennae and wet and crumpled wings, reaching back to me but emerging . . .*

A Fine Young Man

So it is with all our adolescent boys, especially in the first half of adolescence: They appear to be emerging from a womb, and we are called to give them direction as they emerge. Just *who* is called to give them that direction? Let us explore this question with care. It sits at the heart of our redefinition of a male's crucial passage. Adolescent boys seek a lot of personnel, a lot of caregivers, a tribe to help them through their crucial passage; they seek the talents and inspiration of parents, mentors, and educators in ways they never have before, and ways they themselves often, unconsciously, resist.

Adolescent Boys Need Clans

We asserted the purpose of adolescence, we asserted ten goals of adolescence; let us now assert the protectors and nurturers of a boy's adolescence: *For the adult male core self to fully emerge, the adolescent male needs a clan to lead him through adolescence.* Wherever the boy and whatever the features of his culture, an adolescent boy needs a clan of caregiving personnel to help him through the second birth and into the adult masculature—the core self by which he will not only survive in adult life but flourish with passion and dignity.

In the ideal the adolescent boy needs father, mother, grandparents, uncles, aunts, older friends, mentors, coaches, teachers, friends, compatriots, legendary figures passed down in family lore, relatives alive in pictures and even perhaps old videotapes, brothers and sisters of many kinds, either blood or nonblood, cousins, partners, provocateurs, challengers, initiators. These people—living, breathing people—are his clan members. When we say "clan member" we do not especially mean some media figure or sports figure the boy doesn't know at all, has never met, has never been "intimate" (shared affection and respect) with. Those figures will become role models to him as and when he himself bonds with them, but if they make up the bulk of his "clan," then his clan is made from virtual reality, not the real world in which he lives, thus its lessons don't create much long-term confidence in the boy. And though the son may have a biological link to an absent father, the father who sees him once a year barely qualifies as a clan member. Nor is a clan member a Jesus or Moses or Allah or God unless the boy and his immediate family have made them so.

A clan member is a person or "entity" or spirit or model who loves the adolescent boy.

For the boy's core self to develop, he must not attach just to Mom or one or two other caregivers. For it to develop fully he must attach to his tribe or clan, and they to him. Anthropologists have watched for centuries how males and females tend to form groups. While females tend toward pairs and tri- ads, males tend toward fives and tens—sports teams, "gangs" to walk down the street with, hunting groups, and so on. Males who don't have a larger, nourishing group—whether filled with blood kin or nonblood kin—have less ability to prove themselves, something they are biochemically, neurologi- cally, and culturally wired to do, especially in adolescence. Males (and of course females, too) flourish when loving clans, mentors, and friends help them along. The less clan the child has, the more isolated s/he feels. Despite the stereotype of the "loner" male, in fact it is a rare adolescent male who doesn't naturally and instinctually seek a trustworthy clan in which to be loved.

Given what we know about male brain development and the paucity of words so many adolescent boys live in, it is even more essential that we give them clans to relate to. Without clans, they have few people in their lives who can stimulate self-development that is not dependent on conversation with one or more parents.

If the boy has a clan in place before he enters adolescence, he'll ma- neuver adolescence much more easily, suffer less emotional disadvantage, and, most likely, become a man on schedule—i.e., by the time he's in his early twenties. If a boy has no real clan in place before he enters adoles- cence, he's very likely to go out and find one that consumes him, tribalizes him, redirects him, even brainwashes him—a formal gang, a peer group that disaffects him, a cult, a media obsession, If he has no real clan in place by the time he's ten, he's more likely to become a "problem adolescent." If he has no real clan in place, he's more likely to suppress some key part of his core self, if for no other reason than that he could not develop a relationship of love and respect with someone who could recognize that hidden treasure in him and help bring it out.

The Masculine Nurturing System

One of the areas of deepest confusion in our culture today is the role of men and masculinity in the raising of children and nurturing of human culture. This confusion has deeply affected the development of a clan to nur- ture each individual adolescent male. Men opt out, and are pushed out, of child and adolescent care.

However, if a clan is essential for the healthy development of the adolescent boy, a masculine nurturing system within that clan is even more essential.

In order to build a new design of adolescent development for our males, we must retrieve and refine one of the primary nurturing structures in male adolescence: the masculine (or male) nurturing system. By this phrase we mean a nurturing system, male-driven, in which discipline, morality teaching, and emotional sustenance are provided *by* males, *for* males. We mean elder men, with women alongside, helping high-density male groups—as in a classroom or sports field or community program. We mean older boys nurturing younger boys in male peer groups. We mean younger boys seeking both challenge and kindness in environments full of male energy. We mean fathers, male mentors, coaches, teachers, older boys, grandfathers and other older men, male leaders, male role models, male heroes, male sports figures, and male peers.

We do not mean that women are unimportant in the clan. They are and always will be essential. We mean simply that there is a lot women can't do, especially when it comes to adolescent boys. There are some things men must do, and for men to start doing them again, all of us, including women who are afraid of or hate men, must open up the culture again to the sanctity of the role of masculine nurturing systems in the lives of adolescent boys. To open ourselves again to it, let us understand what we mean by *masculine nurturing systems.*

Any social system dominated by the presence of males is technically a male or masculine nurturing system—two or more males together are going to form some sort of bond and through that bond nurture each other. The long-term, in-depth social usefulness of the male nurturing system depends, however, on the variety and multigenerationality of the male personnel. For instance, without elder men involved—fathers and mentors—the nurturing system is male in population but its ability to nurture males in the goals of male adolescence will be very limited. Perhaps it can teach toughness and attractiveness, things peer males are good at teaching one another, but it will probably teach little of depth regarding social codes and family commitments. Perhaps it can teach an avocation, but the boy will never get enough stimulation from vocational elders to learn a real vocation. Boys can't nurture boys into men.

One of the most profound functions of the male nurturing system shows up during the difficult times in middle adolescence. Adolescent males need multigenerational male nurturing systems during the years of "adolescent rebellion," when it appears elder males are despised by the fifteen- or sixteen-year-old. In fact, the elder males exist during this time as the wall to push off of, a job in masculine nurturing systems that is just as important as the job of hugging a boy who has fallen and needs embrace.

There is a wonderful African saying: "The mother has the boy for the first half of his childhood, the father for the second." Our boys are like boys in Africa or anywhere—they will, somewhere toward the end of the first decade of their lives, begin moving with full force toward male systems. Even those boys successfully raised by single mothers gravitate toward male peer groups and hunger for elder male attention. This is hard-wired into our boys in the same way that our girls are wired to seek female role models. About her fourteen-year-old son, one mom, a *Baltimore Sun* reporter, Susan Reimer, said pragmatically: "What I say these days means nothing to him. He just wants his dad now."

The son's growing need for more intrusive, more omnipotent male nurturing systems as adolescence begins is a difficult one for moms, and each mom has a different response to it: some deny the need for elder males; others acknowledge the need and feel isolated, in our culture, from available males. The mother's inherent difficulty in any culture is one of the reasons why most tribal and ancestral cultures inculcated some form of forced separation of boy from mother as adolescence began. It was believed that if the boy and mother are forced apart, and that "apartness" is sanctified by the culture, the mother won't have to feel so much of the guilt moms feel when they have to let go of sons—"Did I do enough?" "Am I still responsible for him if he fails or gets hurt?" With forced separation, the mother knows when her time is up and when the men now become responsible. This is good for the mother, and it is good for the men. The men are forced to do their full job. Among some tribes, like the ancient Hopis, boys live in male encampments for months, even years, as they move through adolescence.

The boy's hardwired drive to engage in masculine nurturing systems is hardly supplied software in our culture. These days, the lack of time and responsibility that adult and fathering males have and take, and the plethora of social attacks on male nurturing systems have combined to injure male adolescent development. Because male nurturing systems are in disarray, more and more of our adolescent boys are either traumatized or emotionally neglected. It is useful to consider a male who grows through adolescence without a strong masculine clan in place to be "developmentally disabled." His core-self development is derailed by the lack of the masculine nurturing system in his life. It would be similarly derailed if he had no female nurturing system either, so the presence of elder men is not to be considered the only essential element. In our culture, however, we see far fewer cases of adolescent males traumatized, neglected, disabled, or derailed by lack of intimate female nurturance than by lack of intimate male nurturance. Our culture's economic stresses, family breakdowns, and forgetfulness of the developmental needs of adolescent males have made it one of the only cultures on human record that gives adolescent males so little intimate nurturing by elder males.

When we do give the attention, the results are quite amazing. When fathers are in the home, for instance, as David Blankenhorn, in *Fatherless America*, showed us, both our boys and girls are less likely to suffer poverty, bad grades, high-risk behavior . . . on and on the list goes.

Big Brothers and Big Sisters of America, which serves children of single parents, commissioned a full-scale independent study in 1995, which showed that boys who go through their program test out better than their peers on every indicator, including academic achievement, emotional maturity, job security, and self-esteem. They were less likely to use drugs and alcohol than non-BBBS peer youth, less likely to hit someone, missed fewer days of school, felt more competent, and felt *more* bonded with parents and other primary caregivers. Additionally, boys who went through BBBS programs were less likely than peer youth to feel peer pressure. Therapist Terry Trueman commented on this finding: "Adolescent boys have to know that they're at the center of the lives of one or more men they respect. If they know they're at the center, they'll be okay."

The Boy Scouts of America commissioned a Louis Harris & Associates study to discover the effects of Scouting on participants and alumni. The results: Scouts with five years' tenure—i.e., who continued scouting into adolescence—were more likely than non-Scouts to graduate from high school (98 percent, compared to 83 percent), graduate from college (40 percent, compared to 16 percent), more likely to assume a leadership role in school, more empathetic to the needs of others, more able to make difficult decisions of integrity, more likely to value the natural environment, more likely to earn higher incomes (33 percent, compared to 17 percent, earned incomes of $55,000 or higher), less likely to use drugs or abuse alcohol, less likely to turn to criminal behavior. Former Eagle Scout Terry Howerton, who spent his entire adolescence in the Scouts and who now runs *Scouter Magazine*, put his experience in simple terms: "I attribute much of the man that I have become to my days in Scouting . . . Many of the most successful people in this country would echo that sentiment."

In educational environments, masculine nurturing systems show very positive results. In New Jersey, male-only classrooms had fewer discipline problems, lowered at-risk rates for boys, and showed greater academic achievement. In her 1992 study, researcher Marie Tickner found that there were fewer discipline problems in boys' schools than coed schools—a conclusion that negates the unspoken cultural assumption we have that when boys get together they'll create more problems. Educator and researcher Cornelius Riordan, in his study "Girls and Boys in School: Together or Separate," found that in many boys' schools the level of learning was higher, the climate of values more substantial, and academic achievement more emphatic than in comparable coed schools. This finding is important especially in the face of the fact that adolescent males are falling so far behind adolescent females in academics.

The military, for all of its high publicity and reprehensible power abuses, remains one of the most studied institutions among male nurturing systems and one of the most successful at decreasing at-risk male behavior and male criminality, refocusing male energy, raising fine men, and protecting our culture. Male sports activities change boys' lives. Sports advocates point to studies and surveys that show that boys who participate in extracurricular sports are twice and sometimes three times less likely to take drugs than boys who do not.

The reinvigoration of male adolescence as a crucial stage of growth requires that we reevaluate our attitudes toward the kind of care males give and can give to our adolescent boys in our civilization. Often, it won't always be the kind of care a woman or groups of women would prefer.

A recently divorced mom came to me, hoping I could convince her ex-husband to stop teaching their son about hunting and firearms. It turned out, however, that this activity was one in which father and son not only bonded but transmitted to each other some of life's deepest lessons.

Another mom, who had been single for some time, told me about how she wanted to pull her son out of basketball practice when she heard the high school coach's authoritarian attitude and voice. "It seemed to me he treated those boys with no respect at all. Just because the boys were in high school, it didn't seem to me they should be treated like they were in the military." When she confronted the coach with her misgivings, he asked her to get out of the way of his work. She pursued it to the principal. What she learned from the coach and principal and, finally, from her son was that the son felt at home in the harshness. It frightened him, too, but he welcomed it, for it challenged him to become a teammate, not just an individual, conditioned him to learn respect, and helped him to get ready for the even greater pressure of living life, both on the court and off.

A father quite affectionately recounted a list of chores his wife wanted him and their son to accomplish. Eventually (later than she wished!) the chores got done. More important, from the father's point of view, was the "value of puttering with my son." While puttering around, such important notions as whether the son thought the father stuck his tongue out like Michael Jordan or what kind of screwdriver was needed for a particular job got well resolved—silly and small pieces of puttering that, in total, built a bond of love between father and son that ultimately meant much more to the mother than their finishing the chores quickly.

As we embrace the immense strengths of masculine nurturing systems and the men within those systems, we treat all female points of view with respect, but simultaneously we come to rely on men again to raise our adolescent boys. It is, after all, very much their job. In order for them to do their job, and in order for masculine nurturing systems to be refined for use in the contemporary world, cultural attitude shifts will have to occur in which, for instance, girls don't sue to join the Boy Scouts but instead Girl Scouts are better supported so that both girls and boys have their own places of development. Economic and structural shifts will become essential for families. More divorced women will have to give custody of their adolescent sons to their ex-husbands, more court decisions and social pressures will have to support the husband's claims to adolescent males, and in intact families more women may want to return to workplaces during the sons' adolescence so that fathers are more free to spend time with the boys.

Recently I took my children to get a snack at a cafe and met a woman who recognized me from *The Wonder of Boys*. "My husband," she said, "tries to tell me things about raising our two boys that he can't really explain. He'll say, 'Just trust me, honey, I know this will work.' Often they're things that seem so strange to me, raised in a home of three girls. But usually he's right. As I read your book I finally found reasons in the brain, in biology, and in male culture, reasons for these things my husband is so good at suggesting but so bad at explaining. I've come to the point where I know more than I can handle about how we *women* do things. I'm hungry to know how *men* think about their kids. I have two sons, no daughters, and I know that unless I understand this stuff about males a lot better, I won't feel like a good mom."

What an honest voice in the center of a time in our civilization when life is so confusing. Her call to herself is, I believe, a national call to reinvest ourselves in understanding the masculine and the masculine nurturing systems males create. We are just opening the doorway again into a fascinating world that, despite our rhetoric to the contrary ("We know all we want to know about men, it's women we need to learn more about"), we have in fact never really understood. Opening that door does not close women out; it makes their lives easier. It does not rob women; it spreads the responsibility.

We have experimented over the last few hundred years with taking adult males far away from their children into workplaces that often sap males' hearts and souls. We have tried to right the imbalance inherent in industrialization by giving 90 percent of the job of child-raising to mothers and women. Women have rebelled against this, especially when it comes to raising, alone, adolescent boys who are already taller than they are and seem to come from another planet! We are ready now to redefine the way we raise adolescent boys so that men do more of what they were always meant to do, women are not disenfranchised but instead aided and respected, and the adolescent boys grow up into strong core selves, filled with energy, vision, and love.

The next three chapters of this book will detail a program by which to accomplish this redefinition of male adolescence in your home and community. Though we have emphasized here the role of the father and other males, this three-stage program is as much about mothering as fathering.

A Three-Stage Program for Raising Boys into Men

The next three chapters of this book divide male adolescence into three developmental stages and provide information, wisdom, and strategies for nurturing males through each stage. We will discover what happens in the developing male's body and brain as he traverses the years from nine to his early twenties. We will explore how to help shape the interior experience into a positive one, and include specific ideas for communication techniques, discipline, and rites of passage.

Developmental psychologists tend to classify the adolescent half of a boy's life this way:

Stage 1: nine to thirteen

Stage 2: fourteen to seventeen

Stage 3: eighteen to twenty-one

A Fine Young Man

I recently heard the adolescent development expert Jim States, M.D., argue that Stage 3 ought to be defined as seventeen to thirty-five. He argued that because our technology is so vast now, it takes a young person until at least age thirty-five to actually prepare himself or herself for life in the adult world. Some specialists put the beginning of Stage 1 at ten, others at nine, others at eleven. Because so many of our boys are already conscious at nine of adolescent imagery in the media and in the lives of older siblings, and because in some cases boys are experiencing wet dreams at nine, it is a good and logical place to begin looking at our boys as beginning explorers in adolescent life.

Despite disagreements on when to end the third stage of adolescence, and disagreements on when exactly to mark the end of Stage 1 and the end of Stage 2, there is general agreement on the fact that both female and male adolescents go through three stages and that there is a first stage marked by the mental and physical transition out of childhood, a second stage marked by the near full ascension of the body into adulthood, and a third stage marked by the near full ascension of the mind into adulthood. In general, the body begins its change in Stage 1 and perfects it to about 90 percent in Stage 2 (e.g., acne can still last well into the twenties, but the body has basically become a man's by age eighteen); it also begins its mental changes in Stage 1, hones them in Stage 2, and brings them to near full completion in Stage 3.

One of the reasons Jim States argues that Stage 3 adolescence now lasts till thirty-five is his sense that the mind does not in fact move to near full completion by twenty-two, but in fact needs till middle age to do so. I am going to resist his argument in my presentation because I think that while it is descriptively true for some in our generation, it also brings with it significant dangers, not the least of which is this: Should we come to general agreement that it's okay for our young people not to become mature adults until they are in their mid-thirties, we will continue turning out immature adults.

It is essential that we come together to create a staging model for our males (and our females) that *requires* them to become adults by twenty-one. We will not be perfect at it, and of course all of us continue to grow psychologically well into old age. But we must have cultural agreement on when a boy becomes a man; and we must lead boys through the staging process and make them into men before the majority of them marry, enter the workplace in earnest, have children, build businesses and community ideals, and take on the adult burden of caring for all those who need adult care. Letting a male elongate his journey to maturity too far ends up making him emotionally immature, and his emotional immaturity kills marriages, ruins his children, and destroys his own soul.

So we will work with a three-stage process as described above. I encourage you, however, to develop your own inner sense of the stages your boys are going through. Let the one in this book serve just as a model.

The Value of Suffering

Often, as parents lead their boys and youth through the stages of adolescence, I hear, "If I were a good parent, my child wouldn't suffer so much." When mentors, and educators don't say it outright, still many are thinking, "Why does he have to struggle so much?" There is an instinct to protect our children from suffering. There is an instinct to protect our boys from suffering, but by doing so we may not fully serve their core-self development.

Birth is a process of suffering. Our joy in being born is all the more powerful because we have suffered through the process of coming alive. So it is with the second birth of our adolescents, both male and female. Specifically in the case of our boys, tribal cultures have known since the beginning of time that girls automatically suffer as they move through second birth—i.e., when they menstruate. Every month, girls suffer. Boys, on the other hand, have no natural link to ritual suffering. Their birth into adulthood requires a different quantity and quality of attention from its society. It is a rare culture that puts its girls through as rigorous and painful an adolescent initiation process as its boys.

When we help our boys through adolescence, I hope we'll realize the value in some of the suffering we put them through, the suffering they find in everyday life, and the suffering they ask for as they seek to make the second birth. If, always mindful of their fragility, we lead them carefully through the pains of adolescence, we can expect them to live less painful and more joyful lives in adulthood. If we try to keep them from suffering the pains of adolescence, we put them at risk of living very confused adult lives. Adolescence is a time of new discovery, discovery of the adult core self. No discovery of this magnitude is not filled with deeply valuable pains and sorrows. Our job is not to save the boy (unless his behavior really has become inordinately dangerous) but rather to *guide* him through suffering, even if he doesn't notice our guidance consciously, and even if he doesn't always agree with it. Being the parent, mentor, or educator of an adolescent boy is, in my mind, a more difficult task than being the same for a little boy; confronting the value of suffering is a primary reason.

I hope the staging process I present in the next chapters helps you to help your son or another boy in your life experience joy and suffering in valuable ways. The staging process is meant to help *any* adolescent boy. I invite you to join me now as we begin the practical journey of creating a fine young man. Let us discover together specific, concrete ways to love and care for our adolescent boys, ways that honor each stage of change in their lives and ours, ways that challenge the boys to become exceptional young men and us to become exceptional caregivers.

CHAPTER FOUR

Stage 1

The Age of Transformation
(Ages 9–13)

"What do you want from life right now?"
"I don't know."
"What do you need from life right now?"
"I don't know."
"What do you think is most important right now?"
"I don't know."
"What DO *you know?"*
(With a grin:) "I don't know."

WORDS BETWEEN A TWELVE-YEAR-OLD
AND HIS MOM IN A COUNSELING OFFICE

In 1971 my father got a teaching exchange in Laramie, Wyoming. Our family moved from the wet-beach warmth of Honolulu, Hawaii, where we had lived for four years, to the dry mountainous world of Wyoming, where we would spend the next year. It was culture shock of the most powerful kind. Instead of living in a world of kids dressing year-round in shorts and multicolored shirts with no socks and shoes, I'd moved into a world of cowboy boots, long pants, a certain stiffness in the air. Instead of the "aloha spirit," this new world mastered another kind of energy, more austere.

The boys I met as I entered seventh grade were different from Hawaii's boys: Their interests lay more in hunting and lake fishing than in swimming and surfing. They were generally more homogeneous, thus more prejudiced. They intrigued me, and I came to seek their love as much as I had sought the love of my Hawaiian peers; but they found me exotic because I was Jewish. Some of them found my ethnicity reprehensible. I got beat up more than once for being a kind of mouthy, idea-charged, Jewish twelve-year-old who had, I must admit, a little too much attitude.

For most of the first stage of my adolescence, which I spent in Honolulu, then Laramie, then Durango, Colorado, I was a typical boy seeking early manhood—I wondered constantly when it would come, I masturbated a lot, I found girls increasingly magnetic, and found my body reacting physically— sweats, wet dreams, tingles—to my findings; I began to dislike my parents with a strange intensity, yet hated to stray far from their known world; I desperately wanted to belong. Like most early-adolescent boys, I believed that a few key boys would know the rules of the game. Where were they? Who were they? I had to find them.

I had a friend whose name I forget now, a kid who hit puberty at thirteen. To me, he was kind of a man. I wanted his blessing constantly, and rarely got it. He and I went shoplifting, got caught once, ran away. My brother, two years older, paid little attention to me. We feuded a great deal anyway, so I pretended in my heart I didn't miss his shows of love.

When I met the mother and son of the "I don't know" story, I recall looking at the boy and remembering Laramie, remembering myself saying "I don't know" a lot, recalling that I really did know what I wanted—I wanted love, but couldn't admit it. Childhood innocence and certainty were dissolving. A hug from Mom used to bring me such comfort and electricity, and now it confused me a little. A few minutes of talk used to seem welcome, but now I noticed I wanted more control over those minutes; when I didn't get it, I felt a certain laconic resentment. I used to enjoy "looking up" to older boys, even my brother, yet now I felt a deep impatience to be much more than I was. It felt as if I had been asleep in childhood. Now, as I woke up, I needed help more than I knew, or could ever admit to my parents and caregivers.

For their part, my parents weren't well aware of the kind of material about adolescent males that we're looking at in this book. They lived in a time in which when a boy hit ten or twelve, he started to find himself, and the parents, though still setting limits, just let his energy wander around in the world. They were busy and distracted and didn't direct too much the life of their young men. They were Bahai's on my thirteenth birthday, so they didn't put me through the bar mitzvah ritual. Instead of standing before my community in achievement and prayer as I entered manhood, I shoplifted again.

My parents did their best and gave me a life that has led me to where I am. I can only thank them. But I wonder how different my life, my brother's life, and the lives of my friends would have been had my parents and their peers known that Stage 1 adolescents need very special attentions.

Adolescence Can Begin at Nine Years Old

It also would have been very helpful if my caregivers knew how early adolescence can begin. Young males already start to look into the window of adolescence by nine years old, prodded by the media, by older peers, by internal psychological and developmental urges. At nine we are on the threshold of the second decade of life. In recent years, the beginnings of menses for girls and physical sex characteristics for boys have appeared in younger and younger kids. While most kids don't show these signs of puberty till later, more and more do now. One explanation for this phenomenon is that the growth hormones in the foods we eat—for example, in dairy products—have affected the human biochemical/hormonal system.

Even if the boy's body is going through no changes at all at nine years old, it is still a good time to begin making ourselves conscious, as his caregivers, of adolescent development. It is the time to read books, talk to friends, even to talk to him. Many parents will notice that already at nine he begins his psychological pull away from his mom—the normal psychological separation process by which he asserts that he wants to be an adult and a man. By the time their son is nine, many parents notice him talking back to Mom more, or just not listening to her as much.

There are really two phases in the first stage of adolescence. Nine years old marks the onset of prepuberty. A boy's first physical changes mark the start of puberty, which occurs somewhere around thirteen or fourteen. Some boys don't start puberty until fifteen (if their bodies haven't begun the change to manhood by fifteen, a doctor should be consulted). But despite the natural variety of boys' experiences, it's fair to say that by nine or ten a boy's brain is beginning to look forward and deeply into what a man is; by thirteen or fourteen, on average, his body is joining the brain in making the change.

As we explore Stage 1, we'll cover all the material for the prepuberty phase in this chapter and some of the puberty material, and save some of it for the next chapter on Stage 2, since most boys go through the brunt of puberty during the years thirteen through sixteen, a time of overlap between stages 1 and 2. Remember in this chapter and in the next two that *everything* we say has to be adjusted to fit the boy or boys you know and love. Some nine-year-old boys still are focused completely on childhood games. Others are already more curious about girls.

The Formative Years

People often say that the first five years of life are a child's formative years. They say this as if there is no other time period in the child's life that comes close to being as important. This is an inaccurate assumption, for there is a second set of formative years which occurs in a child's adolescence, and it wants to be treated with as much care as the first set.

In general, when we nurture an adolescent male through these new formative years, we observe some primary categories of change in him:

Physiological growth

Hormonal restructuring

Cognitive growth

As you review the material I present on these formative years, seek the inspiration to treat them in the same systematic way you treated your boy's birth and early childhood over a decade ago. As much as possible, it is useful to talk strategy with other parents, mentors, extended family members, and educators in study groups and community councils; to share your fears, confusions, exhilarations, humorous moments with teen boys. *Connect* with others so that you approach this material as a clan approaches the birth of a baby. Helping a boy through the second set of formative years ought to be one of the great joys of living.

In these pages, I won't go through every possible change in the boy's body, psyche, and world; I'll focus on those I think are very important and often missed. Certain other kinds of nitty-gritty information about physiological changes can be found in Steinberg and Levine's *You and Your Adolescent*, one of the best books I've read on adolescent development in general.

By the time the boy moves into Stage 2 of adolescence, the "rebellion" stage, his rebirth will become much more his own business than ours (though, as we'll see in chapter 5, we must remain *very* active in his life), so it's even more important that we notice some of the intricate body, hormone, and brain changes in his chrysalis between nine and about thirteen. This first stage of adolescence is a time when he's less hardened to us. He's less focused on *me* and, as adolescent-development trainer Wayne Pawlowski once put it, "he's less focused on Peers as the primary 'P' in his life. His Parents are most often still the capital 'P' in his life."

What to Expect from a Prepubescent Adolescent Male

(On Average, Between Nine and Twelve)

As we come to notice the complexities of our prepubescent males in the beginnings of a "second birth" or "second set of formative years," it may not be too surprising that our minds think of the wonderful *What to Expect When You're Expecting* and *What to Expect in Your Child's First Year* books that so many of us used during our boys' births. In the same spirit, let's look briefly at what to expect from the fifth- or sixth-grade boy who is moving into Stage 1 of adolescence.

He'll be conforming a little more to his "maleness" and seeing its difference from "femaleness." So this is a good time to go a little more in depth with him on what we think a man is.

He'll be seeking some independence, acting on that impulse in little fits and starts.

He'll develop a passion to belong in peer groups, but he'll also want to feel self-sufficient. These competing passions will create a confusion. He'll resolve it again in fits and starts, sometimes pulling away from parents toward peers, sometimes away from peers toward parents; in each tug and pull he'll be trying to find out who he is in between the two Ps in his life.

He'll seek out opportunities to make his own decisions, and he'll show, in small ways, that his parents don't have the power over his mind that they used to.

He'll do things parents tell him not to do when he's away from home. I remember my parents forbidding me to watch television after school. Of course, I went to my friend's house and watched TV. The more rules parents make for him *outside the home*, the more chance he'll try, over the next years, to break them.

He'll appear to "not need" parents and family, but that is only an act.

He'll need the emotional safety net of the parents as much as ever. He just won't show it as much, as frequently, and as clearly.

School Life

He'll have a little more difficulty handling failure now, especially in certain academic or athletic areas he cares most about.

He'll become a bit more competitive as the challenges of his peers gain new importance.

He'll enjoy taking on responsibility in school as it's appropriate—tutoring another kid in an area he's strong in; being coached to help younger kids along.

He may need a good deal of the teacher's time and even affection.

He'll question authority a little more, especially authority of ideas. In other words, he'll debate things a little more than he did because he'll want to "think for himself." Until his abstract intellect develops more fully, he probably won't be able to out-think his teacher (not till middle to late adolescence), but he'll still try.

He'll disagree with authority a little more also on how he should behave. These disagreements are great opportunities for adults to look at whether they are transitioning with the boy into the next stage of life. The adult authority may want to bend now, bend not toward permissiveness but toward further responsibility on the boy's part. "Teacher, I don't want to do that." "Okay, then, what do you want to do? You have to do something."

He'll want more choice now, and when he's given it he will learn consequences more harshly than before, but grow from the learning in ways he now can handle.

He'll need more challenge now, and less protection.

He'll transfer a lot of his urge for a clan, a social safety net, to the school environment. This is why school, especially the transfer from elementary to junior high, can be so hard. He wants school to be a safe tribal experience, but emotionally it's unknown. We do best when we make sure he has a home/clan safety net well in place so that school can be eased into as the focus of social life rather than grabbed ahold of by the boy because he has little else of a tribal nature.

Peers

As the first-stage boy moves toward puberty, he'll get a lot of information from his peers, information about sex, sex roles, cigarettes, drugs, and so on.

He'll imitate the behaviors of his peers in more major ways than before, wanting nose rings if peers have them, drinking similar drinks, wanting the same shoes (in our very materialistic culture, a lot of this materialistic imitation happens much earlier than Stage 1 of adolescence).

At eleven or twelve, he'll begin some sexual experimentation, with both male and female peers. His mild experimentation with males is *normal,* in fact less worrisome for parents than his experimentation with girls (beyond kissing).

He'll hope to find something of an "important" role within his peer group or clique.

In all this he'll feel the confusion inherent in Stage 1 life: the urge to be in one clique, then another; the sense of never quite knowing where he belongs; the pull to do what parents say but also what peers say.

Our first-stage boys (and girls) experience the confusion more than perhaps any other society's adolescents for two reasons: our family system is perhaps the loosest, the least extended, the least clanlike, so to find the clan in which he belongs, our boys have to go outside the family; and two, our media and its effect on peers is so various and profound that adults can't keep up in many cases.

The solution to excessive media and peer influence on Stage 1 boys is rarely to forbid contact. The solution is most often to provide so profoundly interesting a family clan (even one that includes nonblood "relatives" and friends) that the youngster does not need to wander too far to find most of himself. He can find a lot of it in the clan we make. In Stage 2 it is more appropriate for him to spend less and less time with his nuclear family unit. But in Stage 1, if you are raising a boy who measures 70 or 80 percent of his self-worth according to peer standards, you will probably want to seek help. That is too much for a ten-, eleven-, or twelve-year-old. His chances of causing great harm to himself or others during the remainder of adolescence skyrocket.

Emotions and Behavior

As he moves through Stage 1, our boy will probably become either more boisterous or more subdued, or vacillate between these poles. Perhaps with peers he's more boisterous, but around us, he's a silent lump. Much of this is normal.

He'll become pretty self-conscious about his skills, his appearance, and even become anxious about his behavior.

He'll become more sensitive than before about being criticized, and a little paranoid (in an adult's mind) about ridicule. Much of this he may, if he's stoic by temperament, keep to himself.

He'll develop a kind of introspectiveness he may not have had before.

He'll often surprise parents by becoming more rigid than at seven or eight about tolerating differences. Whereas he used to adapt to any playing partners, now he's just more critical of everyone. His cognitive development is moving forward, and he uses his new cognitive skills to be a little more critical.

He's especially critical of himself, but he may hide it in criticism of others. With eleven- and twelve-year-old boys I like to say, "You're dissing Joe, but let's face it, you're really talking about yourself. It's *you* you don't like." Confronting the hidden self-criticism can't hurt, not much, at least.

While he's going inward, he's also developing some ability to care for others, which may surprise us. He'll become more sensitive to himself and therefore, if well-directed by elders to *see* others' pain, increasingly sensitive to others.

He'll become something of a worrier in general—he'll worry over the years of Stage 1 about everything from the world falling apart to how he's appreciated. If there is a tragedy of some kind in his life, a parental death or divorce during Stage 1, he will take it very, very hard, no matter how he covers up. He's in a very vulnerable emotional state.

He may engage in lots of reading, television watching, or other kinds of activity that secure aloneness and fantasy and provide lots of images by which to measure and find himself.

His Thinking Process, Including His Sense of Values

He can keep his attention on something for a longer period of time now than he used to. This increased attention occurs the more his cognitive changes occur (to be discussed in depth in a moment). He comes to love long-attention tasks. He likes applying his mind to them, his logic, his ethics. He likes looking at lots of alternatives.

He can see cause and effect better now, so teaching him the deeper logics of ethics and morality becomes easier now. He won't accept our saying

"That's bad." He wants to know *why*. It's our job to keep teaching why. Though he won't say "Why, Mommy?" as much as he did when he was a toddler, he's thinking about it far more now.

He is discovering the line between fact and fantasy and needs our help. If his clan doesn't provide the line, his peers will. For instance, he may be involved in lots of fantasizing about violence. If his parents and clan don't constantly show him what aggression is okay and what violence is not—i.e., the line between aggression and violence—he'll learn from peers where the line is. The line peers teach is very often one that allows much more violence than parents or clan want from a young male.

He seeks out one or two good friends to "think" with. Though he may ride bikes and do athletics with them, he also wants to think with these people, reason with them, be challenged by them. He wants thinking mentors now, too.

He's increasing his vocabulary.

He's also swearing a little more now, too. As always, he lives in confusion. On the one hand, he wants sophistication. On the other hand, being smart doesn't always feel as powerful, in a peer group, as using the word "shit."

He's becoming more and more group-oriented, even in thinking, so that he's susceptible to group-think. As much as he's developing his own intellectual powers, he's quite capable of giving them over to a more powerful thinker, even a parental figure who is an authoritarian thinker. Our job is to help him develop his own gifts, not just become a thinking machine in the model of Dad or an "alpha" (leader, usually older) peer. On the other hand, sometimes finding him an alpha peer who will guide his thinking process can keep him away from other, worse temptations. The developing mind of the Stage 1 adolescent is a fragile, powerful, seeker mind. It is a small and beautiful cygnet that has found itself in the nest not just of swans but of carrion birds. Every move we make to mentor it and help it grow is rewarded by later beauty.

In brief, these are the sorts of things we can expect from our nine- to thirteen- or fourteen-year-old before puberty and during early puberty. Now that we've looked at prepubescence, let's dive deeper into puberty itself. Let's continue to profile our growing boy, and as we do so, it's useful for us to remember that we can expect some of his Stage 1 characteristics to expand as adolescence proceeds, and some to contract. We wouldn't want to be wedded to one mood of the boy's, even one idea, vision, mode of his being. In fact, if he weren't ever-changing during puberty, we might want to worry about him. Puberty is a trial-and-error experience. Don't be surprised if your "sweet little boy" becomes aggressive, especially as the physiological changes take place. Don't be surprised either if the "aggressive little boy" becomes more introspective, more sensitive over the next few years. Hormones and cognitive development, combined with social influences, explode the little boy's nature, allow it to experiment with new selves, and help it find its new, adolescent nature. The boy is like ore, and adolescence is a very complex tempering process. Mother Nature looks for gaps in the masculine spectrum and tries to fill them. Hopefully, armed with practical knowledge, we attentive caregivers guide the filling-in process.

What to Expect from Adolescent Boys During Puberty

I met Brenda on an airplane on the way from Salt Lake City to Atlanta. She was a demure woman, blond, a gentle spirit, about 5'6", a native of Idaho heading to Atlanta for a forestry conference. We got to talking about children, sharing stories. She told me about her son, just turned thirteen. "It's starting!" she said. "Puberty's happening in our house like a locomotive. He passed my weight last month. I won't tell you what my weight is, but I'll tell you that he's now 145 pounds. He became as tall as me a couple months ago. He's only thirteen! He's mouthing off all the time, although mainly when his friends are around. When we take long road trips and it's just us, or when we have all the cousins and relatives over for a party, he's more himself, even a little apologetic for how he acts with his peers. But watch out when it's just him and his peers: I'm just his mom—I better get out of the way."

Here is a boy, thirteen years old, as tall as his mother, weighing as much or more. Thirteen years old. This kind of situation is just one of the reasons why mothers used to say, "All right, you men, now it's your turn to raise these boys. They can break me like a twig."

When I asked this mom how she handled the son's puberty, she said, "I try to take nothing personally." Good advice.

When she and I talked about testosterone and its effects on the boy, we agreed that testosterone is like the Nile river running right now through her backyard.

Physiological Changes

When we consider a boy's physiological changes during puberty we think very much about the hormone testosterone, which forces increased testicular size, a deeper voice, body hair beginning mainly under arms and in the crotch, and the most profound physical growth spurt he'll ever experience in his life, one that will last around two to three years. A boy can gain up to 50 percent of his adult weight in his adolescent growth spurt. Testosterone stimulates red blood cell production in the body, which makes ongoing aerobic activity a staple of the pubescent boy's life. The more red blood cells in the system, the more oxygen in the system, so endurance is now much less a problem than before. When you notice adolescent boys running around everywhere, or riding bikes, or chasing soccer balls up and down the field for hours, you're seeing, in large measure, the endurance and enjoyment of red blood cells and oxygen coursing through the system.

The average age when a boy goes through his growth spurt is thirteen to fourteen. It's useful for us to remember that the average girl goes through hers between one and two years earlier. In all the primary parts of the adolescent journey, the female on average matures earlier.

The boy's sexual physiology will change in five distinct steps. He'll watch each one carefully, with wonder, anticipation, confusion, and fear, from the tiny bit of hair and sexual organ growth all the way to full beard, full organ size, and full height. We truly cannot interact with him enough during these years of growth. As we answer his questions and volunteer our time, experience, and wisdom to him, we follow his lead, but we must also just come right out now and then with words that say, "I notice you're becoming a man. My job is to help you. Here are ways I know how to help. You will have to teach me other ways you need my help."

He needs us to talk to him about puberty before puberty starts (which is why sex education in schools occurs in fifth and/or sixth grade). He needs a lot more sex ed from us than the school provides. He needs it especially from elder men. Puberty needs to be put in a physical as well as spiritual context. Later in the book we'll delve more deeply into this subject.

When I was a boy, my father had one conversation with me about sex and my body growth, then another when he taught me how to shave. The shaving conversation was mainly about mechanics. The sexual conversation occurred while we were watching a tennis match on television. It was brief, and I learned very little.

While I was growing up, my body change was one of those areas of freedom and privacy that parents gave kids, whether for puritanical lessons ("Oh, I just can't talk about those things") or social-revolution/permissiveness reasons ("Let kids have their bodies to themselves"). A child is neglected when he goes through early adolescence with only a few hours, in five years, spent on what is, in his life, the most profound change happening anywhere in the world. He needs years of conversation about his body change.

To put in perspective the timeline we have to help boys negotiate their physiological changes, remember that it can take a year or more for a boy's growth spurt to occur, two or more years for his hair to come in, a year or more for his voice to change, three or more years for the penis and testes to grow to adult size. In other words, many years are needed for the adult male body to be fully born. We have to be with him every step, in the same way we were with doctors, nurses, midwives, relatives, and other caregivers to give birth to the boy in the first place. We have many years to accomplish this boy's second birth, not just a few days in the hospital.

More About Testosterone

One of my favorite teaching tools at conferences is to ask the adult men to confess how many times a day they masturbated or wanted to masturbate when they were going through the massive body change. Generally, we end up with an average of one to two times. There are usually one or two men who laugh and say, "Once a day? Try five times a day." And of course there are some men who recall masturbating once a week, or even, though rarely, not at all. ("I was raised a strict Catholic," one man joked. "We *never* masturbated." His grin told all.)

Once a mother of two sons told me a wonderful story. Her husband had back trouble and tossed in bed furiously on one particular night. Her sons slept in bunk beds, but her eldest son, who slept in the bottom bunk, was gone at an overnight party, leaving her younger son, thirteen, in the top bunk. In the middle of the night, this mom left her bedroom and sought some sound sleep in her eldest son's empty bed. Around five in the morning, she awoke to the bed shaking, and some startling sounds. It took her a few seconds to figure out what her son was doing! Mortified, she held her breath, silently playing the role of her sleeping eldest son. When her second son had climaxed, she thought he was going to climb down from his upper bunk. "I just wouldn't have known what to say!" she said, laughing, in retrospect. In fact, her second son fell back to sleep after his early morning masturbation, and she snuck out. He's grown now, and she has never told him this story. She did tell her husband, however, who "couldn't stop laughing. He was hardly sympathetic. 'Welcome to the world of boys,' he said with a grin."

I am truly convinced that the reason religions like Catholicism and Islam have ritualized prayer at various times of the day—for instance, in the late evening and early morning—is to present males with an alternative spiritual activity for those moments when the testosterone is surging. If it's going to surge—which it will do five to seven times a day, and often at those very times—let's give the boy spiritual occupation and discipline.

A boy's interest in masturbation is in self-care, in quick physical tension release, in the new kind of power the body possesses—in many things that need, for the sake of the boy and his healthy journey, to be fully understood and, finally, enjoyed.

The hormone testosterone is like a prime mover in male puberty not only because of the hormone itself but because it washes through the male brain, which is already a testosterone-friendly system. In other words, when we refer to "testosterone" in this chapter and elsewhere in this book, we mean also the brain system set up to receive it. Let's understand the link.

Parents of young boys will say, "Why's my two-year-old boy bouncing off the walls and hitting so much? He doesn't have testosterone moving through his body yet." Or: "I've heard about research saying testosterone *doesn't* make males more aggressive." It is useful for us to remember that though the little boy doesn't have his testosterone yet, testosterone surges in the womb caused a male brain to be formed, and that brain is setting up already for the male to be "male" during puberty, when the boy will experience testosterone surges directly. If people think only testosterone creates aggression, they will say, "What about those people who are aggressive who don't have high levels of testosterone, and vice versa?" The important thing is for us to look at testosterone *and* the brain system when we make "gender" statements about aggression: A high-testosterone male with a "male" brain is more likely to be physically aggressive and pursue higher levels of sexual activity than a low-testosterone male with a more "female" brain.

To realize the importance of seeing testosterone and the brain as united principles, imagine if the brain were not set up to handle testosterone surges that come in adolescence and adulthood. It would be like a car without a gas tank. The gas would just get thrown all over the car with no container to manage it. Similarly, imagine if the female brain weren't set up to handle estrogen/progesterone surges. We would be in a kind of neurological and physiological chaos, the kind nature abhors.

A Fine Young Man

As your boy moves through puberty and beyond, his testosterone increases up to twenty times the adult female's level. He'll bump into things, he'll masturbate, he'll become more physically aggressive than before. He'll see the world in something of a "testosterone wash," as a place of hierarchies and dominance systems and pecking orders. He'll be driven to prove himself. He'll cry less than he did when younger (socialization against male vulnerability and against male tears adds to this biological proclivity). He'll tend to become more territorial. While much of this behavior will become tempered over the next stages of adolescence, much of it also will become only more solidified.

He'll become a teen with, on average, a 40-percent protein to 15-percent body fat ratio. His female peer, who moved through an estrogen/progesterone puberty adventure, ends up with, on average, a 23-percent protein to 25-percent body fat ratio. Is it easier for postpubescent males to lose weight than it is for their wives? On average, it certainly is. Because testosterone is an anabolic steroid, it increases the body's capacity to store calcium and phosphorus, which is the primary cause of the male body's larger bone size (on average) than female. Calcium storage, as we know from studying elderly females, has a great number of effects on quality of life—especially in osteoporosis-risk females.

Testosterone is not something to be trifled with. A culture that does not consciously, carefully, and intricately stage its male adolescent journey through the testosterone years is in some danger. Hormones are brain chemicals.

The Emerging Adolescent Male's Brain

Let's focus for a second on the intriguing brain changes testosterone spurs, changes that create in the adolescent a well-emerged male brain. Of course, since brain activity exists on a male/female continuum, some of what we'll notice happens to girls, too. But you'll discover some things that explain your boys in ways you may not have imagined or understood before. Anne Moir and David Jessel, authors of *Brain Sex*, have this to say: "As children, the way the hormones set the minds of boys and girls apart puts a certain distance between them. At adolescence, that distance becomes a chasm." *Chasm* may seem to some an overstatement; nonetheless, some of the male and female brain differences that kick in at puberty are quite substantial.

Let's look at some examples. We mentioned some of these in chapter 2, when we explored some of the ways the adolescent boy develops emotionally.

Let's delve more deeply now into the development of the male brain system during and beyond puberty. While the male and female brains are well established in kids long before puberty, puberty acts to enhance some of these circumstances:

SENSORY DATA.   Have you noticed that Stage 1 adolescent females often seem to hear better than their peer males? If you watch closely, you may notice that they tend to smell with more subtlety, taste with more subtlety (care more about how what they eat is prepared), even observe more culinary detail (while the males care more about quantity!). You may notice also that the females enjoy more prolonged touch activity and sensation. They like to hug and touch one another more, for instance.

The female brain takes in more sensory data: more sight, sound, smell, taste, and touch data. One reason is the hormone estrogen. It promotes the brain cells to be more active, especially when, during a girl's menstrual cycle, the estrogen is heightened. Testosterone does not heighten brain cell activity in the same way. In fact, it tends to limit male brain use more toward task orientation and sensory data relevant to a specific task, as opposed to heightening general brain cell activity. In other words, a male concentrating on a task might hear extremely well the sounds of that task but might not hear background noise, including his mother's voice.

Often the adolescent male whom we do not think is "listening" is in fact not hearing. Often the Stage 1 boy who seems to be less interested in touching us (hugging us, etc.) is simply not as connected to the tactile sense as we are. Often moms will say, "Wait a minute, my thirteen-year-old still loves to hug me." He may continue to love to hug and cuddle for quite a while, but the chances are that *especially* when his hormones come in, he'll cut back on the hugging, touching, and other tactile activity that is not focused on a task.

EMOTIONAL LABILITY.   The words "emotionally labile" refer to up/down emotional moods. We might substitute the phrase "emotional volatility." Judith is the mother of three sons, seven, ten, and thirteen, and two daughters, twelve and fourteen. "Are you kidding?" she said to another mom at a parent roundtable. "Adolescent boys aren't half as hard to raise as adolescent girls. With my boys, I always know where they're at. With my girls, I never know. One second it's one thing, one second it's another. Their emotions are always on their sleeves. I just tread on eggs with the girls." She was referring to something many parents talk about, the fact that so often a boy's emotional response is less complex than a girl's.

While this statement is a huge generalization, the truth in it becomes clear when we remember how the male brain tasks out its emotional work. It doesn't expend as much neurotransmission on emotional work as does the female brain (on average). So if you have noticed that boys seem more "simple" in their emotional responses, that is a reason why. Combine this information with the up/down nature of the female hormone mix (estrogen/progesterone), and you have a picture of Judith's point of view. While estrogen makes brain cells more active, progesterone makes them more inhibited. Progesterone has been compared to anesthesia because it seems to "put the brain to sleep." A girl can seem "high" one day and then "depressed" the next, especially during the days of her cycle, in which first estrogen may rise, then progesterone.

The boy's emotional cycle is not controlled by these hormones. Testosterone, his dominant hormone, is not as "emotional" a hormone. He also has less brain activity circulating around emotional issues because of the way his brain is formatted. This does not mean he won't be up/down. Many social and cognitive factors, as well as personality traits, control mood. But it is worth knowing that his brain simply may not process emotion during puberty with the same self-awareness and verbosity that many pubescent and post-pubescent girls possess.

VERBAL EXPRESSION OF FEELING. By now, if you've wondered why your average adolescent male talks less than your average adolescent female, you know much of the answer is in the brain. Especially in Stage 1, as the body changes and brain changes emerge, the male brain's structural differences from the female emerge even more clearly than when the kids were seven or eight. The smaller corpus callosum, the biochemical differences in brain cell activity, the lesser quantity and area of brain use in the male during verbal and emotive tasks—these and many other differences conspire to make an early adolescent male (on average) less verbal, especially about complex emotive data. In other words, he might be very verbal about a cognitive puzzle or debate problem, but he'll be less verbal about how he's feeling. He'll talk about his feelings as if they were asides or not so important. He's more likely to say "I think" than "I feel." This will probably continue well through male adulthood. *We are not saying he doesn't feel or doesn't talk about his feelings.* He does and he can. We are just saying that in comparison to his sisters, he will probably emphasize this less.

Males can of course be socialized to speak freely and deeply about their feelings. But if we ever should expect the average male to speak as freely and deeply about emotionality as the average female, we are simply showing an ignorance of, distaste for, or disrespect for brain and hormone activity. I am often saddened when I talk to people or read articles by people who insist male/female emotionality is mainly a function of "nurture" or "socialization." Even when I talk with a mom or female teacher who says, "My son (my student) Joe is just as able to talk about emotions as any girl," we generally notice that much of why he is "better than the average guy" at expressing complex feeling is because he is already far more "female" on the brain spectrum—i.e., his brain is better able to take in sensory data than many of his male peers', he seems less inherently aggressive than many males around him, and so on. He is perhaps much more a contemplative artist than an active warrior—socialization has some effect on this development, but genetics, biochemistry, and brain structure have more.

That is not to say he or his "more male" peer is in fact more "a man" or better or worse. Words get in the way of the truth, which is twofold: Every adolescent male is an individual, so there's no set type that is "good" or "bad." But, simultaneously, the male brain has certain tendencies, and since the "average" thirteen-year-old boy does not speak as well about his emotions as his female peer, we neglect him if we don't respect his difference. When we accept it we much better prepare him to deal with females, who mature earlier and generally have better emotive/verbal skills, skills that can truly "mess with a boy's mind" (one thirteen-year-old's words). If we want our sons to keep up with female emotionality, we must understand how he processes his feelings and give him strategies for talking to females on his own terms.

Moms who start out denying or wishing away brain differences often have found themselves forced to accommodate it. I remember one mom of three sons saying, "My first boy was not very typically male-brainish, but my second and third were. I tried all the same parenting with my second and third as my first, but they just were who they were. I recall feeling like a bad mom because I couldn't get my second and third to be more . . . female . . . more like their big brother. It was very liberating to get free from the stereotype I imposed on my own kids. Their father and I divorced when they were young, so I had to figure it all out myself, about maleness, and that it's really okay that they're just . . . guys."

What an example of the kind of stereotyping that boys face. Just as much as our Stage 1 adolescents are being forced by certain parts of the culture to become more hypermasculine as testosterone kicks in, so are they being forced by family and society to demasculinize. Liberation for both parent and son comes in letting the boy be who he is.

INDEPENDENCE SEEKING. The male brain, combined with testosterone wash, tends to see itself as a more discrete element in the social flow than does the female brain. The Stage 1 developing brain in the male will, at some point, probably show an increase in the need for independence. It feels more pressure, from its hormonal flow and from its brain system, toward independence-seeking activity. (Remember that simultaneously, it feels very fragile in its isolation from the emotional nurturing systems it is not as good at getting close to as the female is.)

The male brain evolved to become good at independence because so much of its work included lonely vigils during war, lonely hunts even when a hunting group started out together, and work away from home and family in order to provide resources to home and family. To this day, that independence-oriented brain still resides in many male heads, especially once adolescent testosterone levels wash through the brain, reprogramming it to be even more "male" than it was in late childhood.

HIERARCHY. The male brain is a more "hierarchical" brain than the female (on average). What do we mean? It is a brain system built for hunting (often in groups), physical-protection activity, edifice-building activity, and proof of prowess through social ambition. It sees where it fits in the pecking order and makes decisions of importance to self and family and community based first on the sense of "Where do I fit among men?" It looks toward alphas for leadership while seeking to become an alpha. When we watch twelve- and thirteen-year-olds at play, we find the hierarchical tendencies in all activities from verbal sparring in the lunchroom to fights over leadership on the street.

Many studies show us that the best way to decrease violence among teen males is to provide them with a clear sense of the hierarchy they live in. A University of Chicago study involving a summer camp showed this beautifully. Toward the beginning of camp activities, discipline problems existed in large number, as well as spontaneous fights and squabbles. Once the maturing males took their places as leaders of the pack, giving the younger boys males to look up to and a sense of their follower place in the hierarchy, most of the squabbling went away. Friendships also formed more freely now that hierarchy was clear.

This idea that hierarchy provides *more* health to a people, culture, or group than less is problematic in a time when our culture has experimented with the idea that male hierarchy (patriarchy) is the cause of the world's problems with war, violence, oppression, and colonialism. Male hierarchy has been a large factor in creating these things. On playgrounds, for instance, bullies and "bad guys" do often become the alpha males in the hierarchy. However, if we look more holistically at our Stage 1 adolescents on a junior-high playground, we'll see that the hierarchy also gives them safety, even purpose. Our adolescents challenge us to rethink the simplistic anti-hierarchy notions that have been popular in some circles.

Male hierarchy is a very complex organism and has to be handled with immense wisdom and care. A hierarchy is not just a place of giving and taking orders. It is a free-flowing system of complex play, work, family, and teaching that gives a boy a sense of his place but also gives him room to advance, room to "move." An authoritarian mother or father is less effective in the long term with a thirteen-year-old male than is an authoritative mother or father. The difference is in the way the alpha holds his or her authority—like a jewel, not a club.

In a sense, the good parental authority at this stage of a child's life is the "author" of the basic plot of the drama the child lives, but the child is becoming the author of his own subplot. He will want his subplot to fit well in the alpha's plot if the alpha holds a respectable, trustworthy position, for the trusted alpha parent holds on to magic that the boy still needs, magic that is in fact essential in the boy's journey. This magic often shows up in a boy's desire to be with or do things with the alpha. As long as this desire still exists in the boy, the alpha is carrying magic the boy wants. When the Stage 1 boy has absolutely no desire anymore to be with the alpha, the parent alpha has lost his or her authority, and there is reason to worry.

PHYSICAL ACTIVITY.   Because of its spatiality, and because of testosterone washing through it, the male brain tends more toward activities that verge on violence, physical activity, physical gesturing (outside of conversation gestures), and physical play than does the female. All of these behaviors can break physical boundaries between people. (We should note that female behavior seems to break verbal boundaries between people more than the male.)

The tendency toward violence in male brain activity has many neurological sources. Ruben Gur, at the University of Pennsylvania, a pioneer in brain research, has found that just the activity of staying quiet and relaxed is harder for the average male than the average female. The temporal limbic system—which controls action-oriented responses, including violent responses—is more active in males than females. The cingulate gyrus—another part of the brain that controls symbolic responses such as language—is less active in the male than female. With fewer verbal tools available to them, especially in response to intense emotive reactions like anger, males generally will use more physical gestures.

There is a reason why your average boy comes home with more bruises than your girl—there is a vast brain biology behind it. So it is essential that we remember some of the principles we established in chapter 2 about what adolescent males need in order to be emotionally well cared for. They have such an emotional disadvantage during their lives that we must mark our care of them in Stage 1 with profound and clear attention to their brain system. We must give them help in accessing feelings not only through words but also through healthy outlets, like punching bags, martial arts, sports, and thus diminish the chance that they will use randomly other human beings as outlets.

ATTENTION TO SPACE. Territoriality and tidiness are two linked traits of the emerging male's spatially oriented brain. This brain is constantly attending to how far space can expand, how space is used, how much space it can call its own (its territory), how much space it needs to perform a certain task.

Architecture, for instance, is a very male brain activity. (This does not mean women aren't great architects. It just means that on average we'll find more adolescent males wondering about the design and erection of a building than adolescent females. It's useful to remember that only one-fifth of girls reach their peer males' abilities in spatial tests.) Architecture aims to use space to fulfill a design. It sets out what territory can be used, negotiates space qualifications within the boundaries (keeps looking to see if the boundaries might be expandable), and then builds accordingly.

Architectural thinking creates a fine metaphor for how the male brain's territorialty and tidiness work. This is a brain which tends to erect a building, (i.e., its brain functions) in a specific area of the brain, and keep the brain function in that area until the task (i.e. the building) is completed. The female brain is more like a body of water. It spreads out in many places. By this we mean that when we use brain scan equipment on the two brains, we see the male brain as "tidier." It uses less of the brain and focuses the use in particular areas depending on the task at hand. The female brain uses more and various parts of the brain, so it's not quite as tidy. (Don't confuse brain "tidiness" with tidiness around the house! Tidiness in the brain is about using fewer brain cells. Kids or husbands leaving clothes all over the house is much more about liking to spread more things out in more space.)

The architecture of the male brain lends itself toward an intensely focused orientation to tasks at hand. Often parents (and wives) will become frustrated with males who can't do two things at once. Males can, of course, do many things at once—hold a phone in one ear while talking to someone in the room and also pressing a computer key. Let's notice, however, that even when a male does three things at once, each activity is often focused on the task or project at hand. Were the male to be challenged by emotive data, for instance, from the phone conversation, his ability to do the task at hand would suffer. The emotive data challenges another part of the brain, a part that isn't lit up right at that time. He becomes easily angered and territorial about his task and avoids the emotive stimulation until perhaps later, when the task is done.

The female brain is inherently more flexible. The female in a similar circumstance is more likely to put the task aside, "shift gears," and attend to the new emotive stimulation. Her brain is less territorial, less "tidy."

GALVANIZING THE BRAIN.   When our grandmothers or grandfathers used to say, "That boy's got too much time on his hands; let's get him doing something," they knew "that boy's" brain needed what brain scientists call "galvanizing." It needed to focus on a task so that it could get activated. When I hear the old saying "Idle hands are the devil's playground," or when I hear a mom say, "My son sits around doing nothing. I try to get him to focus on something, but he won't," I see a boy who is not being galvanized enough, challenged or interested enough. There is always something out there that he can apply his spatial, territorial, tidy, wonderful brain to. We just have to help him find it. Boys often have more trouble than girls in getting immediately galvanized. Often we consider them lazier than their sisters because they are not as easily galvanized.

Simultaneously, often more than their sisters, our boys have a hard time getting ungalvanized. We watch in amazement at how focused those boys get. We notice how they flourish when they're taking something apart, or putting it together, or being taught how to do this or that. Admiring this helps us be more patient when they seem less "flexible" than we'd like, less able to "shift gears." Both the intense focus and the inflexibility that come with galvanizing a male brain contribute equally to the amazing things our males create and get done.

Along with the formation of a distinctly male brain, there are other cognitive changes affecting how your Stage 1 adolescent acts—his new argumentativeness, his development of abstract intelligence, even his moodiness derive from general cognitive changes that both girls and boys go through (girls generally earlier than boys). Let's save greater detail on these general cognitive changes for our chapter on Stage 2, since it is in Stage 2 when a male usually solidifies the cognitive changes.

What We Can Do to Raise Stage 1 Males into Exceptional Men

We've looked a lot at how the Stage 1 boy acts, both in prepubescence and in puberty. We've looked at why he is the way he is. Let's look briefly now at some strategies for handling his testosterone and his brain. We'll flesh these out even more in the next chapter because, again, in Stage 2 many of our males go through the bulk of puberty.

Stage 1 is a time for men to start involving themselves much more in the lives of boys.

Stage 1 is a time to provide boys with activities that honor both their love of design and creativity and their desire for quick tension release and physical activity. They can't get enough of either thinking or moving around.

Stage 1 is a time to intensify our compassion, sensitivity, and empathy training through all available means, including didactic talk, but also activities like volunteering as a family at a homeless shelter or finding a church project.

Stage 1 is a time to provide peer group structures to males, like Boy Scouts, so that some of their impulses for peer contact are satisfied by structured, disciplined social systems.

Stage 1 is a time, for many boys, of intensive sport activity and of hero worship of sports idols. The more involved the clan is in the boy's sports activities and emotions, the closer the boy will remain with his family and clan.

Stage 1 is a time of media saturation and especially imagery that is testosterone saturated. When we allow our younger Stage 1 boys to see violent movies, it is essential that we discuss the movies with them. "If you want to go see Schwarzenegger's new film," we say, "the deal is, we talk about it later. Be prepared to give me a report, and be prepared to really think about that show." We say to a ten-year-old, "Let's talk about *Hercules*. What are we supposed to be learning from it, do you think?" We don't wait to talk to boys about violence till they're fifteen.

In Stage 1 we benefit if we stop anything else we're doing to talk to the boy about his physical transformation whenever he brings it up. Whether he talks about acne, growing pains, whether girls like his body, anything . . . stop and interact with him about that body's changing life. Whether you are the boy's dad or another elder male in his clan, recall with and for him your own adolescent journey—not like a lecture or a boring egotistical story, but like an adventure. If you are a woman, talk to him about your body changes and what you've observed among men and boys.

Stage 1 is often a time of silence for boys. If your boy tends to be silent about his body changes, find innovative ways to get him activated. Use jesting, joking, ribbing, teasing if need be of course, always within the proportion that fits the emerging self-esteem of the boy. Nearly every boy can take some ribbing to get him activated to deal with something important.

In Stage 1, nearly anything the boy goes through physiologically fits within the spectrum of "normal." Let us constantly show and tell him that, even if he doesn't always ask. For a Stage 1 boy, this effort on our part reveals, even when he appears to resent it, our deep love for him as a forming, newly born young man.

The High and Low Ends of the Testosterone Scale

There are many reasons Stage 1 boys can become very, and continually, angry. Testosterone is one of them. A recent study indicates that males with higher testosterone levels tend to be more moody and distant than their peers. Testosterone has effects on male emotionality that we are only beginning to discover. Thus, if you have a very angry pubescent male, high testosterone may have something to do with it.

When this boy is in an angry state, getting him to talk about it at that moment is generally the *wrong* thing to do. The best thing to do is *not press*. Usually, handling his anger with serenity and detachment is a better course than escalating his anger with anger of your own. There will be times, however, when you should "match" his anger. For example, if he gets angry for the umpteenth time about a limit you have set, you may need to get angry back, show him your power.

For high-testosterone males, we find lots of *team* efforts in which to tribalize the flow of testosterone and, in tribalizing or in "teaming up," to find the other forces, especially coaches, mentors, and teachers, who will help the individual male both prove himself and blend in, both be "the leader" and, more often, "the follower."

As much as we may be able to see clearly our high-testosterone Stage 1 boy, we will notice our low-testosterone Stage 1 boy. Even after he's moved through puberty altogether, he's still uninterested in sports, his muscle mass may never be very large, he may lack social ambition, and so on.

We will most likely find some area, whether video games or verbal one-upping, in which he is ruled by testosterone, but there are many boys who just don't fit the "testosterone type." We nurture them, of course, for their beautiful natures as they are. They often find themselves in smaller groups that accept them, avoiding larger male groups (larger male groups require more aggression/testosterone), and they often become spokesmen for others who do not fit a type. Often moms will wonder whether their "sweet, sensitive boy" ought to be pushed into sports. The best wisdom I know is to follow the Stage 1 boy into the activities *he* chooses.

Having said this, if the boy is facing social, emotional, or other problems, sports and other "testosterone-type" activities may be the best thing for him, giving him a group and an activity on which to focus. I've never seen a "sensitive boy" ruined by playing on the tennis team. Or perhaps martial arts, like aikido, would challenge and nurture him well.

Psychosocial Changes in Stage 1 Males

Identity, Autonomy, Morality, Intimacy

Throughout our explorations of physiological changes, brain and biochemical formation, and school and peer adjustments, we have been finding, without specifically calling attention to them, four psychosocial changes the boy's core self experiences as he traverses Stage 1. He measures himself against these same four in the later stages of adolescence, and so we'll call attention to them again in the next two chapters.

During his adolescence, this newly formed young man asks four primary questions concerning core-self development:

Who am I?

When will I be independent?

What is right or wrong behavior for *me?*

What is love, and how do I do it well?

These are questions of identity, autonomy, morality, and intimacy: I AM I.

The adolescent boy is crying, "I AM I. Pay attention to me! See me as a person, an independent person, a person who shapes his own unique moral vision out of the traditions he has inherited, a person who is lovable and knows how to love!" Throughout adolescence, the boy is trying to develop an identity, show he's autonomous, manipulate the rules to fit his unique being, and bring all that identity, autonomy, and integrity to his relationships with others in such a way that everyone will mirror hidden parts of his core self.

The Search for Identity

The Stage 1 boy's crucial questions of identity change over the years of this stage. Early on, at nine or ten, he's not very conscious of caring about identity—he begins to model and experiment with new identities by watching friends and family members, but he doesn't push too hard. By the time puberty comes, his biology pushes him hard from within to become his own man. He starts wondering in earnest, "What do people think of me now?" He starts trying to figure out what parts of himself to hide and what parts to bring out if he's to become an effective adult.

This is another way of saying, "Will people know who I am, who I really am, in all my potential weaknesses? If so, will they love me? What should I do?" First-stage adolescence is a time when a boy's natural (this goes for girls, too, of course) inner insecurity goes from being unconscious to conscious. The boy loses a great deal of self-esteem as he consciously realizes all his flaws. Five years before, he might have felt like an imposter in a social situation, but then a hug or a good explanation would have mollified his pain, mainly because it would have distracted him and helped him forget. Now, he forgets almost none of the emotional pains his identity suffers.

If we can help our boys *consciously* address their searches for identity and the self-esteem fluctuation that accompanies its adolescent beginnings, we can make the whole male life journey much easier. To help, we must increase our male-on-male time with the boy in early adolescence; increase self-confidence-building activities (like teen challenges, camping and hunting with greater responsibility); encourage his participation in one or more achievement groups (e.g., orchestra, Debate Club, Chess Club), through which boys and elders achieve goals while bonding together; and increase his household duties and freedom rewards, which will be very important when he negotiates his new desire for autonomy.

The Search for Autonomy

"I want to be my own person!" the boy hisses when we tell him what to do.

"Leave me alone," he snarls.

"You don't get it. You just don't get it!" he yells.

Or he simply, and quietly, does not do what we ask, asserting his independence.

A boy moving through Stage 1 is realizing that he can't "become himself" unless he becomes, by the end of adolescence, an autonomous self. He can't find his identity unless he can free himself first from those people and systems that have kept him from full, adult identity—we are speaking, of course, of parents and their ancillary systems, i.e., their traditions, even religions.

So we start seeing rebellion against authority in Stage 1. It is not normal for out-and-out rebellion to occur until Stage 2. That is, harsh rebellion against parental and clan authority from ten years old to twenty is not normal and generally indicates a boy in significant distress. More normal is for the rebellion behavior to begin in Stage 1, amplify in Stage 2, and taper in Stage 3.

If we can remain serene as the autonomy seeking begins, it is beautiful to watch the boy assess our values, our school's values, his peer's values, female culture's values, the media's values.

We can best help him toward autonomy by making sure he has a constant safety net of clan personnel to talk to, figure things out with, measure his progress with.

We can remain very active in his life while allowing him more decisions.

We can trust him with ever new responsibilities and freedoms.

We guide this Stage 1 boy's search for autonomy by allowing autonomy as he needs it, but never allowing him to remain lonely too long or overcontrolled too long.

Autonomy and the Mother-Son Relationship

Mothers face a special challenge with their boys' autonomy development. "Mothers of sons have long had to tread carefully," journalist Barbara Meltz put it. "Too much closeness and you'll raise a mama's boy; too little and you've got a serial killer." While Meltz uses sardonic terms, at some point the mother of an autonomy-seeking son feels the dilemma. Am I loving him enough? Am I overmothering? Am I neglecting him? Am I controlling him too much? Often the mother won't be relieved of her self-doubting questions for years on end. Then, when the boy becomes a man and makes the mistakes he is fated to make in life, the mother asks the questions all over again—an endless retrospective on her parenting.

What are the appropriate "boundaries" between mother and son? While the question is one to be explored throughout a boy's life, it is essential to do so by the time he is moving through early adolescence. Stage 1 is the time when his normal psychological separation from mother becomes clear, in less talk with her, less vulnerability with her, more interest in worlds other than hers, more judgments of her, sometimes verbal abuse of her, and the discovery of moral choices other than those she would make.

In the cultures of our ancestors, the boundaries were clarified for both mother and son in early adolescence. The boy started spending much more time with the father and the other men, and less with the mother. The boy was also mentored by the father and other men and would practice setting boundaries for his future adult-male relationships with the mother and women. For the most part, these were boundaries of chivalry, respect, and provision of financial support. The son, in other words, was *directed* in making his journey of autonomy. He moved from the mother-son bond to father-son and mentor-protégé bonds, replacing one set of psychological bonds with another.

Life has changed, however, and our mothers and sons are not getting much help in figuring out how to accomplish the natural separation that must occur for both mother and son to move on in their lives and yet also realize the boy's natural need to continue his emotional development in bonds with his mother and other females. Especially in a culture in which adolescents do not bond enough with fathers and other men, sons can separate from mothers without a safe psychological world to move into. Especially in a culture that sends many chauvinistic messages to boys, adolescents can end up filling emotional voids with media stereotypes and sexist and chauvinistic attitudes that cloud healthy masculine development.

How can a mother help her son (and herself) with the mother-son separation? Here are some suggestions for mothers.

1. See the mother-son separation not as merely a relational "issue" between mother and son but as a passage that involves *the whole family and clan.*

2. Though emotional separation is occurring, be constantly available to nurture the son's vulnerability. If he's upset, allow him to delay his reaction if he needs to, let him go into his room, but then when the time's right, help him process his feelings. This can go on between mothers and sons very late into adolescence. It is best done with little lecturing from the mother. Her role is to ask a question or two and then listen.

3. If fathers or other mentorial males are not around, the mother should adapt to the son's changing emotional structure when necessary by masculinizing her emotional method. The mother often can't help her son develop emotionally during adolescence if she's still talking to him the way she did when he was five. Now he may need her to be more of a jester with him, or more confrontative, or more subtle. Mothers watch how their sons' relating styles are changing, and they change their own to accommodate the emerging men.

4. Get the boy to read as much as possible because reading helps develop emotional vocabulary. Similarly, use media to encourage emotional responses: "What do you think that kid was feeling on that show?" "I started to cry when I watched that episode of 'Party of Five' with you. I think maybe you were tearing up inside a little, too."

5. Verbally reward the son's moments of emotional conversation or insight seeking. If the son says, "I think you're sad," admit you're sad. Don't hide your own feelings. This is an area where there is great confusion for mother and son. The mother doesn't want to burden the boy with her feelings. But if she lets him know she's sad, she's not burdening. Burdening comes when she does not take personal responsibility for her own feelings, e.g., "I'm sad because you're dad's such an asshole." If she expresses her feelings as *her* feelings, he admires her honesty and expresses his own more often.

6. When it comes to "helping your son do things," help him mainly when

you're asked, and even then you might refuse to help if he could be more independent. Exceptions to this—besides logistical ones for younger males like use of the car!—generally lie in decisions we make to blur the lines of independence in order to increase emotional access to each other. For instance, if your boy could ride his bike across town to his friend's house, you might say fine, unless you really need the car time to talk to him about something or just to relate.

7. Watch the boy's signals about smothering. A boy needs his mother's love. When he's getting too much, though, he'll make it clear in either words or nonverbal cues or moods. Once you see that he's distancing himself in his room, or through abusive language, or through grimaces and other facial clues, confront the boy with what has now become a moment of change and passage in your relationship. The more verbal and conscious you make the mother-son-separation process, the more you will love your boy, help him continue his emotional development, build trust in him for both you and himself in his process of change, and help him journey toward autonomy in a way that will feel, once he's a man, like his mother blessed him with not only life itself and care of that life, but also the bloom of manhood.

The Search for Morality

The search for a moral center is a trial-and-error process for an adolescent, especially a Stage 1 adolescent. He will experiment with lying, not only to see how it feels but also in order to decide when lying is okay. He might cheat a little to see if it feels good or bad. He'll now be able to understand the difference between guilt and shame. Guilt, he'll understand at some deep level (even if he can't articulate it), is a necessary function in the self in which one feels bad because one has done wrong. One feels guilt in order to do surgery on the self and improve in the future. Shame, he'll discover, is a whole other issue—a crushing blow to self-esteem and core-self development.

He'll discover that morality is somewhat malleable, fitting whatever group he's with. Most adolescent males do not stray too far from their clans' morality. Many more, however, do stray from the morality system of a single parent or loose caregiving system. It is, as always, essential that some sort of clan structure be holding a moral center in the boy's life.

As the boys discover the malleability of morality, we talk to them as much as possible. We teach them the difference between values we consider sacrosanct, bedrock values, and values that we consider malleable. We don't pretend that all of our values are absolutes. They'll see through this very quickly. Nor do we become so permissive that all values become relative. They'll see through this too and lose their respect for us. In their universe, if there are no core or absolute values, they don't feel safe.

When we look closely at morality systems, we find that no adult, no matter how old, ever feels safe either without some absolutes in his life. Our job with a Stage 1 male is very much to show him not only the absolute values that will keep him safe the rest of his life but also the relative values through which he must journey now to find himself.

The Search for Intimacy

When we say the word "intimacy" these days, we think mainly of adult coupled relationships. But for our Stage 1 adolescent male, coupled romance is not a very active form of intimacy. Best friends, social groups, relationships with parents and other family members, and relationships with mentors or coaches are where the boy makes his search for love. When a Stage 1 boy does not have enough of the variety of intimacy experiences, or when one or more of those important ones is problematic in significant ways, we find him moving to romantic intimacy too early for his developing brain and emotional structure to truly handle. When, for instance, he just can't wait to get free of a domineering mother or cruel father, romantic intimacy is an escape from the pain, an alternative structure set up by the core self in order to give it a refuge. Thirteen or fourteen is too young for a boy to be neglecting other friends because he's spending all his time with one girl. An adolescent male who becomes seriously involved before fifteen or sixteen is most likely not capable of maneuvering the involvement without serious risks, not only sexual health risks but also risks to the core self. Even many Stage 2 adolescents aren't close to ready. Their physical, cognitive, and emotional changes have not advanced enough. They stand to lose themselves in romantic love rather than gain themselves.

"My son's in love," a father once told me, "but he hasn't hardly reached puberty yet." He was right to worry. His son was very shy, had great difficulty in athletics, made few friends, and used romantic intimacy as a way of feeling okay about himself.

In Stage 1 of adolescence, some kissing might happen, even a hickey or two, but generally much more physical intimacy is too much. Stage 1 is a time when hugs with parents are still sought and beloved, and parents best help the boy by talking to him—for now his developing mind can understand better—about what love and intimacy are. Putting intimacy into a spiritual context is often very helpful—focusing on God as love, for instance, and on spiritual activities that build compassion in the boy.

A good rule of thumb for American culture is: No dating till sixteen. If we all shoot for it with our adolescent boys, we'll be allowing their body and brain changes to reach positions of advancement that make the building of romantic love a help rather than a hindrance to core-self development. In other words, if we help them to mature the core self through other intimacies first, they will be more likely to love a mate without becoming emotionally dependent on that one mate for their core-self development.

The Stage 1 Rite of Passage

Rites of Preparation and Confirmation

All humans have a primal need for their transition from one life-stage to another to be ritualized and acknowledged by their community and clan. When a male is not provided with rites of passage to mark each of his transitions through adolescence, we can expect him to create rites of passage of his own. If we as elders in his clan don't devote a great deal of our time to helping him engage in rites of passage, he'll create superficial ones that just propagate stereotypes. For example, he might use a girl as a sex object, sleep with her, and decide that now he's a man, he's got a notch in his belt; or he'll take up an adult habit, like smoking, and figure he's made it now; or he'll seek out a gang and vandalize or do other high-risk, antisocial behavior to prove his passage into manhood.

The male adolescent rite of passage is as much a developmental reality as is menstruation or menopause for the female. Male puberty, testosterone surges, brain development, and psychosocial pressures all build within the male the natural energy and instinct of passage, whether that passage is killing his first deer himself, going to the mountain for five solo days of prayer without food, lying on a bed of nails, killing his nation's enemy, going to work, or another set of life-defining events.

What rites of passage shall we provide our males? I have some suggestions, and I hope you'll use them in your communities not as stone tablets but as magnets, not as prescriptions but as possibilities that attract communal dialogue in your family, clan, and town about what rites of passage would work where you are. While there is a certain universal skeleton to rites of passage, the flesh of each can be different.

The rites of passage I suggest for all three stages of adolescence will appear at the end of each of the "stage" chapters (chapters 4, 5, and 6). They can be pursued at whatever the appropriate time in your boy's life. A general suggestion would be to pursue a rite of passage (RP) toward the *end* of each stage. I have based my suggested rites of passage on research among some thirty historical groups and tribal cultures, by ascertaining feasibility in our present culture, mostly, by personally instituting these rites with youth themselves over the last decade.

It is my hope that our clans will provide *two* rites of passage for our Stage 1 males, the first when he's ten, in which to say, "You are entering the adolescent journey now." This is a rite of preparation that ends his childhood and brings him to conscious contact with his threshold of adolescence. It may be simple, like taking him out for dinner and talking about adolescence and manhood with him, creating a new chores or responsibility list, increasing his allowance, and so on. This rite or series of small rites of passage prepares him for the next stage of life—early adolescence—and the whole adolescent journey to manhood.

His second Stage 1 rite will occur toward the end of the stage. This more complex rite for Stage 1 is the rite of confirmation. This Stage 1 rite of passage takes place when the boy is around thirteen or fourteen. (Each family and clan must decide, based on watching the boy's development, the exact time.) Among other things, this rite confirms that the boy is becoming a man. A Jewish bar mitzvah is a rite of confirmation, as is a Catholic or other Christian confirmation ceremony. As always, I will present models that are not restricted to one religious or ethnic group but take the core of a ceremony, add to the core wisdom and ceremony from other tribal and modern cultures, and combine that with secular ceremonies that are being used around the country right now.

Community educator Stan Crow has directed rites of passage in the Seattle area for some twenty years. He puts the "skeleton" of a Stage 1 rite of passage very simply. The key elements are: mentors, ordeals and tests, rituals, and community celebration.

For the Stage 1 male the mentor might be Father. It might also be one of Father's best male friends. It might be single Mom or her male friend with whom the boy has bonded. The mentor might be "assigned," through a church system. At one church I know of, mentors volunteer and the boys pick, giving first, second, and third choices. All the mentors are picked, and all the boys get a mentor. Once the mentor is established for the boy, the rite of passage starts getting planned.

A Stage 1 boy who is being led toward an RP and mentored in it becomes a curiosity to his friends. He likes to brag, even though he's a little uncertain about what is going to happen to him. Gradually he can report to them that his RP is going to take place in the woods or mountains, that it is going to involve some solo time, that he'll have to prove himself capable of certain things he used to be afraid of, that he'll have to show his ability to be caring and compassionate. He'll report that while he and his clan have decided on the intentions, some of the experiences, and some of the hoped-for outcome, his elders are starting to get a little secretive, not telling him all their plans. They're making him a little nervous. He and his friends will wonder what is going to happen. Before he knows it, his friends are not just curious about his RP, not just dissing him as boys do, but also downright jealous that so many people are paying so much deep attention to his manhood.

When we plan a Stage 1 RP we want to do it with that kind of energy, the kind of energy that says, "We're devoting ourselves to this boy's journey to manhood."

Here are some basics, or staples, of what could happen in the RP of a thirteen- or fourteen-year-old.

1. Have him toss out his old life in some way, in order to symbolize his understanding of his rebirth. The Maasai in Africa have their early-adolescent males give away childhood possessions. We might do this by holding a garage sale in which the boy sells all (or most) of his old toys.

2. Have him create a set of essential questions he wants answered by the elders of his community. Tell him he can ask absolutely anything. Try to answer anything he asks.

3. Have him prepare himself for a solo trip in which he accepts that his boyhood is dying and his manhood is emerging. The Maasai elders shave the hair on the heads of the initiate boys, and replace the hair with ashes to symbolize death, the first stage of rebirth. Most of us might find this too "tribal." Still, we must remember that the boy wants boyhood to die and manhood to emerge. So we need to find something in our community that is like head shaving. Hair is, in most traditions, including our own Judeo-Christian (remember Samson's hair), symbolic of personal power, also of wildness. Covering our hair is symbolic of humility in the eyes of God.

As our boy prepares for a solo trip, we make humility an object of the trip. We ask the boy and the community how he will incorporate the need for humility, the need to sacrifice wildness for community, and the need to give up to elders, for a time of passage, his personal power.

One boy I helped through a rite of passage told me that he could think of no other way to symbolize all these than to shave his head. He asked his mother's permission to get it done. Without my mentioning it, he made the connection between what he was doing at fourteen and what his eighteen-year-old brother had to do when he joined the military. He saw how his brother had to give up his wildness, let himself be sacrificed and rebuilt by the military. He shaved his head in large part because his brother modeled it, and he felt very important doing it at fourteen, not eighteen.

Another boy I met at a church group said that he used intense prayer as his method of giving up personal power for the greater good.

Few boys in Stage 1 are well able to imagine themselves dying and being reborn. Except perhaps for Catholics, putting ash on the head doesn't carry the energy it carries for the Maasai. So I've suggested to boys that they go to graveyards of ancestors and spend time among the dead, contemplating the lives of the dead, especially dead ancestors if those graveyards are available. I've asked the boys also to contemplate their own lives as if dead. I've told them to watch Charles Dickens's *A Christmas Carol,* one of the finest death-rebirth stories we have in our literature of male (and human) development. It is a journey of maturity for a male who, though old in the story, has clearly not matured into full flower. *Scrooged,* a 1990s version starring Bill Murray, is very well received among adolescent males. They find it funny, poignant, and can use it to wonder aloud about ghosts in their own lives, ways they have not been humble enough, and the power of getting close to death to find one's desire to really live.

4. Let the RP include some way of experiencing the life cycle. Rebirth is symbolized in various cultures by various fertility symbols. For the ancient Christians, certain fish carried fertility. For the Maasai, a bird's nest worn on the forehead symbolizes rebirth. However this experience is integrated into the lives of our boys, their RPs must involve some way of experiencing the life cycle.

For one boy I worked with, the birth of his baby sister became this element. He thought that because his father, after his parents' divorce, had nearly abandoned him, he would hate his father's new child (conceived with his father's new wife). But I asked the father to let the boy be there for the birth. The father agreed, reluctantly. However, when he saw his son's tears of joy at watching his half sister born, the father embraced his son as he had not embraced him in years. An uncle got it on videotape. It was a moment of passage that happened spontaneously, in which the life cycle touched a man's love for his boy and a boy's journey toward manhood.

5. What physical challenges will we give the boy at the end of Stage 1? Will he lie for a night on a bed of nails like a South Indian initiate? Probably not! But maybe he can manage for twenty-four hours alone in the woods. Even if he gets hungry, is scared, and does not sleep, he will still have managed, and will feel proud. Of course, we lead him to this kind of "survival" experience with preparation, care, and his consent. Perhaps we camp near enough by his own campsite that we're available for emergencies. He can blow on a whistle, perhaps, if the going gets too frightening for him.

6. What artistic challenges will we give the boy at the end of Stage 1? The boy must create something, some object of art or spirit, that will go on an altar he keeps in his room. It will carry energy for him. Trophies for certain successes, like a debate championship or chess championship, might qualify as an object created. But still he must create something that is very spiritual, too, something unique to him, showing his connection to his natural, even dreamlike inner world.

7. What community celebration will welcome this boy into the next stage of life? A party? A dance? Definitely some kind of clan event in which the boy's "rebirth-day" is celebrated. His mentor will present him, after his RP, to the community, let him talk about all the experiences he's gone through, and give him the reward of social admiration.

8. The RP for any stage of adolescence ought to begin about a year before its climactic activities (or even earlier). The Jews have it right, I think, when they begin their students on their bar mitzvah Hebrew a year or more before the public bar mitzvahs. The one-year rule is, by the way, not stringent at all compared to certain tribes, like the Ndembu of Africa or Shavante of Brazil or the ancient Hopi, who took many years of continual RPs to mature their Stage 1 males.

Always when we are preparing RPs with boys we must notice the natural, spontaneous rites that occur, as well as the institutional ones already in place. We must integrate them as much as possible. The move to junior high could be integrated—it's an institutional passage already set up for us. A boy's first shave is a spontaneous passage, not enough on its own to teach what manhood is really about, but something physical to be integrated.

Religions and religious leaders can help provide grist for RPs. If every church spent part of its budget on rites of passage, we'd raise a nation of healthier, more spiritual males. These RPs don't require huge structural changes in a church or community. They require that church, community, and clan set aside certain times, for instance a specific weekend every year, for these RPs. Educator Peter Wallis, of Seattle, led a weekend rite of passage in which a Stage 1 boy who had until then been unclear on what to do with his life found himself listening as never before to elder men telling their stories, and he realized he wanted to become a doctor. Six months after this weekend, this same boy (and his family) reported that his impulsivity and his bad temper had toned down considerably. It was not an exaggeration to say that the weekend had "changed his life."

9. What gestures will end the RP? At the end of the rite of passage that Stan Crow facilitates, he has the boys wash the feet of their parents. Every RP needs some powerful ending gesture of this kind. The respect, the intimacy, of the feet gesture will never be forgotten by either child or parent.

A rite of passage is a fluid, adaptable thing. Traditions create them, modify them, destroy them, resurrect them. Every one of us now who creates rites of passage for our boys is involved in traditions that are age-old and is adapting them to our time. Each of us is empowered to do this work. There is no capital city of Rites of Passage wherein lies the secret and only code of staging male adolescent passages. The best code lies in the conversation of the boy and his clan, and then in the risks his elders take to make for him a rite in which his core self blooms, a flower bending upward toward the radiance of his community, his sun.

By the time a boy is around fourteen, he officially enters Stage 2 of his adolescent journey to manhood. Let's now look at Stage 2 with as much vigor as we looked at Stage 1.

CHAPTER FIVE

Stage 2

The Age of Determination
(Ages 14–17)

"Don't tell me what to do. I'll figure it out myself.
I'm a searcher. I'll find my way."

ME, AT SIXTEEN, TO MY FATHER

Jeremy was a fifteen-year-old whose body had advanced more than halfway through the change, a tall blond youth, well-shaven, lanky yet muscular, and prone to dressing neatly in button-down shirts, blue jeans, and name-brand tennis shoes. He was the oldest child out of three (a sister fourteen, and a brother ten). He got good grades, played soccer, and stayed relatively close to home. He evidenced no high-risk behavior—drugs, alcohol, sexual activity. He liked to help out, whether around the house or in the community. He was one of those kids good things seemed to come to, and he seemed to make the most of them.

"He's hyperresponsible," his mother, a single woman, told me. She added, half in irony, half in seriousness: "I hope he's a normal boy."

Frank—Frankie, to his friends—was also fifteen, short, skinny, just beginning his growth spurt. He couldn't eat enough these days. He fidgeted all the time, "like a dynamo," his mother said. He loved his little sister but also loved to wrestle with her as if she were one of his neighborhood friends. She didn't mind it, until she minded it and told him so. He was on Ritalin because he had been having problems in school "since I was a kid." His words.

"I can't get him to settle down long enough to pay attention to anything," his mother told me. "I worry that he'll never calm down."

Layton was sixteen, a black youth from L.A. who moved to a relatively small Midwestern city. "What does a guy *do* in a place like this?" he complained. He wore his pants baggy and black; his shoelaces were always untied. He knew he scared people a little, and he knew he liked it a little, but it made him sad, too. "I'm big and I'm black and I'm from L.A. and I thought I'd like seeing people scared, but I don't." Layton seemed lonely to me when I met him, lonely and wondering what to do with his life.

"We had to move," his mother told me. "I got a good job here, hoping it's good for my son. He can go over the edge quick. He's naive, he's never been good at seeing through his friends. They can con him into anything. I hope they're different here. God, I worry about him."

To raise a middle-adolescent male is to worry. If he is experiencing lots of success, don't we worry about the house of cards falling down, or that maybe we don't know what's *really* going on in his "other" life, the life he doesn't tell us about? If he's having trouble focusing in school or finding friends, don't we worry that we've got to solve the problem *now*, or his adulthood will be tainted? If he's *too* friendly with peers, don't we worry that some of them will lead him astray?

Sometimes we have reason to worry. Each of our middle-adolescent males probably knows someone who uses hard drugs, has brought a gun to school, is sexually active before he should be, or drinks too much. We remember the temptations when we were fifteen and sixteen and know it's a lot worse for kids now. We can't control some key elements in our middle-adolescent's life, and we yearn to, and so we worry.

A logical impulse is to talk to our middle adolescent males, yet many of them won't help us. They become more and more silent. They seem to get angrier more now, or more withdrawn, or both. They fight us a lot more. They appear to hold different values than we have. They want the world to be *theirs*, not ours. They become know-it-alls in certain areas, like their music, their hobbies, their sports. Simultaneously, they pretend ignorance about things we ask them to do.

"Did you wash the car?"

"Huh? Did you ask me to wash the car?"

"Don't you remember how important being on time at the play was to your sister?"

"Who cares?" They like to cuss more now, and they're sarcastic in hurtful ways. They know our weaknesses and how to pounce.

We know deep down they're good kids, but sometimes we'd like to wring their necks.

If parents are going to have problems with adolescent males—high-risk behavior; episodes of rage, rebellion, and/or general intransigence—they are most likely to happen during the middle of adolescence, somewhere between fourteen and eighteen. If it has happened to you during another time, remember we're just averaging here.

This chapter is about these middle-adolescent years, which are made to be a little tough. A kid is supposed to rebel some. If your son is rebellious and intransigent in uncomfortable ways through *all* the stages of adolescence, there is something going on that needs professional help. Kids aren't developmentally supposed to rebel during *all* the stages of adolescence. But in the middle stage—well, that's a different story.

Myths About Stage 2 Youths

There are some myths about these years that we might want to start out debunking. The most predominant is that our middle-adolescent males, rebellious, insolent, or just distant, have different values than we do. In fact, study after study shows that they share most of our basic values!

Another myth is that they don't need us anymore (i.e., that they're being rebellious in order to show us they don't need us). The truth is, they need us desperately. They are like boxers who yearn, outside the ring, to be good friends. They want to box hard with us while we're in the ring, but later they'd like to shake hands and share life with us. Who else knows a boxer's life rhythm as well as another boxer? By the same token, who else knows a middle-adolescent male's life rhythm better than the family or clan members who make the passage with him, side by side?

A third myth worth debunking is that *every* middle-adolescent male is a problem. Many are far less of a "problem" than their sisters or other peer females. Some don't rebel much during Stage 2. They just move through the middle years with only a few bumps. Stage 2 males who come from large and close clans tend to fit more in this category.

A fourth myth is that a middle teen becomes very different in middle adolescence from how he's been. In fact, his personality was established long ago. He will probably do one or two primary things differently (for instance, maybe he never used to get real angry, but now he does), but basically he's the same kid (we are excluding here the appearance of a mental illness or the circumstance of a profound trauma, both of which can alter his personality). Who he has always been—for instance, where in his birth order—is who he will be, in the main. Jeremy was a firstborn, somewhat typical, responsible, neat, and so on. He continued as such. Frankie was a kind of Huck Finn. He had been for years, and continued to be. Even Layton, it turns out, had been easily bored back home in L.A.

What to Expect from Our Middle-Adolescent Males

As we look at what to expect from these ever-emerging male creatures, once again remember that the chronological years may not fit your son. He may go through some of this Stage 2 transformation later or earlier than fourteen through eighteen. If you haven't read the previous chapter, it's worth taking the time now, because much of what we detailed in it—the boy's changing sense of himself with peers, schools, and emotions; his hormonal changes, physiological changes, and the solidification of the male brain—only gets more pronounced through these middle years. For many boys, these subtle changes we detailed in Stage 1 won't show clearly till Stage 2.

During the middle-adolescent years, the world is opening up for Jeremy, Frankie, Layton, and all their brothers. They're scared to death, and they're brave as hell. They tread carefully on some things and seem to push forward like maniacs in others. A fire inside them motivates them and then seems to go out suddenly, leaving them exhausted and able to sleep until noon. They both crave structure and despise it, sometimes leaving their parents, mentors, and educators breathless. They seem to save up all their words only for television shows or ideas or activities *they* care about. They seem to need their friends more now than their families. They even stink a little bit. Is it the constantly dirty socks, or is it the testosterone-induced body odor that they wear now like a badge?

In middle adolescence, the boy becomes even more peer-activated and less parent-activated than in Stage 1. There's a twist to this, too, though. During or after his year or two of hanging on what his peers think and wanting to be like them, it's very common for the male (and his female peer, too) to start becoming critical of peers and thinking maybe the peers don't know so much. We see in the middle adolescent a tendency both to need peers and to need to be an *individual* no matter what peers think.

In addition to the hormonal, physiological, and male brain changes the Stage 1 male experiences, there are also specific cognitive changes that solidify in Stage 2. They are a primary reason he becomes who he is, in both the crazy-making ways and the brilliant ones. They augment the changes we detailed in the last chapter, so our analysis of them here will be much briefer.

Cognitive Changes Through Middle Adolescence

There is a vast difference in cognitive ability between prepubescence and postpubescence. Chronologically, a ten-year-old boy (on average) has a very concrete mind. A sixteen-year-old boy has a much more "intellectual" mind. The ten-year-old thinks of *this* place, *this* time. "The future" is pretty vague, except when it relates to "going to the soccer game on Saturday." The sixteen-year-old thinks *everything* out! He can become like a little lawyer. When I was fifteen and sixteen, my parents called me "the fastest mouth in the West." I could debate a decision they made with a second's notice!

The "legalistic, argumentative" boy may drive you nuts while he's coming into his abstract intellect. It will affect not only his conversation but his mood. Sometimes he'll think things out for so long, seeing so many permutations of a thought, that he'll exhaust or scare himself or become very angry or sad. He'll realize after a particularly interesting day in physics class that the world is actually disintegrating, molecule by molecule, and he is, too!

As his abstract intellect comes in, he may have trouble making decisions. He may seem immobilized by all the possibilities he can now see. It may seem to you that his intuition is nonexistent as he strives to think everything out.

He will also have thoughts that don't fit actions. He'll say he believes that kids his age shouldn't smoke cigarettes, but he'll experiment with them anyway. When we confront him with "But you said you would never try cigarettes..." we're trying to get him to stop an experimental behavior by holding him to a *thought* he had about it. Beginning at about age twelve or thirteen and continuing well into Stage 2, he will say (either aloud or within), "I can change my mind, and I did." If straight talk isn't working with him, a better tack might be to show him what's wrong with cigarettes—e.g., show him a picture of a black lung and let that picture lead to his exploration of the whole body system and what the cigarette does to every piece of it.

Early in Stage 2, he will have trouble connecting theory to practice, but that will gradually get easier. While he's having trouble, he'll *see* the theory but not quite know how to *do* it. This is why good schoolteachers *show* rather than *tell*. The adolescent years are great years of cognitive growth in which to relate to boys by *showing* them *hŏw* things work and then *doing* the things with them until they are ready and able to do them themselves. This means, of course, spending *time* with them.

Stage 2 is, because of cognitive development, a very active period of self-consciousness development in the male. By the time a boy becomes a seventeen- or eighteen-year-old youth, he can know the bulk of his strengths and weaknesses. All his thinking about the world and himself begins to pay off in clarity. His clan is especially useful in helping him build this clarity.

What We Can Do to Raise Exceptional Middle-Adolescent Males

The boy is becoming a man—his testosterone has pretty much finished its job on him by the time he's eighteen, his brain system has emerged well enough to perform a great deal of adult thinking. He's still confused a great deal, and will need another stage of adolescence in which to refine himself before he can be called an adult, but he has shown us now a lot of sides to himself that he needs our help in focusing, structuring, developing, and accepting.

Here are things we can do to make sure the confused, searching, emerging Stage 2 male develops his core self in healthy neurological, biochemical, and social ways.

We give him visionary ways to expand his consciousness. We get him involved in the science or hobby of astronomy, perhaps, get him stargazing; talk to him about space, God, hidden worlds, and ideas. If he reads science fiction, we talk with him about the plots, characters, and messages, testing him and following him in his searching.

We take him deeper than before into his interrelationship with nature, the outdoors.

We direct him to myths and legends that now are not child's play but interesting ways of looking at the development of the world. When teachers teach Greek mythology to middle adolescents, they do not teach just the story. They teach archetypal psychology. They show how the story is really about inner life and about hidden parts of ourselves. They teach the cosmos, both external and internal. This approach also keeps religion fresh and interesting to middle adolescents. When religion is about both the inner and outer cosmos, it's more compelling than when it's just an old, droning, repetitive set of lessons.

We give him a deep sense of his ancestral roots. As the youth's cognitive development occurs, his abstract intellect needs constantly to fill in gaps about himself in the family and other systems in which he belongs. We give him a lot of clan and family stories. "Your great-grandma did . . ." "Your great-uncle was . . ."

We give him more responsibility for thinking out his position in his home and community. We let him take on more of a caregiving role. "Neighbor Joe is just back from the hospital from his stroke. What do you want to do for him or his family?"

We let him know we want to talk to him about anything, even his deepest fears. As always, we rely more on our own life stories than on lecturing. "When I was fourteen I remember thinking . . ." We constantly help him understand how he's developing by telling our own stories.

Often with middle-adolescent males (and males in general), "What do you think . . . ?" is better than "What do you feel . . . ?" It's easier for him, with his brain system, to access what he thinks. Later in a conversation we might try "What do you feel . . . ?" Or we might find that he gets to his feelings on his own by beginning with thinking.

We make sure he has a profound sense of spiritual connection. Part four of this book will help inspire and support this effort with boys. When abstract intellect comes into a growing mind, it asks: "How do I as an individual being fit in the life-and-death cycle of the universe?" If it does not get an answer, it stresses out with ontological insecurity.

We train the youth toward compassion and empathy. One of the best ways to handle adolescent egocentrism and remodel it away from selfishness and toward compassion is to point it out as it happens—usually not with shame but with observation. "Did you notice when you talked about Mrs. Billings that you pretended yours was the only point of view here? What is *her* point of view?"

As much as possible, we relate to the mind-changing boy with humor and serenity. We take very little personally. We know that this boy is going through a mental rebirth that is so confusing, so insecurity-causing, so filled with changing social systems (e.g., moving from elementary school to middle school, then middle school to high school), with other kids at different maturity levels (e.g., some boys at fourteen already are pubescent, some not; some girls are way beyond boys), with new stimulations from without and within that very little the boy does is "about" us. Most of it is about his feeling like flotsam on a vastly unfamiliar ocean.

At a recent teen pregnancy conference, a man who had raised four kids told me a wonderful story in this regard about his son and his wife. The son, fourteen, came to Mom and said, "Some boys are showing books with dirty pictures." Mom said serenely, "Have you seen anything in the books that you haven't seen at home?" "Nope," the son responded. And the Mom: "Then it isn't much." This son is now grown. According to the man sharing the story, this incident with Mom has been a metaphor for the son's adult life—he gets curious about something, thinks critically, makes some comparisons, and remains serene. The mother has been a great teacher of serenity in this regard.

We utilize *his* media to teach *our* lessons. Chapter 8 details strategies in this regard. It is essential to remain connected to what your boy likes to watch and read, go to movies with him, learn about his music. Even more so, it is essential to utilize that media to teach what you want him to learn. "How many times did they have sex in that movie, son? What do you think? You think those two sixteen-year-olds were ready?" I have heard many very fine results from parents who went out and bought *Penthouse* and talked to sons who were developmentally ready (thirteen, fourteen, fifteen) about the centerfolds. There's nothing quite as powerful as an adult honestly and serenely looking with the boy at a taboo picture and talking about sex, the body, and objectification of the female. This is a risky suggestion and must be handled with great care. It is also scary for the boy who can feel very embarrassed. Yet it is the kind of in-your-face parenting that sometimes can work.

We provide the boy mentors as much as possible. A single mom told me about how much she had come to rely on her fourteen-year-old's nineteen-year-old brother. She noticed that her young son was going through a growth spurt and a lot of confusing changes while the older brother, a college student, was home for the summer. She noticed how he came to rely on the older brother as a father (the biological father lived 3,000 miles away). It was a healthy alliance, in which the older brother mentored his younger sibling. When the older brother went back to college, the younger brother felt it as a tragedy, as did the mother. We worked out a system whereby the older brother would spend two or more hours a week on the phone with his younger sibling. It worked beautifully over the months. The older brother was able to help the younger brother maneuver the changes that marked his body's second birth.

We give him lots of physical exercise and lots of stuff to do. The male hypothalamus, a crucial part of the brain, is like a thermostat that controls testosterone. When there's too much testosterone in the system, the hypothalamus sends the message out that the system needs cooling down. This is a primary reason why adolescent males tend to need quick tension release and constant tension-release. Quick physical gestures, like banging doors and tables, release tension. Athletic activities release tension. A game of chess, the accomplishment of a science experiment, release tension. A boy releases tension by hitting, moving a ball through space, playing a game, building something to its conclusion. We provide these outlets to boys as much as we can throughout middle adolescence, and the youths generally seek them out.

Intense competition also *increases* testosterone, so we need to be aware of that fact. If you find that your boy is *only* competing, then you need to help him find other outlets. As parents, mentors, and educators, we are striving to handle his testosterone in a balanced way by helping him find activities that give outlets for its release without focusing him singularly on one or two of those outlets. The parent who forces his son to become the best football player and let everything else slide is, ironically, doing the testosterone no favors. He is compounding it in the boy constantly and creating a cycle of testosterone increase that is healthy only for a boy who plays football or hockey every minute of his whole life. This boy's system gradually accommodates the constantly increasing testosterone flow, and then we have a testosterone-saturated male. In the end, this male will crash somewhere, perhaps in violent behavior.

When Does Aggression Become Violence?

As we inspire and challenge one another to delve deeply into the effects of testosterone and the male brain on our individual males, their relating styles, and their communities, we must at some point discuss the aggression we see among some of our adolescent males.

I was working with a school in which the following incident occurred:

A Fine Young Man

During cross-country practice, five teens, fifteen to sixteen years old, lagged behind the rest. The coach noticed them missing and retraced their steps. The team did some of its warm-up and cool-down running in some rural land near the campus. Around a bend on this land, the coach came upon the five boys. Four of them were swinging the fifth and smallest one back and forth, dissing him and generally threatening to toss his body into rough grass and a pile of cow manure.

The coach yelled at the boys, breaking up the prank immediately. He also called the incident before the administration. The behavior-review committee at this school is composed of both faculty and students. The committee heard from the five students and the coach and ended up deciding that the aggressors would get written up but not suspended.

This incident of hazing brought up many days, even weeks, of discussion in the school. When I came in to consult on a number of different issues, some of them concerned this situation. When interviewed, the boy who was hazed said that he was a little scared, but he was laughing, too, and he himself had been the aggressor in similar incidents previously. And all the students involved agreed that there had been far worse hazings of the kind at the school than this one.

Nonetheless, to regard the incident as just a passing moment during cross-country practice wouldn't do it justice. It raised, for both students and faculty, the gray-area question: When is aggression "between guys" violence? If we can't define the line between aggression and violence in an incident like this, how do we define it anywhere?

Aggression is natural to the human being. Aggression is quite natural to males and male culture. Aggression is especially natural in a testosterone-driven group of males who use it to determine pecking orders. Hazing is a natural form of toughness training that males put one another through to constantly test one another's resolve, strength, courage, belongingness. It also helps show who the alphas are, the leaders, the strong ones, and separates them from those elsewhere in the hierarchy.

Aggression is one person or group's physical, verbal, or institutional attempt to control and direct the person or behavior of others.

When does it become violence?

Violence is one person or group's physical, verbal, or institutional violation of a person's core self or a group's sovereignty.

Were the four boys involved in destruction of another boy's core self? Were they "normal boys" who were, in the words of all five, "just having some fun"?

In the case of these five, especially given that the "victim" agreed that everyone was having fun, the act was not an act of violence, when we use the definitions I've given here. It was undoubtedly an act of aggression.

Our culture is faced with a very difficult job in its care of our aggressive male youth. We have to use each incident of aggression as a teaching moment without overreacting to it as if each constituted violence. If we overreact, the kids learn very little except that we're "tripping out about something that's normal." Boys especially learn that we don't understand certain core aspects of their male relating style. When we approach them about their hazings, we have to be able to explain to them that we've drawn a line between aggression and violence, we've got to be able to show them the line, we've got to justify it, and it always helps if we can honor the males even while we are reprimanding them—in other words, if we can explain to them what's going on in their bodies and social systems that creates the aggression and violence and thus necessitates the drawing of a line.

Which Middle Teen Behaviors Should We *Really* Worry About?

Many of our interactions with the middle-adolescent male are "trust moments." They are moments in which he is measuring whether he can still trust us, and we are measuring whether we can still trust him. Because he is psychologically separating from us and physically spending less time with us, we are worried that he's going down roads we don't know about or don't like; he's also worried about whether we still love, respect, and trust him in the deep ways he needs once we discover who he really is, flaws and all.

A Stage 2 male often feels that we can't be respected anymore or don't respect him; he feels we don't love him (if we did, we would *know* what he's feeling); he feels we don't trust him; and he is cognitively able now to realize many of his own and *all* of our flaws, so he has to develop new, nonchildish, noninnocent ways of trusting us—he just can't trust us the way he used to when he was a boy. All this passes in a moment within the psyche, a thousand neurons trying to find sense in this new semiadult relationship with us.

The trust moments within the youth and our family are normal. When do they show that a teen male is becoming "troubled"?

In chapter 1 we covered troubled-teen males in depth, emphasizing those who are high risks in the home, in school, and on the streets. In chapter 2 we covered the many teen males who suffer emotional neglect and therefore find themselves gravitating into listlessness, excessive anger, stoical repression, and emotional confusion. If you passed by those chapters, you might want to revisit them. They show how much of what teen males go through now ought not to be considered normal, but instead troubling, even dangerous, not only for themselves and their families but for the culture as a whole. They also show that the teen male in your own home might be suffering emotional neglect and confusion in ways you did not realize, ways that you may notice more overtly now, in Stage 2.

Simultaneously, many Stage 2 males will appear troubled or "on the edge," and they will confuse us more than we can say, for they don't seem to fit a category. They commit one or two very troubling acts but often, otherwise, seem fine.

Stephen was a sixteen-year-old whose parents reported him to be sullen and angry. It had begun, they thought, back when he was ten and his grandfather died. Stephen was an only child, very bonded to his grandfather. The death hit him hard, though he stood it stoically. Now, at sixteen, and following a troubling incident, his parents recalled the death of the grandfather.

The troubling incident was this: Stephen had taken his parents' car for a joyride, but it had mechanical trouble. It stalled; he got out, went to a house near the car, and knocked, hoping to use the phone. No one was home, but the door was open, so he went in, found the phone, and was using the phone book when the owner of the house, a woman in her thirties, walked in. She was scared, he was scared; she called the police and, as you can imagine, Stephen was in a lot of trouble. Trouble not only for taking the car without asking but for trespassing.

The woman saw her way not to press charges, a very wise move, and Stephen returned to his life. However, his parents trusted him less now, and he was ashamed; his father forbade him to drive the car, and Stephen became more hopeless than he was before. His father felt that treating him harshly would teach him a lesson. He instituted a system whereby he picked Stephen up from his school, took him back to his workplace, and had him sit in a room doing homework, then watching TV and playing video games. The father set no limit on how long the denial of car privileges would run.

As we looked carefully at Stephen's temperament, his issues, and his problems, we noticed a number of things: First, he was feeling alienated, alone. He didn't have many friends. He had switched schools and, an only child with an introspective temperament, didn't make friends quickly. Second, he tended toward the stoic in his handling of emotional pain, shame, and guilt. Many boys, when they tend toward the stoic anyway, will use sullenness and anger to process pain, shame, and guilt. Third, he had done nothing *intentional* during the technically criminal episode except the somewhat normal rebellious behavior of taking Dad's car without asking.

Stephen had made a mistake and was paying for it in a way that exacerbated some of his other emotional issues rather than helped. His parents and I explored some things Stephen might need, things needed by many Stage 2 males who confuse us with amoral acts or at-risk choices.

Dad and Mom would present him with a deal. He would get car privileges back, but he had to practice as much responsibility as he did freedom. Specifically, for three months, every time he used the car, he would fill it with gas. Every time he needed the car for his own use (and at sixteen that was not endless—he still had to ask to use it, and not too frequently, and parents had right of refusal), he also had to use it to do something for the family. In six months the strictness of these conditions would be reevaluated.

He would use the car at least one afternoon a week to do something social with one or more friends.

He would stop complaining so much about how much his parents annoyed him. Rather, he would communicate with them about what he liked about them, what he wished would change, and what he was willing to give so that they would make some changes.

Because Stephen wasn't very good at verbalizing feelings, especially in one-on-one confrontative conversations (often he either shut down or got irritated), he would write a letter to them about what he loved and appreciated about them, what confused him about them, how he had changed over the last months and years, and what new freedoms *and* responsibilities he needed.

Stephen's case is a good example of a youth who does something wrong and at risk, scares his parents and even others in society, but is consequently treated in a way that hinders rather than helps. The parents' intentions were good, but, without realizing it, they had participated in doing something so many of us do: A Stage 2 male is sullen and angry, making us think he's on the brink of going bad. Once he does something that is untoward, we figure he *has* gone bad. We cut him off from new freedoms and responsibilities because of our own fear of his descent into teen madness.

The Teen Male Who Seems to Be Suffering and We Just Don't Know Why

I vividly recall a conversation with my mother in my middle adolescence. It was relatively one-sided.

"What's wrong?" she asked.

"I don't know," I answered.

"You've been so . . . down lately." (This same conversation had occurred in the past with "You've been so angry" or "You've been so out of it.")

"I have?"

"Of course you have. Haven't you noticed?"

"I guess."

"What do you mean, you *guess?* You're driving everyone nuts."

"Uh-huh."

There was something bugging me. I didn't know what it was; she didn't know what it was; I made the world suffer for our general ignorance. I was processing something grave, something painful, and I couldn't do it alone. The way I reached out for help was to keep my family stimulated by being difficult. Constantly stimulated by me, my family connected with me (not successfully if our standard of success is "solving Mike's problem," but very successfully if our standard is "letting Mike know we care").

Many parents live through years with sons who just don't know what they feel and why they feel what they feel. Something has happened, but they either can't remember it as any big deal or repress thinking about it as a big deal.

Much of what we must do to support them is lower our standard of success from "learning the details and then helping them solve the problem so they'll feel better" to "just being there for them." This is spiritual detachment in the best sense of the word. We let the youth work it out. Most things he can work out if we get out of the way and let him *but show we care.*

Simultaneously, we can also try to direct a boy's thinking process by focusing on the four key areas where "problems" generally occur. Confusing emotional states usually grow from inner conflict in psychosocial areas of identity, autonomy, morality, and/or intimacy. If we direct the boy toward these four, we increase our chances of helping.

"Are you not fitting in anymore with the _____ clique?"

"Is it about stuff happening with me or your dad?"

"Has someone done something wrong? Have you?"

"Are you having a problem with Sue? with Joe?"

Certainly there can be medical and psychiatric problems, but most normal kids going through normal "strangeness" fall into one or more of these four key areas. Let's look at each one and how it might work for your middle-adolescent, whether he's having a problem or just negotiating the normal psychosocial development of a middle-adolescent male.

Psychosocial Development

Identity, Autonomy, Morality, Intimacy

As we noticed in Stage 1, the Stage 2 youth focuses on asking "I AM I" questions of himself and the world regarding his developing identity, his growing sense of autonomy, his much-expanded sense of what is moral, and his increasing need to be intimate, now especially with potential mates. Let's briefly explore these questions.

The Search for Identity

In India, where I lived as a boy, there is a proverb that loosely translates this way:

Treat your son like an emperor till he's five.
Treat him like a slave till he's ten.
Treat him like a friend till he's fifteen.
At fifteen, give him to a guru.

It is an interesting saying, one that culminates with middle adolescence. Wisdom about the early years of a boy's life is the wisdom of attachment—the wisdom that says, "Lavish his identity with an inherent sense of its importance, its regality, its essentiality in the center of the culture."

Wisdom about the late-childhood years is the wisdom of discipline: "Train up this child's identity carefully now, so that he knows his place."

Wisdom about early adolescence is the wisdom of new trust: "Let the emerging identity know it is gaining equality with the adults."

Wisdom about middle adolescence is the deep wisdom about identity I saw all over India: Once a male is in the center of his "change," his rebirth, his emergence into manhood, his identity needs the shaping of powerful, already formed forces.

Many of our Stage 2 boys will, somewhere in the middle-adolescent period, sing out, whether in words or deed, to one or both parents:

"Leave me alone. I'm myself, not you."

"You can't tell me who to be."

"You don't understand *me*, who *I* am."

"You don't care about *me*."

Inside these songs is another song often unnoticed:

"You can't help me, but please show me who can."

Herein lies the need for the guru. As much as the youth wants no one to tell him who he is, he wants someone special to tell him who he is.

Perhaps the song will be sung to Mom, and so Dad must become the guru. In some cases, just the opposite. The divorced mom, for a period of middle adolescence, is the boy's best friend and guru. In almost all cases, the youth also wants a guru who is not just Mom or Dad, a guru who joins them in raising him. If we apply the Indian proverb to our lives, we gain by noticing how we can evolve from being parents to gurus, and how we can bring more nonparental gurus into the youth's life, elders who mirror for the youth his hidden, evolving identity.

Uncle Ralph will say, "You have a seriousness in you that you've had since you were born. It is going to take you somewhere incredible."

Mom will say, "You have a warmth about you that reaches into people's hearts. It's just who you are, no matter how you hide it."

Dad will say, "You're becoming like me in the way you bottle things up, but I hope you won't become like me too much."

Many of the teaching moments we enjoy with our middle adolescents need to be "mirror moments," moments when we mirror for him the depth of himself that only we can see. Much of the mirroring will occur because he has asked a specific question of us, or he has performed well at something, or he has grown in a way we want to call attention to.

Native Americans, as well as African, Australian, and other indigenous tribes, have a tradition of "renaming" the middle adolescent after he has been through certain rites of passage and initiations. In India, after the boy has shown his abilities at certain spiritual levels, he is renamed, often by the guru. This renaming process is a cultural way of honoring the youth's identity development. The culture says to him, "You were once _____, but now we see you as _____."

Many adolescent males rename themselves in this culture. When I was a boy living in Honolulu, my parents called me "Meka," a Hawaiian nickname. One day in the middle of my adolescence, I told my father, "Don't call me Meka anymore. I'm not a kid. I'm Mike." In the inner city, many boys get renamed by their "homies," going from Nate to P. L. T., or Jim to Ice T. Some boys seek the renaming in Stage 1 of adolescence or earlier, some not till Stage 3 or later.

There is in the male a deep need to be renamed—to be known as something new, something identifiably different from who he was "as a kid."

Later in this chapter we'll look at how to ceremonialize the renaming and create a rite of passage for the Stage 2 youth that includes the renaming. It will require us to think carefully about who our son's gurus are.

The Search for Autonomy

How much independence should a Stage 2 male have? What rules must he follow, and what rules are meant to be broken? Let me share a story from a mom, Sandra, that helps answer these questions.

All through my boys' growing up, Jack and I made sure they knew the rules. They always knew there were some rules that could be bent, but they also knew there were some rules that were solid.

In the high school years, the rules showed we cared:

They weren't allowed to have a party at our house when we were gone until they were eighteen. We didn't set this rule to be ogres. We set it because we didn't feel it was right for them to have to have paramount responsibility over our house.

They weren't allowed to date until they were sixteen. This was for their safety: We didn't feel they had developed enough to understand love until that age.

They had to let us know where they were headed at night.

They had to come home at a set time. It got later and later over the years, but it was always set.

If plans changed in a big way, they had to call us. These rules were for their safety, not just our sanity.

They couldn't use our car or anything we cared about to engage in activity we did not want them involved in, for instance in drugs, or disrespect of girls, or aiding in something criminal. This was a good way of helping them cut down on the possibility of getting into trouble.

A Fine Young Man

They had to get their work done before their play, or work out a deal to exchange times, and there could be no nagging by us about getting the work done later. We taught them that a person who didn't do his work first was a person who couldn't succeed later in life.

Every year through high school, we increased the boys' responsibilities and freedoms, we gave them more and more independence, and we stood by as they took more and more. But the solid rules couldn't be broken, and they knew it. If they broke those key rules—the "trust rules" is what my oldest son called them—the consequences were swift.

I don't know if our rules were for everyone, but they worked for us. Now I hear my son say to his kids, "As long as you're living in this house, you'll . . ." I have to grin. He sounds just like Jack and I did with him.

Sandra and her husband's wisdom is great for dealing with normal middle adolescents who are searching as much for independence and autonomy as they are for a safety net of set and core principles. They want independence, yes, but they want to know we care about them enough to keep them toeing the line, and they want to know where a good, sound line is so that when they are faced with temptations they fear, they can fall back on "Sorry, can't do that, it's breaking a 'trust rule.' "

What Sandra's son called "trust rules" might also be called "core rules" or "sacred rules." Our sons need these in place so they can navigate the search for autonomy. Without that sense of a family's/clan's sacred line or code in place, they feel quite lost.

A dad once told me about overhearing his son Aaron talking on the phone with a friend who wanted Aaron to drive the car that night in order to pick up an older brother of the friend, in from out of town, who would buy booze for everyone. Aaron at first said he would drive the car, then came and told his dad what he had said. He said he felt pressure to comply—among this group of friends, he was the only one with a license—but he also felt like he couldn't break a sacred rule. "My conscience would kill me," he told his dad. His dad asked him what he felt about getting drunk and driving. It scared him, he admitted. He was no stranger to alcohol, but he didn't want to drive. His dad said, "Remember, I can't stop you from the drinking—you're sixteen and I can't follow you around—but I can give you a good excuse to tell Blake, and you won't have to drive." The guys ended up having no car that night, Aaron got to blame his dad for needing the car and messing up the plans, and though the young men did drink, they remained safely ensconced in a backyard.

The choices for middle adolescents and parents are hard, without too much black and white. A dad has to give in on one thing to keep something else sacred. The son may seem to want to be independent and do whatever he wishes, but really he doesn't want it, and he shouldn't have that freedom. It is more appropriate later in Stage 3 adolescence, and then adulthood. If in Stage 2 we give him *carte blanche,* we are showing we don't know how to love him. Freedom without responsibility doesn't help build autonomy in a boy; it builds confusion, disrespect, and egotism. The boy knows it deep down—and we know it, too—but there comes into us a kind of fear that if we're too strict with the boy, he'll rebel too furiously for us to handle, or he'll remain too dependent on us and not be liked enough by friends and not grow well enough into a free-spirited man.

The great lesson adolescent males have taught me is this: There is no such thing as freedom unless it takes place within the limitations of responsibility to higher powers.

The Search for Morality

Stage 2 males, especially as they go further into this stage, are very moral creatures. One mom said to me, "I really picked my battles with my teens. I chose to do battle with them about issues of *morality* and *justice.* Other things were smaller things to me, and I let most of them go." This mother got to the heart of where most middle-adolescent males are doing so much of their growing: in their search for a moral center. We can tell how moral these middle teens are because they so often criticize the actions of others, and of parents.

The hard things in morality teaching are: (1) to get him to criticize his own actions, and (2) to get him to criticize actions the way *we* want them criticized. We want him to remain a student of *our* morality. We also want him to fight his egotistical, self-centered Stage 2 urges and become a good self-critic.

Let's look for a minute at how his psyche works. When he doesn't quite know what he thinks about himself, he's very likely to project himself onto others: "Jim is being a dork with Ted. He's not listening. He's just acting like a jerk." Often this is 100 percent about Jim. Just as often, this is 50 percent about the one who is doing the criticizing, the son.

"Mom, you're wrong. You think you're so high and mighty. You think you're so right all the time. Well, you're wrong." Often this is about Mom. Just as often this is about the son, unconsciously telling himself he's being high and mighty.

In these situations, the boy is saying, "I don't really know what I think or feel until I find an object out there to project my inner life onto. Once I see it on the object, I can critique it."

The great gift Mom gives this son is the gift of "Okay, maybe you're right. Maybe I'm being high and mighty. Here's how I'm probably being high and mighty. How are *you* being high and mighty?" What a gift to admit one's flaw and, in admitting it, challenge the youth to push through his veil and really see himself and take ownership. So often he can't do it when we say, "I'm not being high and mighty, you are!" Or, "Don't talk to me that way."

Whenever we see a Stage 2 youth criticizing, moralizing, value clarifying, we ought to help. We and our clan are still the most essential sounding board for his moral center. Although we are the object of his psychological separation as he searches for autonomy, we are the most stable moral center he knows. His peers and the media, despite their huge influences, are not stable. His peers are constantly changing their minds, doing crazy things, taking little moral ownership, blaming others. The media is, if the youth has a discerning mind at all, filled with stereotypes that he, at sixteen or seventeen, revels in seeing through and not "buying."

Whenever possible, we ought to engage in moral/philosophical discussion with Stage 2 boys. A mother and sixteen-year-old son debating each other bond with each other. Of course, for it to be bonding, it can't always be a moral debate about what he did or she did. A lot of the debate has to be about themes in the physical world, the community, the human condition, the spiritual world.

If we decide to invest in moral debate and in moral development in general for our Stage 2 youth, we will have to be ready for him to end up on the other side of some issues. We will learn the great life lesson of patience as we watch him vacillate between one opinion one week ("I won't change my mind!") and another the next week ("Well, *this* time I won't change my mind"). Sometimes we will have to wait twenty years for him to come around again to our way of seeing it. Sometimes he never comes around, and we end up seeing it his way.

More important than the exact moral taught is the process of trying to help the youth learn it. Process, not product, is often the key.

Having said this, we would be unrealistic to think it holds true if our youth is what we call a "troubled teen." That youth needs a much harsher, rule-oriented, domineering approach to morality. He needs moral intervention, not moral debate.

The Search for Intimacy

"But I love her! Don't you get it? I love her!"

The words scare us. He's just a boy. He's still got some fuzz on his face, not a full beard. He's sixteen; he's seventeen. He's not ready.

"No girls return my calls. No girl could like me. I'm ugly."

We look into the budding young man's face and try our best to console him.

Late Stage 2 is an appropriate time for coupling, especially for those boys who have moved through puberty relatively early and are, by sixteen or seventeen, physiologically developed.

As we said earlier, a boy coupling with a girl at thirteen is something to watch *very* closely. That is *very* early. But a boy coupling at sixteen is more developmentally normal.

Just as normal is for the boy not to couple at all. The mystery of why one kid falls in love at sixteen and another not till he's twenty is just that, a mystery.

Bill was the father of a popular fifteen-year-old, Tony. Tony got a call or more a night from a girl. Bill admitted to me, in a joking but very honest way, that he was envious. When he was fifteen, no girls called him. "Why are you popular?" I asked Tony one day. "I don't know," he said, as if I asked a stupid question. "I guess I just let them talk, and they like that."

In another conversation, Tony admitted, though unenthusiastically, that the "Can't date till I'm sixteen" rule felt okay to him. It meant he didn't have to commit to one girl or date one and make another jealous.

Boys and youth in the middle teens are doing trial-and-error work in the area of intimacy as much as they are in learning how to drive or think out calculus problems. They're learning what makes girls mad, what makes them happy. They're learning how far they'll go to get a response from a girl that makes them feel good. They know the rejections and responses that make them feel bad.

Middle-adolescent males are experiencing continually the deep-seated male fear of the feminine. It is natural. It is complicated. And we must address it as parents, mentors, and educators. Males are inherently afraid of the feminine in the same way females are inherently afraid of the masculine. Adolescent girls will say, "He's so aggressive!" When we listen closely, we'll notice adolescent boys saying, "Girls are so aggressive."

The teen male is afraid of both rejection and domination. He will be for some time. A girl will begin to devour him psychologically—"She's trying to control me, like she's the only one in my life"—and he will abandon her in order to protect his own fragile, developing identity. A girl will reject him—"I adore her and she thinks I'm just a piece of shit"—and he will be scarred for life. Many men in middle age still remember the rejection of their first love. One man, telling me about it, touched his cheek and said, "It's like I just kept getting slapped. I can almost feel it, right here on my cheek, as if she really hit me."

The more you become your son's ally in his search for intimacy, the more you point out to him that being afraid of girls is real and part of life, the more you call him on self-destructive and also female-dominating behavior that he's involving himself in as a result of his fear, the more you help him through the middle adolescent years. When we see a son who is dominating a female, we must confront him with his own fear of her. "You think it's cool to possess her and treat her like shit. You think you're so strong 'cause you can do that. When I was your age, I did it, too. I did it because I was scared to death of her." When we see our son self-destructing after a rejection, diminishing his grades, checking out of peer friendships, becoming withdrawn, we allow him time and space to grieve, but then we show him again what true love is—the love of family and clan, the love of self. We take him away from his present circumstance on a trip somewhere else, where he can renew his spirit and regain his sense of inner safety and esteem.

The Emergence of the Homosexual Adolescent Male

Stage 2 is a time when most youths who are homosexual become relatively sure of that fact. Homosexual orientation can begin early in a boy's life—that hidden inner sense of being somehow different emerging during gym class. It can wait until early adolescence to become a conscious part of the male's life. It can also wait until during or after puberty to profoundly change the boy's sense of himself. Generally, boys know they are homosexual by early adolescence but don't fully admit it until later, often in late Stage 2, after their bodies have changed and their cognitive abilities have developed enough for them to begin to understand their sexual orientation.

In *The Wonder of Boys* I presented what I consider to be overwhelming and commonsensical scientific evidence that homosexuality is, in most cases, something innate. Since the publication of that book, evidence supporting the "genetic base" point of view has grown even more overwhelming.

Homosexuality among males, we now know, runs in certain family lines more than others, *even when the children are given up for adoption.* In other words, environment is not generally the cause of the homosexuality.

Not to accept the biological base of homosexuality, especially if the adolescent boy is or feels he is homosexual, is to cut off an essential element of caring for him. The psychosocial development of any teenager is difficult, but the psychosocial development of a homosexual adolescent boy is profoundly difficult.

Bruce Bawer, author of *A Place at the Table,* tells the story of standing in a New York bookstore and watching a sixteen-year-old male edging through the mainstream magazines, picking one up, leafing through, putting one down, then another, then another, and then finally, very furtively, picking up the magazine for which he had clearly come in the first place, a magazine about gay issues. The gay adolescent boy's awkwardness and need to conceal himself was like a living metaphor, for Bawer, of the condition of the homosexual.

There is perhaps nothing more difficult for the teen boy or for his family to navigate than the announcement, by the boy to his family, of his sexual identity. There is no magic act that makes this action easier, no two or three "tips" that make the boy's life easier and the family's life ever the same again. Unfortunately in our culture, to be a homosexual male is to be not a second- but a tenth-class citizen. There is no logical reason for this discrimination—homosexuality does none of the harms to the society for which it is condemned. The vast majority of sexual predators, for instance, are heterosexual males, not homosexual males. The AIDS virus is not a "gay" virus but something everyone in the world faces. The Bible barely mentions homosexuality; our culture's great historical teaching book has much more to say about eating habits, for instance, than homosexuality.

The irrationality of homophobia makes the boy's life even more confusing and dangerous, and all we can do is love the boy. He is who he is. If we have raised him to be honest and forthright and to face life's challenges as they come, then we must embrace his honesty and help him face this challenge with our love and acceptance. If there is any magic to dealing with homosexuality in a boy's adolescent years, it is completely in that. To inspire ourselves, and to help us navigate our own conflicted feelings about a son's homosexuality, we might read *The Wonder of Boys, A Place at the Table,* and other books that provide insight and current research.

Biological evidence tells us that if an adolescent male is "wondering" about whether he is gay but in fact is not biologically wired to be homosexual, he will find himself to be heterosexual after a brief experimental period with homosexuality. If, however, the youth is gay, and if we suspect he is suffering self-esteem drops, bad grades, deep personal conflicts, alienation, or depression because he is gay and cannot admit it, we must, in order to give him the care he deserves, help him navigate through his own fear of who he truly is.

Creating and Finding Rites and Rituals with Our Stage 2 Males

A Stage 2 male's psychosocial development is wrapped up around rituals and rites in ways we often do not notice. High fives, sport traditions, rites inherent in studying music and the arts, family traditions, rites involving driver's licenses, purchases of first cars . . . The list is endless, and we as caregivers enrich and guide our Stage 2 males' lives the more we involve ourselves in appropriate ways in the rites and rituals our sons naturally gravitate toward.

Family Rituals

All eras in a boy's life are enhanced by rituals, yet Stage 2 is a time when family rituals often fall apart. Because the boy is pulling away from family in order to become a man, we often let him disappear from family life. This is a grave mistake. He doesn't want it, and neither do we. When he pulled away from us as an infant or toddler, neither of us wanted less love. The same is true with a middle adolescent.

Studies show us that moms talk to, cuddle, and keep eye contact for shorter periods of time with infant boys than with infant girls. The primary reason is that the infant girl holds eye contact with the mom for longer periods of time than the boy. The boy's decreased eye-contact time is mainly a result of his brain system—for instance, it loves objects moving through space, so it is more easily distracted by any other movement in the room. It breaks eye contact to look at the mobile or the new person coming in. Because eye contact is broken, the mother often puts the boy back down in his chair, breaking the cuddling, ending the holding time (a boy's squirmyness is part of it, too).

We want our little boys to be held as much as girls, so once we're armed with the knowledge of why we put them down more, we change our behavior. We notice the boy's eyes moving away from eye contact, but we hold him anyway, and soon his eyes come back to us and the rewards of loving him flow through us.

So it is with boys during the middle-teen years. They are, as it were, breaking eye contact with us, looking elsewhere than at us. But we want to love them and be loved by them as much as before. They want to be loved by us as much as before, just somewhat differently now.

In adolescence, the "holding" is not as physical as it is *ritual.* What holds the boy's eye contact are routines and rituals of family and clan activity that he is required to attend (and truly enjoys, quite often).

Eating together is one such ritual. Families of middle teens ought to try to eat together at least three nights a week. If this means one less sport or activity for the boy, then that's okay. Eating together and loving one another and communicating during dinner is worth one of those sports. Even better, if possible—depending on parents' and kids' schedules—would be to eat at least one meal together a day. For many homes with middle teens in them, it is not possible. But it's worth trying. It's at least worth thinking about why it's not possible, and how that impossibility came to be, and what priorities are now more important than being around a table together.

Family outings are essential. Consider the "going to church" ritual. Even if a youth hates church, at least it's a ritual time when the family's together. Maybe a deal can be struck. "We go to church, then we do what *you* want." This way you get *two* bonding activities out of negotiations surrounding one ritual.

Ritualized clan time is essential. Not just at Thanksgiving and Christmas, but lots of events, picnics, clan soccer or softball games where everyone gets to flourish and be seen.

Ritualized father-son time is essential. Maybe father and son play racquetball or tennis together every Saturday afternoon. Maybe father and son work out at the spa or gym, not doing the same exercises, perhaps, but driving there and back together, and meeting for a little while in a hot tub afterward. A few words are exchanged.

Ritualized mother-son time is essential. A lunch at a restaurant together on a Saturday? Often the son is separating from his mother too harshly for the two of them to do something public together. Nonetheless, some mother-son rituals need to exist. Maybe mother and son play racquetball together!

A Fine Young Man

One mom, a feminist, taught me something about the necessary flexibility of any ideology. She said:

> *I work, I train my kids to respect women as equals, I taught my boys how to fend for themselves. As soon as they were able, they did their laundry. If they wanted something for dinner and I was busy, they made it themselves.*
>
> *Then one day when my oldest was about sixteen, I realized that I was almost never making them dinner. My son would say, already knowing the answer, "Hey Mom, what about some dinner, huh?" It was like a joke. I would say, "Yeah, right. Get it yourself." He did; so did son number two. The result was we didn't eat together, we didn't talk as much. I kind of missed making dinner and sitting everyone down and making an hour of time together.*
>
> *So, I changed. Both my sons and husband were a little surprised at first, but loved it. A few nights a week I made dinner (I've always liked to cook anyway), and we sat together, and they admired my food, and I admired their appetites, and we were more bonded than before. To this day, my sons remind me of "when you started to cook again." The memories we have are precious ones.*

Rituals are essential not only for their moment of transpiring but also for the safety they provide. If a middle teen is having trouble figuring out when to tell his parents or mentors something, he always knows the ritual time exists. If he doesn't even know he's bothered by something, the ritual time provides challenges, closeness, opportunities for the hidden to surface, perhaps as he loses his temper during racquetball with Dad and the real reason he's tense comes out.

Protect your family rituals like they are gold. They are truly as important as money in providing for the welfare of that middle-adolescent male.

The Stage 2 Rite of Passage: The Quest for the Self

A Stage 2 male has many spontaneous rites of passage: getting a driver's license, getting his first car, bonding with that car, perhaps having sex for the first time, doing dangerous or risky things, asking the girl out whom he knows is "too good" for him. Each of these is a spontaneous rite, carrying with it the energy of personal challenge, achievement, and community celebration or recognition. Many ritual activities and moments surround high school life and graduation—many moments of athletic and academic recognition, decisions about college or vocational school, prom nights, dances, falling in love.

Jim Kershner, an accomplished newspaper columnist, once described in print a rite of passage traversed by his sixteen-year-old son, in the company of a peer friend. The two youths decided to roam; they drove from Spokane, Washington, to Big Timber, Montana, 900 miles. Some of Kershner's friends thought he was crazy to let his sixteen-year-old hit the road with a friend for spring break, when anything could go wrong. Other friends, in Kershner's words, said, " 'Good for you! . . .' This opinion was held almost entirely by middle-aged men, and their philosophy, if you can call it a philosophy, goes like this: 'You need to give a boy his freedom. Hell, back when I was sixteen, I drove all the way to Reno one summer, and let me tell you, that was the best darn week of my life. I never did so much growing up as I did on that . . .' "

It was risky for Kershner and his family to let the young men go on their travels, but a great deal happened to those two youths, including an unexpected blizzard that brought them up against harsh conditions, their own fears, their own joys. The families weathered the fear, too, watching the news and seeing the storm build and going through its own rite of passage along with the boys. No process of this type, wherein the human is reduced by Mother Nature's indifferent affection, is not filled with spiritual content. For all involved, issues of heart and soul rise from the vapors, and then return. Lives are changed.

Kershner made a wonderful ending comment about the trip's importance not just for his son but for himself: "In the days since, I have decided that this trip was indeed an important rite of passage. . . . It's called 'letting go,' and it's going to be a long, icy road with reduced visibility at times."

Just as much as we help our males notice the rites they are naturally going through, we need to create a rite for Stage 2, and use it and reuse it (adjusting it, with the male's input) over the years. In other words, sometimes we don't want to do it just once, say at seventeen, but we want to do it every year, like most Indian tribes who regather for a rite at an appointed time annually. I remember an Indian colleague telling me he thought a male adolescent ought to experience some sort of spiritual rite every month. "Doesn't a young woman?" he asked rhetorically. "She experiences her body-held spiritual and generative ritual of menstruation once a month. So should he."

The Vision Quest Model

As we search to build meaningful spiritual rites for our youths, we need not look too far from home for inspiration and technique. Many Native Americans practice the "vision quest" tradition. It is profound and powerful; one that requires our immense respect and admiration. We can use it to help all people, especially our young.

I was first introduced to this tradition during my adolescence, when my father worked on the Southern Ute reservation, in southern Colorado and northern New Mexico. Since then I have made my own vision quests and, as a professional, combined them with therapeutic techniques to help young people, adults, couples, and families. Many others around the country are similarly combining traditions—Western, Far Eastern, and Native American—to develop new rites of passage. I will describe here some of the material that has worked for me with youth.

It is important in laying this out here for me to be honest and say that while I've enjoyed learning and sharing techniques with many Native American friends, there are others who despise it when Caucasians modify their sacred rituals for the care of non-Native Americans. These individuals feel that Caucasians have slaughtered their ancestors and then pilfered their traditions, too.

While I respect my colleagues who dislike the Caucasian use of Native American rites, I follow the statement of a Northern Cheyenne colleague, Clayton Small, who said to me, "It has come time for us to forgive, move forward, and share with white people."

If you are a person deeply involved in a church or other spiritual community and have good rites of passage in place for your young people, I think you still will find much to emulate in the vision quest tradition. If you have no deep involvement in a spiritual community, I hope you will find this description of a quest useful as you *create* a new ritual for your clan and family.

Creating Your Own Vision Quest

A youth joins a few others on a rafting trip with his father and other male friends of his father's. This trip lasts perhaps a week. On it, the river provides challenge in nature. The men provide the mentors. The night and the day provide visions. Stories are told, some of them spontaneous, some of them planned, some even mythic or biblical. Memories rise up and disappear. A journal is kept. Specific ritual celebrations are worked out by the group, some developed before the trip, others developing spontaneously during the trip. The object of the trip is to "have fun," but also to change the lives of the young men. The elder men are always focused on their spiritual work: the mentoring of boys into manhood.

Much of what transpires involves each youth's search for vision (i.e., insight, dreams, hopes, self-perceptions, career directions). Each is a middle-adolescent male, fifteen, sixteen, seventeen, eighteen—his mind is filled with the glory and confusion of the world, his past, his future, nature, time, death, peace, war, pain, grief, health, sickness, reverence, absurdity, indecision, shame, inadequacy, power, hope, justice, truth. A mind filled with all this needs vision. Who am I? What can I hope for? Where shall I go? Who will help me? Why am I alive? What is life? What is death? These questions need vision. Quest is the root word of "question." Here is a model for providing a quest for answers, a quest for vision, in the life of the youth you know.

The community will want to start the youth on his quest a few weeks, even months, before the actual weekend or weeklong rite of passage trip. We ask him what texts he finds especially sacred. He collects these. One might be a psalm from the Bible, a passage from John, a novel by Hermann Hesse. We ask him to begin a journal. If he already keeps (or wants to begin) a journal for day-to-day expressions, we encourage this, but we make sure he begins a different journal for the spiritual material that surrounds his quest. He is asked to write for a few moments every day about who he has been, what his strengths are, his weaknesses, his hopes, his dreams, his memories. In chapter 5 of *The Prince and the King*, I included many sets of appropriate journal questions parents and mentors can use. If you have not read that book, you might refer to it in the context of the vision quest—I provide many descriptions of specific episodes.

As happens, for instance, during Lent, we ask him to challenge his body through some form of fasting. This does not necessarily mean he doesn't eat at all, but it does mean he goes without some toxin or poison he is presently taking in (e.g., cigarettes, beer, other drugs). If he's taking in no obvious toxin, it will mean some diet change. This diet change shows his physical commitment to becoming a responsible adult. Perhaps he stops eating chocolate. Perhaps he stops drinking coffee or eating so much fat.

We invite him to challenge his body and his mind in other regimens that he and we agree will be heightened in his life. If he has avoided certain athletics out of fear and shame, we focus with him now on pursuing one of those. If he has avoided an academic area, we focus now on that one, understanding the spiritual philosophy that in order for a mind to discover its vision, it must do everything possible to complete its unfinished tasks, right its sense of inadequacy, cleanse itself of intimidations and areas of fear.

All of this, and whatever else we need to challenge him with, takes place over a period of one or two months, as "prequest," or preparation for the quest. During this time also, we talk with him about what we're doing, answer his hard questions in life, tell him to write down any questions he wants to ask but can't yet and will ask once he gets out onto the river, or into the hunting trip, or into the wilderness challenge, or onto the road trip, or onto whatever journey he will make in the actual quest.

As the trip itself nears, we get to know the area to be traversed or the location—perhaps a camping ground—to be enjoyed by studying maps and learning about that area of the world. Or, if it is a family cabin already familiar to us, we decide whether we can create a new experience in such a well-known spot. If we decide we can, then we get to know the place itself better, recalling memories of other times there, contextualizing this new quest as unique despite the fact that it fit into an already established family place.

"Threshold" is the word we use to represent crossing into the actual time and location of the quest. The preparations are done. We are ready. Filled with some apprehension and excitement, we cross the threshold. We drive to the scene. We begin our road trip. We set out on our rafts onto the river. This threshold is celebrated, perhaps with a dinner together on a riverbank in which everyone present must offer a toast. One tradition I use is for every boy and man to stand up and name their male ancestors as far back as they can go. "I am Michael Gurian, the son of Jack Gurian, who was the son of William Gurian . . ." Thus we name our lineal inheritance as we enter the quest for ourselves. Perhaps we will talk a little about each of these men. The youth may not, but the elders certainly must. The youth must know where he came from.

During the trip itself the youth must face challenges and tasks. Each family and clan works out their own. Here are some key suggestions:

1. If possible, let the youth set up camp away from everyone else for a day or some other set portion of time. Remember of course to make sure he's trained to face the ordeal.

2. Provide spiritual rituals during the trip that involve prayer, meditation, contemplation, and spiritual story, whether from the Bible or other spiritual texts and practices.

3. Provide constant mentoring as needed, especially mentoring that involves sharing with the youth what vision you see in him, what vision you have in yourself, what visions in the community seem healthy to you, which ones unhealthy; ask him to talk about the visions he has of past, present, and future, of health and illness in the culture. For many men and youth, debate and argument are great receptors and transmitters of vision. Boys and men will argue about the Talmud, the Bible, a movie, a story, anything with deep content, and in arguing form their own visions. "Being right" isn't really the issue. Raising issues of the soul in the company of men is the great learning experience.

4. Focus on inheritance. The boy is partially becoming a man along his family line of men. Especially if the boy's father is helping to lead the quest, the quest is a good time to discuss with the youth what he's inherited, not only in family but in culture. Along with legacy is purpose. "The tasks before you, son, as I see it, are these . . ." The youth describes his sense of those tasks and why they lie before him.

5. Share stories of manhood—sad stories, happy stories, scary stories. Adult men give the youth the gift of their own shames and guilts. "When I was your age I slept with a girl named Joan and then told her she was bad at it when it was really me who was scared and bad at it. . . . I've never forgiven myself."

6. Heal wounds of the family. Often on quests, father and son delve into their mutual pain, utilizing the alone time or, if they need help, asking for the camaraderie of the other men, especially perhaps one trusted man, to help them heal the pain they've caused each other. Apologies are made.

If this quest is not done in the presence of the father or another by whom the youth is substantially angered and pained, the fellow questers nonetheless provide role play and safety in which the youth can try to work out his feelings. I have used this method with young AIDS victims who had only a few weeks or months to live. Some of them had much to heal with parents who had never accepted them as homosexual, had abandoned them even as they were dying. As they made the quest toward death, role play and other techniques helped facilitate healing. So it does also for youth who have normal separation issues with mothers who, though not on the quest, nonetheless can be brought to the river in spirit and spoken with.

7. Encourage the youth during the quest to find sacred objects—rocks, a feather, a letter he writes in his journal, pictures, memories written down—which he will place in a sacred place, box, file, altar at home. He will have these as emblems to remember his growth and experience years later.

8. Give the youth tasks to accomplish—physical, mental, emotional, and spiritual. "Your task on this trip is to set goals for the next year of your life." "Your task on this trip is to finally learn to swim." "Your task on this trip is to figure out this riddle." "Your task on this trip is to become closer to God." "Your task on this trip is to forgive your father." Not all tasks will be accomplished on the trip. Many will be inspired by the trip. Growth is ongoing, continuing well after the quest.

9. After the many tasks, ordeals, conversations, and silences (remember that much of the time the youth spends on the quest is his alone, for prayer, journaling, walking, being) of the quest, the youth and his group begin to look toward the trip's end. All must prepare to reenter the world, to cross the threshold back. A "quest review" is done in the company of men. "The most important experiences for me were . . ." Elders are constantly available to listen, help interpret experiences, and help the youth delve into his experiences, respect his own interpretations, and respect also his silences.

10. Once the quest is over, the raft put away, the drive home accomplished, some bits of it are shared with Mom and others in the community. Yet there is no prying. The youth is allowed his experience. The bond between the men is not weakened by others, including peers. That bond continues throughout the year, providing the youth with safe males to talk with, and providing the elder males with young men who are becoming their emotional peers and therefore will be supporting them as they make their midlife and elderly transitions.

Here, then, is a possible way of doing a quest. I've given a mainly "father-friendly" model. If Father is not around, other caring males can perform most of the actions. Similarly, everyone can adapt everything to fit their lives and the care of their young.

If you should not choose to pursue anything like this in the life of the boys you know, at least use the model as a background for the key elements of what Stage 2 (and indeed all adult males) need as they make their journeys through the various doorways their lives present them. I make a vision quest for myself every year, even now in my forties. Every year I also help others make quests. Thus I am either the participant in or the leader of more than one quest a year. These are some of the most powerful moments of my life.

· · ·

Stage 2 males are some of the most passionate creatures we'll ever know. They are angry, obtuse, generous, stingy, heartfelt, talkative, silent, emotional, cold, warm, paradoxical. No chapter on them can fully capture them, and that is their beauty and wonder. And that wonder just grows as they enter Stage 3. In Stage 3, even as they leave home, they become men. Admiring them for that is one of life's great joys. Let's explore it.

CHAPTER SIX

Stage 3

The Age of Consolidation
(Ages 18–21)

"We're high school graduates! Can you believe it? Now we can really figure out who we are."

FROM A HIGH SCHOOL VALEDICTORIAN'S
SPEECH, 1997

"If I try to give them anything, it's this: idealistic expectations of the world, but realistic expectations of people."

FROM A COLLEGE PROFESSOR, TALKING
ABOUT HIS STUDENTS

The day I went away to college was the day of liberation. I remember getting on the plane in Honolulu, where we lived, to head to Spokane, Washington, where Gonzaga University lay next to the Spokane River, across from downtown Spokane, a middle-sized American city in the pine-tree-rich Pacific Northwest. It was the seventies, a strange time to be young and free. (I was going to a Jesuit college, so I wouldn't be quite as "free" as I might have thought!) Nixon had fallen; Saigon had fallen; I had been too young to serve in Vietnam. Disco was in; the world awaited me. I left a troubled family trying to mend itself and set off into adulthood, unclear on what adulthood was or what manhood was, but very clear that I could find out.

I remember that plane ride not only because of the liberation it represented but also because of a conversation that took place as we crossed the ocean. Sitting next to me was a man in his late twenties. He was skinny, short, tattooed, with a wiry moustache and greasy blond hair. His blue eyes looked a little filmy. He wore tattered Army fatigue pants (this was before they became popular). He wore a motorcyclist's leather jacket, also frayed and tattered. He wore a white T-shirt underneath, food stains here and there on the chest. He talked fast, then he stopped talking, then he talked fast. He listened to me and called me an "intellectual." I reminded him of a guy in his company. His mind wandered, his voice rose, then fell. He was, as we said during that time, "on his own wavelength."

Always good at getting people to talk, and strangely unembarassed by this somewhat crazy guy sitting next to me, I asked him questions about the war in Vietnam. I sensed he was a man *because* he had fought that war. I still felt like a boy, an imposter in the realm of manhood, though I was of draftable age, had graduated high school, could legally consume alcohol, had friends who already had kids, and had a man's body. I wanted to drink manhood from this warrior, despite the fact that he looked like a troubled, disheveled, almost frightened relic of a warrior's adventure gone bad.

He talked a little about the war, and then he shut up about it. His reticence added to my romanticization of his manhood and my clear sense of my own lack of manhood. I recall vividly to this day sitting next to this soldier, feeling both happy I had not fought in that cruel war and sad that I had not fought in that fine war. Like every young man, despite my "intelligence" and my antiwar sentiment, I wanted to be a man, to have some positive way of showing I was a man. Like every young man, to whatever degree, I envied the warrior who had given his youth up to become an adult in the refining fires of self-sacrifice.

Over the years, as I've shared tales of late adolescence with countless men, I've heard a similar story: Even those of us who were against the Vietnam war felt a strange, visceral envy for those men who fought it and other wars. We watched with a strange sense of "I wish that were me" when the television showed old men and their World War II reunions. Only the most callous and ideologically obsessed among us fought against the Vietnam war without feeling a strange camaraderie with the soldiers actually fighting it.

What is this feeling about? How can it be that even antiwar activists still felt the call of the warrior like a call from deep inside Nature herself? What are the other deep calls from within the center of the young Stage 3 man's being? To answer this, let us first notice what we might expect from an average late-adolescent male. Then, let's permit ourselves some metaphor, answering our question with a journey into the center of the emerging man.

What to Expect from a Stage 3 Adolescent

The male during this stage of life experiences the leveling off of his physiological, hormonal, and cognitive development. His brain is formed; his body is changed; he's getting used to brain, body, hormones. Things are consolidating. He has learned by eighteen or nineteen or twenty-one how to "manage" or handle himself. The containers for all his energy—his body and brain—have gone through their second births. Though there are still things and images about his body that fill him with uncertainty, he is less confused about his body than a few years before because, like someone who has worn a good pair of shoes for a year or two, he's somewhat accustomed to them. The areas where there's still a great deal of "birth" going on are psychosocial areas: identity, autonomy, morality, and intimacy.

We can expect this young man to search with some clarity inside himself for his full, adult self, and for the skills and contacts in the external social world, which will allow him to make use of his "self" in the society. He knows that it does little good to find out who he is if he can't sustain it in useful work. So he seeks a job or a college education or both.

Some young men are "lazy" in Stage 3. They don't seem to look inward or outward. They just want to hang out or stay home and live off the folks. We call them "immature," and unless they are disabled in some physical or mental way, that label is a fair one. It is often our instinct to be hard on them, to kick them out of the house, get them moving on their way. We'll look more closely at this situation in a moment.

The Stage 3 male is less enamored with his peer group than he used to be. He still needs it, especially the one or two subgroups he feels he belongs in, but he's also able to have relatively self-confident conversations of critique and self-critique within his groups. He measures himself as much now by how he critiques his own social container as he used to by how he critiqued his parents' social container.

He is able to become somewhat reflective now, looking back at his own past, even exaggerating certain events from childhood. He's emerging as a solid self and spends a lot of time introspecting on that self, even if he never talks to us about it. Our job with him is to help him identify the many strands of himself, picturing the self as a web and the strands as vocational, avocational, emotional, spiritual tendrils. We respectfully help him see tendrils he may not notice. We actively listen to his own discussions of himself, listening more than directing. We watch his actions and deeds and help him find deeper and deeper opportunities to get better at his actions, get clearer on his deeds.

Even if he's into something we care little about—like always washing and polishing his car—we realize that much of his "objectification" in this stage and throughout the rest of life are signals of his hidden self. His interest in certain objects and systems is really an interest in finding mirrors for who he is. As he polishes the car, he is seeking to clarify the hidden in himself, and care for it, and have it thought of as handsome, regal, worthwhile. Realizing how this objectification works, we might find him greater opportunities for deepening his experience with cars: paying for mechanic's school, or helping him apprentice with an elder man who can teach him about cars and, through them, life, too.

The Stage 3 male, especially late in Stage 3, is finishing his psychological individuation process in relation to his parents. By age twenty-one or so, he becomes their emotional peer, able to be as passionate as they, as needed in the clan as they. (We are speaking, of course, in the ideal, for many of our twenty-one-year-olds are in fact still not emotionally individuated in relation to parents. Many of them continue to relate to their parents in childish ways, which we'll explore in a moment.)

He may move out of the house or find other ways of being almost completely self-sufficient. About his twenty-year-old, one dad told me, "His needs of me right now are pretty much motivational and financial. I give him the money for college; he earns his own spending money. Since he and I are close, he uses me for motivation when he's down in the dumps. Beyond that, he's on his own. I respect that."

The Stage 3 male has a relatively well-developed moral system. It is somewhat flexible, built not as much on moral rules as on intuition and conscience. In other words, he will most often do what's "right" not because someone told him to but because now he has sorted out the rightness of things, and his conscience guides him to it.

Most of his core values will match ours. The places where we don't match may still cause trauma and friction between us. We may be protecting tradition, while he's seeking innovation. Sometimes the young man's core values are very different from ours, even frighteningly. This generally happens as a result of alienation or severe distress earlier in the boy's family and social life, the kinds of stresses we talked about especially in chapter 1.

One of the most difficult challenges in caring for a Stage 3 adolescent is loving him despite his contradictory values. It is what I call "Civil War Syndrome." The parent is a Yankee, and the son a Rebel. Often, families who have been lax in their religious passions will suddenly find their sons obsessed with a religion that parents find disturbing. Most of the time, the best plan is to detach from argument and live and let live.

Stage 3 males are having sex and falling in love now, some of them mating and marrying. Some of them are having kids. This is the time in adolescence when it is developmentally appropriate for peer groups and parents to be less important in the developing self than one mate, a "partner for life." Best is always to encourage a Stage 3 adolescent to balance the forces in his life, but still most will go through a time of obsessing over a girl. Some will have done it earlier in adolescence. The wonderful thing about Stage 3 is that it is a transitional time, when our young people can experiment with how mutuality, love, self-sacrifice really work. Our most effective strategy is to *keep communicating* with these young people; they will understand that they are still learning. They are, after all, still in Stage 3 of adolescence. This isn't adulthood yet, though it's close. And, of course, there's a world of difference in some young men between ages eighteen and twenty-one, so Stage 3 itself has a range of possibilities. Many of our young men do not leave Stage 3 at twenty-one—many are still in it well into their twenties.

The Warrior, the Artist, and the King

It would be decades before I understood my own youthful feelings surrounding the Vietnam vet. Now, as I watch and help Stage 3 males move into adulthood, I remember my plane ride, and I know that I and other adults, especially other grown men, must provide young males with experiences of sacrifice, adventure, service, and skill-building. These experiences generate from within the male a quantity and quality of energy similar to that which is inspired by going to war.

The Warrior

The yearning I felt during my Stage 3 was a universal urge of the male, growing most probably from the testosterone-driven biochemical system, and laden with socialization. It was the desire to be a warrior. Our culture avoids recognizing the universality of that urge at our peril. By the time the male has become seventeen or eighteen or nineteen, he is a full-fledged testosterone-driven male, conscripted by his biology to prove himself worthy of notice in a dangerous and hierarchical (food chain) eco- and social system. He seeks the warrior's edge in many parts of his life. Even if he despises soldiery itself, he will honor the soldier by emulating, somewhere in his young life, the soldier's journey, whether in sports, academics, or business. The often-spoken adage "Business is war" has deep meaning for young men.

The Stage 3 male feels an urgency about fully becoming a man. It is instinctual and is satisfied somewhat by military conscription, by going away to college, by getting a job in a trade one feels called to. If left unsatisfied, it will haunt the adult male. The years of Stage 3 can last most of an adult lifetime if that urge is not satisfied. For many men of my generation, it has lasted well into their fifties. Many youths did not fully become men during their late teens and early twenties. Their midlife crises in their forties and fifties become traumatic to them and their loved ones because at midlife, as death approaches a male adult, his instinct to know he is a man (capable of challenging and surmounting challenges of humanity and nature) and has lived a man's life (proven himself capable) becomes urgent once again.

As we observe the Stage 3 youth, let us think of that male at midlife. What kind of midlife passage do we want him to make? How can we make sure, by nurturing him well at twenty, that when he's fifty he'll make a passage into elderhood rather than revert to late adolescence?

The Artist

As I rode toward Gonzaga University on that airplane, I was envious not only of the warrior but also of the artist. I sought Gonzaga in order to become a good warrior—I went there on a debate scholarship, which involves intellectual warfare. I sought Gonzaga also because I loved poetry, classical mythology, stories, architecture, esthetics, philosophy, theology—everything that felt rich in imagination, truth, joy, emotion, new interior worlds. I read Hermann Hesse's books, like *Siddhartha* and *Narcissus and Goldmund,* as if I lived in a desert and they were lifesaving water. I read books about spirituality—the Bible, the Perennial Philosophy, the Christian Mystics, the Kaballah. I searched through different religions. I studied poetry and painting. In my own opinion, nothing could stand in the way of my touching the heart of life itself except a lack of stamina and a lack of vision. If the warrior in me would provide the stamina, the artist in me would provide the vision.

In this desire for vision—this need to see what I could imagine develop itself on paper, or in stone, or in innovation, or in service—I was like every youth. Even the most hardened, even the one we have beaten down with crushed opportunity or racism or abuse, has at the center of him the need *to create*—to make something in this world, to touch something with his hands, his heart, and his mind, to see it transformed from what it was to what he imagines it could be.

This need, like the need of the warrior, we neglect, to our peril. Every young man who moves through Stage 3 without economic opportunity, educational focus, and vision and skill building that *serve* society will nonetheless follow his need for each, finding economic opportunity as survival demands it, making an art of survival itself, educating himself on things that may end up frightening his society, and learning skills and ways of transforming the world that end up hurting many people. The artist in the young male is not to be denied.

This is a matter not merely of socialization or culture. It is also, to a great extent, a matter of brain systems. In the same way the urgency to be a warrior rises from a testosterone-driven biochemical system, the urgency to create with mind and hands grows from a spatially dominant brain system. The formed young-adult male is an artist in a warrior's body. His spatially dominating brain seeks to put internal schemes into external reality. He wants to design and build. He wants to dream up a plan and then organize a system to match it. Just how he does this will depend on many things, including what vocations he's given by society, but he will try to do it everywhere he turns. He will design everything from a new efficient way of talking across continents (telephones) to communicating via satellite to managing a crew on a task to painting a picture. He will invent lightbulbs. He will invent telescopes. If his brain system includes a high density of verbal skills, he will become a Hermann Hesse or an Ernest Hemingway. Some young men, like me, end up leaning more toward the artist's colony—college. Others, like the vet on the plane, lean more toward the military. All of us find ourselves somewhere in the spectrum that includes the challenges of warrior and artist.

Are we being too literal and reductionist in saying that our young-adult males are so often artists in warriors' bodies—"testosterone-filled physical structures" housing "designer/builder minds"? Yes, we are, and we ought do so only in order to help us call attention to the needs of our males; we ought not use the biological information and psychological metaphors of artist and warrior to say that females are not both as well. Young females in their own ways can be very aggressive and protective and surge up corporate ladders.

.

They can and have designed some of the most important social and scientific systems by which we live.

Simultaneously, we are faced with young-adult males today who need closer attention to the warrior and the artist within themselves than we give. If it was once in search of guidance for the warrior that we sent young males to the military, it was in search of guidance for the artist that we sent them into trades and to college. The social problem we face today is one in which few Stage 3 males are going into the military and increasing numbers of our Stage 3 males are not even finishing high school. This situation would not be sad or even dangerous if cultural expectations of men were decreasing, but they are in fact *increasing*. We want better and better artists, designers, builders, politicians, systems analysts, creators, and to compete today they have to be *more ambitious* than a few hundred years ago. However, we have millions of young-adult males who are vocationless, who don't finish high school, who can't find jobs, whose hardwired drives to encounter the world aggressively are not channeled, who fall far behind in school, who are learning disabled. Although many of our males are doing very well in Stage 3, we should remember Jason and his brothers, who, when they reach Stage 3, find themselves quite lost—in large part because their culture has forgotten how to train an artist in a warrior's body.

The King

In Stage 3, in the satisfaction of the dual instincts to become both respected warrior and respected artist, is the synthesis of these: the king. A Stage 3 male rarely becomes a king in his few years of Stage 3, but he strives in Stage 3 to set a clear foundation for his own kingship. He decides on a potential career path. He may decide who he's going to marry (or at least, through experimentation, become clearer on the type of person he needs). He is able, by his early twenties, to see himself relatively clearly—with his own strengths and weaknesses—as a physical, emotional, mental, and spiritual being. He feels his own uniqueness and how it is needed in the world.

If he does not accomplish the bulk of this foundational work by the time he ends Stage 3, we all are in some danger, for he will try to steal already established kingdoms. By this metaphor we mean that if he is not guided during his Stage 3 toward the very center of his own power, he will try to steal, exploit, dominate, and suppress others' power—whether other men's, women's, children's, social groups', or random individuals'. Stage 3 is very much a time when a person's sense of his own power must be consolidated into a manageable "package" or "self," and when a lack of this consolidation leaves the male (and his future relationships) vulnerable.

In *The Prince and the King*, I followed the work of many thinkers, going back to Homer and the Bible, to elaborate a concept of the king as a metaphor for what boys seek to become as men. Stage 3 males are highly focused on these aspects of the king—they want to learn life from these kings, and they want to become these kings.

- The king is a respectable alpha. He possesses the qualities of order and integrity.

- The king is expressive in emotion—passionate, emotionally complete, stable, centered, balanced.

- The king is filled with life force, vitality, and joy.

- The king feels solid in his identity. He feels secure in himself as a social being. While everyone will always have bouts of self-doubt, the king returns to self-security relatively fast.

- The king is both firm and gentle in his dealings with others.

We might think of a king residing inside every emerging man as a metaphor also for self-discipline. A boy who learns self-discipline is a man. A person of order, integrity, emotion, life force, identity, and security in balance is a self-disciplined person. A male who has fully developed his ability to combine gentleness and firmness, flexibility and centeredness, is a man—a king.

Some of the finest "kings" in our history, like King David of the Bible, or Alexander the Great, or the Ottoman King Suleyman, were both rulers and poets—explorers in geographical terms and in philosophical terms. They were well rounded. It was in fact their well-roundedness that made them more than either artist or warrior alone, that showed them to be kings who had consolidated their own talents and skills to such an extent that no matter the challenge—whether the conquest of a city or the lyricism of a poet—they were up to it and could turn it into a gesture of personal and social generosity.

While we are not trying to make our twenty-year-olds into Hebrew conquerors, the metaphor of the king is nonetheless a useful one. The goal of Stage 3 caregiving is to help our males *consolidate*: to refine in them the personal qualities and lessons actualized in boyhood and to help them finish adolescence effectively so that they get to twenty-one or twenty-two or twenty-three and can say, with some clarity, "I am a loving, wise, and powerful man."

How shall we practically accomplish the goal of consolidation with our young men? How shall we accomplish it with Stage 3 adolescent males who are living away from us, quite often, or, if they are still living with us, want to spend most of their time away from our shadows? We will do so in the same way that every culture before us has nurtured its young kings.

1. Give the young man the responsibilities of a grown man. He can handle almost any responsibility now.

2. Let him wander far away. He can handle just about any journey. And he will come back.

3. Help him to teach you what you've always wanted to learn. Inspire his search for knowledge with your own hunger to keep knowing more.

4. Be humble with him even while you remain a rock of authority. That means apologizing now and then.

5. Get to know his friends. Welcome them into your life.

6. Send him wherever he must go to touch the land and life of his ancestors. He can't become a man, a "king," without learning who were the men and women who came before him.

7. If you are a man, take him now into the deep, life-giving secrets of your own manhood.

8. Teach him the sacredness of his freedom and thus help him learn how important it is for him to sacrifice it when he is called by life, community, and family to do so.

9. Keep playing ball with him.

10. Teach him to stand by his truth.

The Meaningful Testing Ground

College is a "meaningful testing ground" where much of development of warrior, artist, and king can be achieved. Family life can be a meaningful testing ground, especially if it requires heavy responsibilities of the youth. A fine, challenging, and vital workplace can be a meaningful testing ground. A Mormon's missionary journey can be a meaningful testing ground, as can seminary or any other spiritual schooling. Soldiery can be a meaningful testing ground. Art or music school can be a meaningful testing ground.

Stage 3 youth need meaningful testing grounds—places, activities, structures in which to test themselves.

Testing grounds can feel meaningless, too. That in itself becomes a test. For many Vietnam vets, their war felt, in retrospect, like a meaningless testing ground. They were traumatized by that meaninglessness. For many seminarians who joined their church school for the wrong reasons, seminary seems, in retrospect, a waste of life itself. For many people, college leads nowhere. For many youths, the workplaces they land in challenge nothing in them but the lure of boredom. The testing ground is the place the youth instinctively gravitates toward. We as elders are responsible for providing meaningful ones and helping our youths gain inspiration even when the testing grounds feel meaningless.

This is a bit of a paradigm shift for many of us. Sometimes we think of workplaces as simply jobs. To our youths they are meaningful testing grounds. We care best for our Stage 3 males when we who hire them remember that these young men have entered our employ not just to make money but to be made into men.

Stage 3 is the time when a society that values its youths (both male and female) provides them with meaningful testing grounds. On these grounds they are led through the third and final stage of adolescence, the stage in which they are finally shaped into adults.

What testing grounds are your males headed for or in right now? This question is crucial to his successful second birth. If in Stage 1 we don't guide his newly found physical power, if in Stage 2 we don't guide his newly found cognitive power, and if in Stage 3 we don't guide his newly found self-consciousness of power itself, we do not raise a boy into a man.

The key word here is, of course, "power." A man is a very powerful being. If he doesn't fully grow up, the boy hidden in the man's body will misuse his power. Our goal as a society must be to shape the power of the male throughout adolescence. For the most part, Stage 3 of this shaping takes place mainly in the company of mentors and peers, not the youth's parents. These people teach him about his power in this stage of life, adding to (and sometimes subtracting from) his adolescent power base. If we want to see how a man is going to use his power later in life, we look most carefully at how his mother used it, his father used it, then how his transitional parents used it in adolescence, especially in Stage 3.

Keepers of the Testing Ground

The Transitional Parents

A lmost always, testing grounds come with mentors. In tribal cultures, a boy is often assigned a "third parent," the elder man who carries wisdom, energy, inspiration, and care for the boy, and who leads him through his many years of initiation. If the third parent is assigned at birth or in early boyhood, he is chosen by Father or Mother or Patriarch or Matriarch, depending on whether the culture is patriarchal or matriarchal.

In our culture, a young man is not generally *assigned* a third parent but *wanders* toward him. Sometimes he meets him early in boyhood, other times in adolescence. Sometimes he has more than one. Tragically, many boys have no third parent. By conservative estimates, at least 80 percent of our high-risk and criminal males were brought up without a father and/or third parent.

Like other boys, I had many teachers, coaches, elders in my life—friends of my parents who took an interest in me, parents of my friends who let me come along on fishing trips, and counselors, too. But not until I went to college was I lucky enough to have my "third parent." He was the mentor who, more than anyone else, led me from boyhood to manhood: He was my transitional parent. I formed a bond with him as powerful as my bond with my parents.

He taught Medieval English literature. I had nearly finished my major in philosophy at Gonzaga University, but then I decided I wanted to become a writer, not just a thinker. I decided to double major. Ever the nerd (the "egghead" or "brain," as we were called then), I was in the honors program. Dr. Michael Herzog, the fourth son of Catholics of German-Russian descent, a first-generation American, was chair of the honors program.

When I first met him I didn't like him. He was hard on me. The thirteenth-century Sufi poet Jalal ad-Din Rumi once wrote that we should "pray for a tough instructor." Michael Herzog was a tough instructor. A big man himself, athletic, a verbal provocateur, he made me suffer more than I thought I ought to. When my girlfriend and I went to his house to play pool, he humiliated me verbally. In retrospect, I see it wasn't much ridicule; in fact it was what anthropologists call "ritual humiliation." He had already seen in me something that attracted his mentorial energy to me, and he was testing my strength, my ability to follow him and thus, through him, to master a piece of my fate. A mentor is an alpha—a leader male—and must act like one. One of his acts of benevolence toward his protégés is to test whether they really can handle his mentorial energy.

I withstood Dr. Herzog. Over the months, then years, I became his protégé, and then, once an adult, I became his friend. While still in college, I baby-sat his kids, changed his young daughter's diapers. I became a great debate partner for his wife, Jean, for whom I cared deeply but with whom I disagreed on many social issues. I memorized Chaucer's poetry. I climbed to the top edges of my class, emboldened by Dr. Herzog. I learned soccer from him. I continued to be as much admired by him as dissed by him. I house-managed his home when he took his family to Europe for a year. He brought me into the lives of his siblings and nieces and nephews. I called his mother "Oma" and his father "Opa," just as his own kids did. Dr. Herzog and his clan adopted me, and I adopted them.

If not for Dr. Herzog, I would not be the man I am today. I would be less of a man, of that I'm sure. I might not have fully become a man—i.e., left Stage 3. I had the advantage of having not only teachers, coaches, elders, mentors, parents, but also of having, in Stage 3, this third parent. I had the honor, recently, when he went up for full professor, of writing to the committee, to support his application. I wrote that after my parents I considered him the most important influence on my life.

Whether he finds him or not, every Stage 3 male seeks a third parent. Some of us find him in Stage 2, but most of us, if we find him, do so in Stage 3—through our clan, in college, at work, or by surprise somewhere else.

If we don't find him, we elongate our adolescence until we do, amalgamating him from fragments of other mentors, teachers, coaches, and friends until we get enough of a "third parent" from all these to finally become a man. If we're lucky enough to actually have one man who becomes our third parent, the process of integrating fragments of other men is easier, and can be quicker.

Because an adolescent has this third parent does not mean he automatically becomes a man at age twenty-one. Many of us, in this culture, do not. I did not until I was twenty-five, as I'll discuss in a moment. But still, a young man's having the third parent in his life makes it more likely he'll become an adult before he enters the age of marriage, child-raising, and the work stresses of adult society. Not having one increases the chances that he'll awaken at forty or fifty, his own children half grown, and realize he is not a man, for he has not been taught what a man is by the intimate relationship with not only Father but the man who is like Father and, in some mysterious, magical way, teaches him to be a man.

Bruce's Story

I found my third parent in college; another young man found him in sport. I learned of the story this way.

Bruce, a man in his fifties, recalled his experiences with golf and young men. He began with his son, teaching him golf, taking him out once a month or so. His son took to it, and Father and son found something to do together, something through which to bond, spend time together, enjoy; time there and back to talk, if need be; time and space in which to enjoy the outdoors. They grew up together, enjoying those "ethereal moments" (Bruce's words) when everything just falls together on the green.

"It's a great sport for boys and men," Bruce told me. "It's a sport, but it's not violent. It gave my son and me a way to give each other some verbal jabs, but not be disrespectful or shaming. The game just lends itself to a little bit of dissing. We didn't have heart-to-hearts on the course, but we were together, for hours on end. We liked each other. We knew each other."

This man, through his son, ended up taking other boys out golfing. It became a kind of clanlike thing. Then, when his son went to college, Bruce met one of his son's friends, Hamid, a student from the Middle East, a young man far from home. This young man came over for dinner a few times (the son and the young man went to a local college, so dinner at home was a weekly thing still). From dinner came the decision to go golfing. From golfing once in a while came "the addiction," as these guys affectionately referred to golf. "It ended up," said Bruce, "that my son went to another university out of state, but Hamid became like a son to me. I learned a lot about him, and he about me. There were some things I ended up telling him over the two years of golfing with him that I don't remember telling my son. This young man in my life was very rewarding. I think I gave him a father figure in the U.S., someone to hold on to a little bit. I even helped him get a job after he graduated."

This man, through the vehicle of golf, became a transitional parent to a son of a faraway land. The young Middle Eastern man became a transitional child for the elder man who was moving through the time of letting his own son go.

Psychosocial Development

Identity, Autonomy, Morality, Intimacy

Between the time I flew on that airplane with the Vietnam vet and the time I knew myself as a man, much psychosocial development had occurred in me. In the Stage 3 years there is a wonderful intensity of growth often hidden from us because we and our sons don't interact as much anymore. Let's briefly notice it now, as we have in the previous chapters, where we called it the I AM I—identity, autonomy, morality, and intimacy—questions.

The Search for Identity

My Stage 3 search for identity lasted until I was twenty-five. I vividly remember the end of my adolescent identity and the beginning of my adult identity, my manhood. I wasn't able to "grow up and feel like a man" until four years past the end of the Stage 3 mark. This is not unusual. In our culture, many of our males do not develop adult identities by age twenty-one, though I hope that the knowledge we are now gaining will help the next generation come closer to the mark.

The actual point of my identity consolidation occurred in Germany. Dr. Herzog, with whom I remained good friends even after college, loaned me the money to travel to Europe and, once in Europe, to go to Germany. As an American Jewish kid who had lost nearly every relative to the Holocaust, I had been brought up with anti-German sentiment. For a time, my parents wouldn't even set foot in a German car. Deep within the bag of shadows I carried with me toward manhood was the dark German world, a world of hurt, betrayal, death, and agony. As a boy I dreamed the deaths of my relatives in camps, and always dreamed the same enemy: Germany. It was perhaps no accident that my transitional parent was of German descent. It was not my fate to walk through life hating any people. Though I didn't have the maturity to understand it at the time, I was on a pilgrimage toward mature identity that would be marked by forgiveness.

For me, wrestling with the German shadow meant wrestling with my identity as a Jew, a man, and a survivor. These issues aggregated when I visited the Dachau camp, where my Jewish brethren, and many others, had been tortured and slaughtered. I was so grief-stricken in that camp that I could not weep until hours later. I left after a day of experience, but returned the next day. I felt fear and revulsion but pushed onward toward something I could not define until after hours and days of standing at the racks of torture, walking the yards, and listening to the whispers. I was surprised, in the end, to feel not hatred for the German people but something amazing—forgiveness. I felt a lifting of my own survivor guilt. I felt myself become solid, realizing that I would do whatever I had to in life to help make sure a Dachau never existed again. I committed myself to the human search for truth and peace.

I was a young man in search of a soul, and I found my own. I grew up during those months in Europe—a maturation that made itself most plain during my days at Dachau. I remember standing in the Dachau yard, taking an inventory of my identity. "Who are you?" I asked myself. "If you stop hating and fearing the Germans, who are you?" I wrote in my journal for hours, and indeed for days after that.

Every Stage 3 adolescent must find his Europe and his Dachau.

If we are to help the next generation, we give them testing grounds for identity. We direct them to their own Dachaus. We tell them how to take inventories of their identities. We show them that just becoming a cog in a wheel is not an "identity." They must become unique with as much vigor as they seek to conform. We make sure they have transitional parents to help them move into adult identities.

As we nurture our Stage 3 youths, our call is to think again to the king metaphor. Our young males will be stimulated toward materialism and definition of self through the pursuit of women and power. It is our job, as parents, mentors, and educators, to form intimate bonds with these men. From within those bonds we can be believed when we say, "I see in you more than a salesman, son, I see a real innovator"; we can be taken up on it when we offer, "I will help you travel to the place where your demons are. Good luck to you there."

The Search for Autonomy

A mother of two sons called in to a radio talk show I was doing in New York. She told a story I've heard all over the country.

> My son is twenty-four and still living with my husband and me. He just won't leave! He started junior college but dropped out. He lived for a while with friends, but now he wants to move back in, save money, and see where he lands next year. My husband and I were all ready to get on with our lives. We're wondering whether to let Lance move back in or not.

Stage 3 is the stage most rife with "autonomy events." These events involve a son moving out of the house, going to college, getting a "real job," going to vocational school, living at home but coming and going as he pleases. Each of these events carries the promise of full adult autonomy, but each is also rife with the possibility of disappointment, both for parents and for children.

Most parents and kids are actually riding the same emotional roller coaster. They are certainly going through the same events, even if from different perspectives, for Stage 3 autonomy generally moves in three distinct steps.

1. First separation (moving out)

2. Backtracking (homesick calls or moving back in)

3. Final separation (moving out again for good). This final separation can end up being extended into many "final" separations.

This process of Stage 3 autonomy carries with it the end of child-parent safety for parents and their children. It carries with it a transformation in trust. We and our kids have to become adults who trust each other. This is a different dynamic than parent-child trust, which is built on constantly testing and watching the child. Adult-adult trust is a very detached kind of trust, allowing the flow of life to carry the relationship where it will.

Both parents and children have to give up manipulation and control of each other. They have to develop new lives now, lives not at all focused on each other.

If, however, a Stage 3 male is not moving toward autonomy in a normal way (and we're assuming he is not significantly disabled, either mentally or physically), then he is afraid. What is he afraid of? Perhaps our job during the years of Stage 3 is to address one or more of these fears with our love and our challenge.

1. Is he afraid no one except his parents will ever love him? Sometimes he develops this fear because his parents didn't know how to love him well earlier in life. He didn't get enough love from them, or got traumatic love, and now won't enter the big world until his parents really show they love and care for him. In this case, we need to love him now, for a time, in the way he is asking to be loved, even if it "inconveniences" us.

2. Is he afraid he will not be good enough at anything to make it out there? Stage 3 is sometimes called a time of leftovers. Worries and shadows that haven't been dealt with earlier in adolescence pile up in the refrigera-

tor like leftovers and need to be eaten now. Performance anxiety can be one of these. Our job is to help him find the place where he can flourish, whether it's nuclear physics or hairdressing. What's most important is the discovery with the boy of a social and work container where he'll do well.

3. Is he afraid he'll harm his parents or clan by leaving them behind? If he is, we may be hanging on to this boy too much, and may need to fully let him go, even if that means hurting ourselves a little, and hurting him. In this regard we always remember that there is barely any sacrifice not appropriate to make for a child. If we have been making him feel guilty about how hard life is or will be without him, we stop this crippling behavior.

4. Is he afraid he'll hurt himself if he leaves his parents' sphere? In other words, is his confidence very low? Is he unable to see life possibilities that don't involve himself making terrible mistakes? We do what we can to build his self-confidence. We get him help if need be. We push him toward work and activities and mentors that will build confidence, which could include giving him a job or pulling strings for him to get one.

5. Is he afraid he will hurt the world, especially loved ones, if he fully becomes a man? If so, we need to get him help in the psychological area, even pay for his therapy, if necessary.

Fear in a Stage 3 adolescent is a normal part of the autonomy process. It is nothing to shame a young man for. It is, in a sense, our last vehicle by which to be intimate with the young man in ways that remind us of caring for him as a baby and a little boy. This vehicle will not last forever. One day he'll stop e-mailing us. We'll catch ourselves, on that day, saying, "Why isn't he keeping in touch? I didn't want him to cut off from us completely!"

The Search for Morality

Most late-adolescent males are becoming very sophisticated moral beings. While there are always the exceptions, a majority of them have lived twenty or so years, been raised in a moral society, know the difference between right and wrong. They may lack the will at all times to do what's right, but then, don't we all at some points in life? They may take unnecessary moral risks, but then, haven't we all? They make terrible mistakes even while thinking they are being very moral, but then, haven't we all?

Our job is to be morality *sounding boards* now, more than *taskmasters* (except, of course, when at-risk behavior is involved).

As Stage 3 progresses, we show these males the increasingly complex moral palette that society is, and help them gain the critical skills and personal will to think out what's right and do it. We show them that we believe in certain basic truths and hope they will too, but we also know that since they are in Stage 3, they must arrive at those truths themselves.

We stimulate that discovery by constant conversation, education, clan life, and moral challenges. Debate around the dinner table, at family reunions, during activities together is a great way to hone the moral skills of the youth. Even if we disagree on certain tenets, a good debate can enhance our bonds, teach us all a thing or two, and ultimately change the world.

One of my obsessions during my decade of teaching college was to inspire colleges to make ethics courses part of the core curriculum. Over the years I've watched more and more colleges cut out their ethics, philosophy, theology, and other morality-challenging courses, replacing them with vocational and business classes. While these latter are essential for preparing males to fully realize their responsibilities as workers, we neglect Stage 3 moral development to our peril. Stage 3 adolescents are absolutely fascinated by their own newly developed abilities to see vast pictures of what's right and wrong, what's chaotic and orderly, what's real and just a tempting illusion. Not to allow the Stage 3 male to explore his own morality is to condemn him to moral confusion for perhaps decades to come. Moral confusion means confusion about his commitments to mates and kids, to jobs and society, and to himself.

One reason why college and church institutions (and hopefully, one day, an awakened, more child-friendly media) must provide morality challenges and morality education is that the young man is no longer much in his parents' care. The larger influences on him are out in the society and the social institutions in which he and his peers live. Thus, the idea that "morality is only a subject for the home" doesn't make much sense for Stage 3 adolescents or for late-Stage 2 males. Even workplace education and human resource planners soon must come to realize that ethics education ought to be part of whatever curricula major corporations provide as in-service training for employees.

.

The Search for Intimacy

During Stage 1 of adolescence, the male just discovers that his body is capable of some forms of love. Much of his emphasis is not on learning about love as spirituality, but rather about love as function, sex, desire, squeamish fantasy.

In Stage 2, the male starts pairing off with female partners but also, most often, holds a lot back, still getting his cognitive abilities, still trying to touch love like it is a fire, pressing at it till he's burned, then pulling away. While some Stage 2 males fall in love very hard, most do not. Most are still willing to play the field, lie about love prowess they possess, delight more in fantasy than reality. They aren't yet fully capable of instituting love as discipline. While the adolescent boy may go to his parents for some help during his experimentations, he is also rebelling and/or just wanting to have something that is his own—he is not as interested in adult views of love.

By Stage 3, however, males are developmentally ready to understand that *adult* love is *love practiced like a spiritual discipline.* They are beginning to see how difficult love is and how important it is to have a common language between lovers, and a long-term (not just infatuation-oriented) vision of relationship.

When we refer to love or intimacy as a spiritual discipline, we mean that it is very much like an artist's discipline, with certain aesthetic rules, energies, signs, signals; it is a discipline like that which a spiritual master teaches his monks, actions that facilitate prayer and the daily fulfillment of commandments; it is a discipline in the same way a healthy warrior master teaches supreme discipline to his young warriors so that they can be servants of the greater good.

In tribal cultures in India, Turkey, and elsewhere, adolescents are constantly forced by their elders to understand love as a discipline, but in our culture, adolescent love generally takes place out of sight of the adults. I find that we in America are the loosest, the least active, in teaching love as spiritual discipline. At the very time, Stage 3, when our kids need it so much, we think: "They're eighteen; they're adults; they'll figure it out." While we don't want "discipline" to imply control and restrictiveness that are not, frankly, possible for us to achieve with Stage 3 adolescents, we do want it to challenge us to teach *more* about love and intimacy than we do. We need to bring to our sons' (and daughters') lives long discussions about love, about discipline, about freedom, about why love exists and how we think it works. I hope we'll make comparisons for them between love and their other occupations, showing them as they train to be engineers that love must be treated as science is treated: a discipline to be mastered. As they train to be artists, we show them that for an artist, discipline is first and foremost: expression of feeling is just paint thrown about unless discipline accompanies that expression. As they train to be social critics, we show them that diplomacy is most often the discipline needed to change the world for the better.

Stage 3 is a good time to model and remind young people that a relationship is a place of politeness, careful conversation, mutual explanation, reasonable expectation.

Stage 3 is just the right time to expose young people to communications courses where they learn good communication and conflict skills:

- How to listen without interrupting

- How to talk without dominating conversation

- How to acknowledge a partner's feelings and ideas before jumping in with a disagreement

- How to finish a "fight" before a certain time (e.g., never going to bed without working things out)

- How to assert oneself if the partner is someone who interrupts a lot

- How to avoid "always" and "never" in fights

- How to stick with "I" statements, like "I feel" or "I think"

- How to avoid the obsession with being "right"

- How to see how each partner has a different perception of everything

- How to allow anger in oneself and others and get help when it be-comes destructive

Because we as adolescents ourselves led relatively chaotic love lives, we often become afraid or numb when challenged to teach the next generation about loving communication and intimate love. I hope that as you face this dilemma you'll find wisdom and companionship from other parents, and that you'll lay *your* own Stage 3 story at the table of your teen boys (and girls). They are ready to hear, understand, and learn from it.

The Stage 3 Rite of Passage

The Pilgrimage

In adolescence, males make many journeys, hunting for themselves throughout these crucial years. They make pilgrimages toward holy places, toward new jobs, toward themselves. The Mormon Stage 3 male may go on his mission. The young man in Turkey may move to Germany, where he can get a better job. The Muslim Stage 3 male may go to Mecca. Our young men somewhat satisfy the instinctual urge for pilgrimage by moving out of the house, if they haven't already, and to another city, or by moving in with a girl-friend and making the life journey now with her.

If your young man has not yet made a literal journey, a real-life, long-term journey—by car, airplane, train, foot; into other worlds, other cultures, other environments—for the sheer search of it, in other words, not because he gets a job as a driver but because he must now fulfill his desire to get away and to move toward, to find out what he's made of, to survive, to flourish, and to grow, by the time he leaves Stage 3 of adolescence, encourage him to do it, facilitate the journey, see it as just as important as college.

In Israel, young people are encouraged (and at least partially funded) to make a two- to three-month trip to Europe (or wherever else is their "old country"). This journey is considered, in many families, a fundamental part of growing up. In Europe they go to their place of origins, origins not only of their families' lines and therefore of much of their present destinies, but origins too of their families' grief and pain. In Europe, they are tested.

I met a young man here in the U.S. who epitomized the psychosocial struggle of the Stage 3 male. He was graduating from college with a degree in political science and wanted to travel the U.S. and the world. "I don't want to get a job yet or go to graduate school," he said. "I just want to find my way around, challenge myself, see new places. My parents ask me, 'What are you after?' I don't know. I just know I want to do it."

His parents were kind people, caring people, who were afraid that if he wandered too far into the mists of the world, he would not find a direct path to success and adult life. He himself, who loved them for their love of him and for the sacrifices they had made, felt guilty for wanting to pursue his dream in the face of their objections. He came to me and asked for advice.

We talked a long time, men who did not know each other before that moment but who bonded immediately because the subject before us was the subject of manhood itself. In the end we determined these things:

The fulfillment of responsibility to parents is a pragmatic subject: If I leave for Europe, will my parents be physically cared for? In this young man's case, his parents were fine. His leaving caused them no hardship. He had to realize that he was not responsible for their feelings about him. He was extending his internal sense of responsibility beyond what it needed to be. In order to be a man now, he had to become responsible for his own self-development.

His fears about leaving safety and traveling would dissipate after a few weeks. He would find that he could do just about anything he set his mind to. He realized he was afraid of the travel itself, even though he dreamed of it all the time.

His guilt about his parents would also dissipate after a few weeks on the road.

He owed his parents some letters so that they could share in his growth while he traveled.

These were things we discovered together, and he became inspired to push through his fear, his guilt, and his parents' arguments. I never met his parents, but I know from meeting the son that in the end they will be very proud of him.

The rites of passage we parents help our Stage 3 males make often do not involve us much in their practicalities. Perhaps they involve us only in that we finance them and help motivate our young men to make the journeys. Perhaps we provide our sons with addresses of relatives to visit, or addresses of potential mentors. Perhaps we go along the way for part of a journey, driving with a son to San Francisco to catch the plane, but then send him off on his own.

I have focused here on the "journey" or "trip" or "pilgrimage" as a Stage 3 rite of passage, yet it may not be possible or wanted in your family. There may be something else that your family or clan uses to show your son that he has *the endurance, stamina, vision, wisdom, will, emotional range, intellectual yearning, common sense, and survival skills of a man.* College graduation, and the whole journey of college itself, can be a rite. Graduating from a trade school, getting a black belt in a martial art, committing to a life work, getting married, having a child—all these can be rites. Stage 3 rites of passage are various, yet some things are basic to all of them: There must be at least one event in which the adolescent male becomes a man; in one of the rites, the clan must bless the young man with his manhood.

"You are a man, now," we say to him. We've said it to him once or more when he was in Stage 1, then a few more ritual times in Stage 2, then a few more in Stage 3, until the adolescent passes some form of clan or family rite in which he is shown that adolescence is over. Much of this "showing" can be done in talk, in elders taking him to lunch or dinner and saying, "Here's the man we see in you." Much of it can be done in trusting him to work side by side with us, without ordering him around. Perhaps after he returns from his trip abroad we have a party for him, accept him as a man, tell him to lead the family toast now.

A Fine Young Man

However we make this Stage 3 rite happen, it must accomplish the development of the king in the man. Afterward, we must want to look up to this male. We must want to follow him into his visions. If we can't do this by the time he's twenty-one, even twenty-five, his adolescence is not over. Our job as parents of an adolescent continues.

*"The task of the teacher is to prepare
a series of motives of cultural
activity, spread over a specially
nurtured environment, without
obtrusive interference.
Accomplishing this task, she will be
witness to the unfolding of a New
Man who will not be the victim of
events but will have the clarity of
vision to direct and shape the
future of human society."*

MARIA MONTESSORI

PART THREE

Educating
Adolescent Boys

CHAPTER SEVEN

Schoolboys

Adolescent Boys and the Educational System

"One who opens a school door, closes a prison."

VICTOR HUGO

I stepped off the soccer field and into the car of one of my teammates. It was a crisp, spring Saturday afternoon. John played forward, and I played sweeper. We hadn't talked much over the months, but I needed a ride and he was happy to give it. I expected just some small talk during the fifteen-minute ride.

Instead, I learned that John, formerly a research chemist, was getting a masters in education so that he could teach high school. It was his second career, a longtime dream getting fulfilled now, in his mid-forties. His wife and his daughter, thirteen, and son, ten, liked the idea of him teaching. He was proud to be embarking on the new adventure.

He had been running into something strange, though. He knew a little about my research and writing and decided to check something out with me.

We're reading arguments by researchers that girls are shortchanged in the educational system. We've been watching videotapes of boys being called on more; we're reading Sadker and Sadker's book (Failing at Fairness). *The big push now is to get more female teachers into math and science to bolster the girls. I have a daughter, so I'm for any bolstering girls can get, but something doesn't make sense. Not in class, but from the Department of*

Education I've read statistics that boys get worse grades than girls nationwide; they drop out of high school more; they make up the majority of behavioral-problem children as well as academic-problem kids. At the school I interned at, almost all the disturbed and special-ed kids were boys. I talked to other interns who saw the same thing. I've watched my own son's struggles. I just read that the majority of college and graduate-school students are female and that most of the valedictorian and salutatorian students are girls.

I know there are unfairnesses to females, but I can't find any way to dispute that the most problems exist with the males—academically, socially, behaviorally—in all categories. What am I missing?

"Have you brought this up with your instructor?" I asked.

No, he said, he hadn't. He resolved to do so.

I saw John a week later, and we talked after the game. He had brought it up, he said, and it felt very strange. While the teacher didn't exactly shoot him down, she did not support his point of view. "Certainly boys suffer," she'd said, "but the real suffering in this society is with our girls. Until we right the wrongs done to them, we can't get anywhere." A female student in the class had said to him, less tactfully, "You're just jealous, as a white male. Women are being targeted for your science jobs, and you don't like it."

John was somewhere between bewildered and angry. He said he had not confronted anyone in class, though after class he went up to his classmate and told her he didn't appreciate being attacked for what was, on his part, a well-researched point.

The next week I saw John again. Things felt different in the class, he said, since he'd brought up his point—polarized between the women and men. He had been a studious, inconspicuous class member until now, but he realized that he was the cause of polarization and he didn't know what to do.

Gender Ideologies and Our Educational Assessments

John is one of many people, both male and female, who are being educated at the turn of the century by ideologies constructed in the 1960s and 1970s, educational ideologies that foster gender polarization. These ideologies are no less aggressive and disastrous than were the Victorian ideologies that polarized men and women against each other, favoring males, oppressing females, and leading finally to the equity feminism of Susan B. Anthony and onward to the victim and gender feminism of Gloria Steinem, Andrea Dworkin, and many others.

The old Victorian educational ideology went a little like this:

Girls don't need to go to school, they need to get married. If they go to school, it's ultimately to get and care for a husband anyway, not to rise to the top of a chosen profession. So girls don't need as good an education as boys.

The new gender educational ideology goes a little like this:

Boys get all the breaks, girls are way behind. If you care about girls, you'll realize that girls are always in more difficulty than boys in this male-dominated society. If you don't take that point of view, you're a traitor to your daughters.

Both ideologies are false.

Girls *do* need as good an education as boys.

Girls are now receiving education as good as or better than boys.

Not accepting the new gender ideology does not make one a traitor to one's daughters or women in general.

We who care about the education of all our children now stand at the threshold of a new era, one in which we can say: "Here are the ways girls are shortchanged. Tell me how boys are shortchanged. Let's work together to fix both." If we do not work together—if we do not start from a point of view of equity—repairs made to female education will cause terrible problems in male education. That is what we face today. We have stressed so formidably the improvement of the lives of our girls that we have neglected the educational world of boys. According to the latest National Education Assessment and the Educational Testing Service Gender Study—perhaps the two most comprehensive educational assessments available—*female indicators are up, and male indicators are dropping, dropping not to a point of parity with female but to a point of disparity.*

If you have not read the statistics and studies on adolescent boys in the educational system that I presented in chapter 1, now would be a great time to do that. They show our adolescent males worse off than our adolescent females in nearly every educational category, from learning disabilities to behavioral problems, from grade performance to professional aspiration. They show that our male children get most of the Ds and Fs and now constitute the minority of salutatorians and valedictorians—they dominate the low end of the grade spectrum and are outperformed at the high end. They show that our males constitute the majority of high school dropouts and the minority of participants in student government. They show that our adolescent females are now taking more math/science classes than our males, and have nearly caught up in math/science performance; our adolescent males, however, are a year and a half behind our females in reading/writing. Researcher Diane Ravitch summed up the situation in this way: "If we want to talk about a gender suffering substantial deprivation in education right now, we are talking about our boys and young men." In the last decade, we've focused on many of the key areas of adolescent-female distress and assumed the adolescent males were doing better. That assumption has been flawed and false.

In this chapter we will explore what's happening to our adolescent boys in education, and suggest powerful solutions for individual families, the educational system, and the culture. We will acknowledge that there are many reasons for what our boys experience, and many cannot be solved by educators. We will recognize also that at the heart of what so many of our boys experience in school is the fact that educational systems are often not well versed in adolescent-male development and needs. *Adolescent boys develop, behave, and learn in boy-specific ways that need male-specific attention.*

As I present this material, I offer the following caveat: Always we must come to center, wherein we know that *both* girls and boys suffer in different ways that need our various, not our singular, responses. If you advocate for adolescent boys, I plead with you not to help the pendulum swing against girls. As we enter the new millennium, we must find a way to care, at once, for all our children. A man like John, a caring educator and father of a daughter, must have the right to bring up a well-documented truth in his class without being labeled antifemale.

Innovations for Educators

Brain and Biology in Every College of Education

The scene was a John Merrow NPR forum on education at the UCLA School of Education. The school faculty and staff were wonderful hosts, providing an audience of professors, community members, educators, counselors, college students, and grad students. The forum was about male development, boy biology, and boy culture. Somewhere in the middle of it,

I asked, "Is there a course in this masters or Ph.D. program on what we're discussing here—brain systems, biochemistry, and male development?" The answer came back: No.

By the end of the forum, we did not agree that a course would be taught, but we had inspired some of the faculty to look more deeply into the need to teach young teachers the nature of their students' development. This hour at UCLA started me on a search to discover whether "Brain, Biochemistry, and Male Development" is taught in any school of education. Thus far I have learned of a very few: one at William and Mary, one at Penn State, and one in Phoenix. There must certainly be others I don't know about, but there are at this point fewer than I can count on my two hands.

This means virtually all of our young teachers go into the school class-room without being trained in crucial aspects of the cognitive natures of the children they teach. Hopefully, in the near future, we'll work together to in-spire schools of education and related graduate programs to provide this class and this training. If every teacher knew more than s/he knows now about brain systems and hormonal systems, they would be able to help both males and females learn better. We would find fewer males in special ed, fewer learning-disabled males, fewer discipline-problem males, fewer male dropouts. Areas of academic distress for male children—like reading and writing—would improve dramatically. Let's explore the different learning modes of our adolescent males and females.

Different Ways Boys and Girls Learn

We've intuited for some time that boys and girls learn differently. Until now we haven't quite known why. Boys and girls measure, absorb, process, and present what they have learned in different ways. These differences begin mainly in brain structure, then the brain's interaction with environmental stimuli. Certainly all are potentially amplified or minimized by socializing factors. While we may discover that some of the amazing male/female learn-ing differences are purely socialized, it is unlikely. Learning, after all, begins and ends in the brain. Here are some of the things we know now about learn-ing differences. They comprise the tip of the iceberg in terms of what is available to us.

EMPHASIS ON DEDUCTIVE REASONING. Boys tend to be more *de-ductive* in their reasoning than girls, who tend to be more *inductive*. Boys tend to begin with the general and apply it to an individual case. Girls tend to look at some examples of something and then build generalizations and theories from them.

When we were discussing this in a school district recently, one teacher said:

> *My God, this explains what goes on in my [sophomore] English class. The males tend to come up with what they're sure the writer is saying pretty quickly. They come up with an example after they come up with the principle. But the girl might say, "Because of this, this, this, and this, and because of this and this too, I think we are led to believe . . . this." The females tend to be less impulsive anyway, and they tend to look at a passage from a novel less as a problem to be solved or generalized than as a series of individual experiences to be understood. The boys see literature much more as a set of problems to be solved than as individual life experiences to be savored. So it seems to me it's about their impulsiveness, their problem-solving minds, and their deductive minds all at once.*

Another teacher agreed, giving an example of her own: "We were reading *The Color Purple,* by Alice Walker. From the very beginning, some of the boys just had to give theories as to why the book was called that. The girls were less inclined. They were almost, if I can say it, just more patient. I wonder if this is the kind of thing we're talking about."

Indeed it was, for both teachers. So many of the impulses of the young male show up in these two teachers' comments: Competition is there, impulsiveness, a tendency toward deductive reasoning first, enjoying the solving of problems.

DIFFERENCES IN GROUP LEARNING EXPERIENCES. Girls gravitate more easily to small group learning experiences than boys. By this we mean they will tend to move to a small group learning experience by self-motivation, whereas boys will tend to have to be directed toward it. Once in the group, girls will spend less time than boys making administrative decisions (sometimes they won't make them), e.g., who's going to lead.

A lot is hidden in this activity: the male push toward personal performance and pecking orders, the male push toward independent action and gain. This is not to say males are not team-oriented. Of course they are, but in many ways they tend toward *larger group teams* than females do—hunting groups, large work groups, sports teams. In the arena of *learning,* we find males holding back a little more than females when it comes to teaming up in small groups. One theory rests in the idea that male biology and culture are based on vigilance about competition and hierarchy, making them slower to form bonds that might make competing with the peer more difficult. In other words, if I'm his friend, can I really beat him?

To check whether you think males and females do indeed fit this model, think about who's more likely in your family to ask for help while driving, or when lost, or when things are unsure. The female members are more likely. One of the new theories about the female proclivity to cry when afraid or alienated (as compared with the male's proclivity to withhold tears) is that males are both hardwired and soft wired not to seek help. Females, on the other hand, are hardwired and soft wired to call attention to their distress as quickly as possible in order to gain help in alleviating the distress.

INTUITION.   In life and in learning areas, girls and women in general are more intuitive and trust their intuition more than boys and men. This is a vast generalization, of course, because there are many intuitive boys. However, you'll find the tendency operative if you study a group of ten boys and ten girls. You'll notice that once a girl has an intuition about something, she'll be pretty confident about it. The boy, on the other hand, will tend to need to back up that intuition with lots of evidence and logic.

You'll also find this intuition superiority operative in marriages and workplaces. Girls and women are better judges of character than boys and men. We know some of why this occurs, and it's linked to structural brain differences. The female corpus callosum, as we've discussed, is larger than the male, allowing more cross talk between the two hemispheres of the brain. The female brain takes in more sensory and emotive data, and more quickly, than the male. Hence, she's got more going through her system, more information, more touch with the world she's observing, and more chance of having a quick intuition and a reason to trust it.

ABSTRACTION.   There is one area of exception to this "intuition" generalization: abstraction. In philosophy, for instance, or mathematics, adolescent boys tend to trust their intuitions more than their female peers. This is not surprising. Boys in general seem to reason more abstractly, making wide leaps between abstract concepts and not needing all the concrete information. Girls usually reason in more concrete terms. Educators of girls have known for some time that when teaching math and science, for instance, they must make sure the material is *concrete*. That way, girls will understand and work with it better. Researchers have discovered these different ways boys and girls reason by studying how adolescent males and females learn calculus. The males were able to understand and apply the concepts on the blackboard more quickly than the females. When the teacher discussed the principles in more concrete terms, the girls did better.

One of the best theories we have as to how this brain difference developed follows the line of most of the other ones concerning historical causes of brain difference: The male brain developed to be better at spatial relationships—which include not only external space but internal space (math and abstraction)—while the female brain developed to be better at concrete, emotive, and sensory tasks.

LANGUAGE USE.   The trail of abstract/concrete reasoning differences gets longer. If we listen to the very language our boys and girls use for explaining concepts, ideas, and even daily plans, we find that boys tend toward more abstract language and girls toward more concrete or "everyday" language. One of the reasons male culture has created the labyrinthine language of disciplines like law and medicine is because the male brain loves the puzzle and jargon of that language. It's very abstract stuff. It leaves lots of room for manuevering. Legalese is perhaps the best example of that.

SYMBOLIC TEXTS.   In general, beginning in early childhood and continuing throughout the human life span, males tend to prefer symbolic texts—diagrams, symbols, emblems, graphs, charts—more than females, and females tend to prefer actual pictorial texts—pictures more realistic, more human and lifelike—than males. In general also, if you spontaneously show a graph and a paragraph to a male and female student, the likelihood is that the female will end up with the paragraph of words and the male the graph.

One art teacher said to me, "I get now why so much art by men is so abstract and why women tend to paint more realistic scenes." He named Jackson Pollock, Pablo Picasso, Mark Rothko, the Constructivists—a list too long to remember. The male brain is very much a symbolizing brain, which is one reason English teachers sensitive to this are teaching literature to males through imagery patterns, symbols, mythology, and metaphor as much as "the story."

EMPHASIS ON HARD LOGIC.   Boys can also like things explained logically. When they ask why, they're looking for *logical* answers: proof, proof, and more proof. Girls in general tend to be more receptive to whatever explanation is given, without needing the whole logical nine yards laid out. People sometimes ask: "So, does this mean girls are just more passive, more gullible?" What makes more sense to me is that the female brain seeks and makes the intuition necessary to absorb the explanation more quickly than the male, and doesn't need as much logic and reasoning to prove the answer. Exceptions for girls lie especially in abstract areas like math.

As we seek to apply what we learn about male/female learning differences, we become better parents, mentors, and educators. We notice where our child, male or female, is frustrated in the learning process and, instead of thinking, "Why the hell isn't he learning?" we think, "How is his brain working, and how can I work *with* it rather than against it?"

Natural Nurturance

Application in Two Areas—Reading and Writing

So much of what males face in the classroom is a result of being normal boys in a setting that is not trained to handle many of our normal boys. On top of that, most educators are not trained specifically to handle the somewhat high-testosterone, male-brain, impulsive, and aggressive boys. These boys enter the classroom crying out for discipline, direction, focus, assistance, and care. Some of them just don't get it and have to leave, labeled, shamed, scared, scarred. Their neighborhoods, their schools, even their families become convinced that they are defective boys, boys who need medicating, boys who can't get along, boys who are troublemakers, boys who can't learn, boys who can't read.

While many of the problems boys face in school are home-related, not school-related, and certainly will not be solved by a graduate-school course on the male brain for prospective teachers, I think it is safe to estimate that about 30 percent of the problems boys experience in school are caused, in large part, by a collision between boys' basic natures and the school systems—teachers, classroom environments, schedules, and administrative attitudes toward males.

The approach I take to parenting and educating is what I call the "natural nurturance" approach. It is based on understanding the way a child is *built*, then forming educational and parenting strategies with that understanding. The ways in which we nurture are dictated by *nature*, reality itself, not our preconceptions. We nurture boys and girls according to their natures—not only as individual human beings, but as girls and boys. I hope the natural nurturance approach will prove fruitful to educators of both boys and girls.

A Fine Young Man

I hope it brings to the educational system an innovation that is, in a sense, age-old but that is now being revived in the wake of stunning brain and biological research and good, clear thinking of many scientists and educators on the impact of genetics, brain systems, and biochemistry on educational environments, and vice versa.

Two areas where we *must* take the natural nurturance approach are reading and writing. United States Department of Education research indicates that at least for the last thirty years, boys have been behind girls in reading and writing, and that the gap is now the worst it's been. Our adolescent boys are on average one and a half years behind our adolescent girls in reading and writing.

The male brain is, from the beginning (as always, we are averaging), not set up to be as good at verbals as the female. Girls use more words than boys when they talk; they read more than boys; they write more than boys; they read and write better, on average, than boys—and this starts early. Some studies show that girls develop verbal skills in early childhood one year before boys. When you listen to little boys and girls talk, you might not be surprised to notice a four-year-old boy still saying "Him go to the store." It is more likely the four-year-old girl will be saying "He goes to the store." With his smaller corpus callosum; with his brain better at symbolics, diagrams, and abstracts than emotive data (which requires more hard language and less diagrammatic thought); with his preference for logic and problem solving rather than long narrative, boys will often depend on more help in reading in order be on par with females.

Reading gender-gap averages continue all through school, finding adolescent boys way behind adolescent girls. To be behind in reading and writing means to be backward in the very stuff of which our culture is made. One mother in Lafayette, Colorado, told me this heartbreaking story about her early teen.

> *In second and third grade, he couldn't decode the language. The teacher didn't know what else to do except to get him to memorize. So he memorized. By fifth grade he was a problem in a lot of ways, from discipline to academic. We had to move him from school to school. We finally found a specialist in male development who told us what had happened. In laymen's terms, he had been taught to memorize and, in memorizing, had filled up his brain. He couldn't take in other things. He got frustrated. This has been a five-year journey now because they didn't know how to teach him to read.*

Her story is just one of millions. While we push schools to improve in this area, here are some things you can do at home to help your son's teachers. They are examples of applying what we know about male disadvantage, and changing a boy's environment to help him surpass the disadvantage.

1. Share with the teachers any knowledge you have of your son's learning style, including diagnostics you've had done on him. For assistance, you might consult Thomas Armstrong's *In Their Own Way: Discovering and Encouraging Your Child's Personal Learning Style.*

2. If you believe your child needs diagnostic tests, but diagnostic tests aren't being done at school, go to your HMO or other care provider and get them done.

3. Set aside family reading time for younger boys and early adolescent males. By the time the male is in middle adolescence, he won't want to be read to, but if you have set up ritual times for years, he may still use them for his own reading or, at your insistence, for reading to the younger children. Early-adolescent males still really like family reading time and still like to read aloud and be read to aloud.

4. Make sure there are books and magazines on coffee tables, shelves, counters. Make reading material an essential part of your life.

5. Home school your boys in reading and writing to augment teachers' work. Teachers love it when we help children out in the areas they are weak. If your son is weak in reading or writing, become a coteacher, giving him assignments, correcting his "homework," sharing with him your own difficulties and triumphs with reading.

6. Use daily life occurrences to inspire research opportunities. If the boy's researching the belt of Orion, he's reading. If you require him to provide you with a one-paragraph report, he's writing. You might think he will refuse to do the report, but if you say, "Tonight at dinner you're gonna read the report to the whole family so you can become a teacher to the whole family," he's likely to love the attention.

7. Make sure all your children have bedside reading lamps and allow later bedtimes in the early years for reading. By adolescence, they'll hopefully be habituated to use it. If you haven't done this in the early years, it's never too late to try.

8. Visit bookstores and libraries with your son whenever you can.

9. If there are sacred texts in your family, the Bible, the Torah, the Koran, the Book of Mormon, the Bhagavad Gita, the Tao Te Ching, read from them and have your son read from them. If you have no such sacred texts, consider finding one and reading it with your son.

10. Be a reading role model. Read in the presence of your son. Don't read just the newspaper, but make sure you're reading something else that's challenging.

When we look at our boys from a developmental perspective, and accept that many of them *naturally* gravitate toward certain educational weaknesses, we can make simple changes. It is up to us also to make larger changes, changes in cultural and educational structures—changes we have to advocate for as parents and educators.

Key areas I would like to look at with you—areas that arise from a developmental perspective—are sex education, after-school programs, and school violence. So many of the improvements we can make in handling these areas depend on understanding a boy's basic, developmental nature.

Improving Sex Education

What we know about our adolescent boys' sexual habits sometimes amazes us. Most startling, by age sixteen, more than half our boys have had intercourse. Also surprising for some is the research that shows that the *more* we talk to youth about sex, the *less* likely they are to engage in coitus inappropriately or in unsafe sex. Those people who worry that if we talk with kids responsibly about sex the kids will go out and do it more are dead wrong.

The finest book I've read recently on sexuality education is Beverly Engel's *Beyond the Birds and the Bees.* She has collected some interesting facts.

- While in the general population the average age when our kids have intercourse is fifteen for males and sixteen for females, in the inner cities it is between twelve and thirteen for males and females respectively.

- One young man out of fifteen will attempt to force sexual activity on a female sometime during his college years.

- On a yearly basis, 2.5 million teens are infected with STDs.

- 20 percent of new AIDS cases are adults in their twenties. Because of the latency period of the virus, we know that these infections were contracted while the young people were in their teens.

- More and more of our young people, particularly in inner cities, are beginning puberty at younger ages: eight, nine, and ten. Girls enter puberty younger than boys, on average.

Our children's bodies are getting ready for sex earlier than ours did, and the kids are having sex at younger ages than we did. Our boys are like the average male of our generation or any other: wired to seek sexual stimulation once the emotional structure of the brain gets courageous enough to pursue the contact.

Are boys different from girls in this regard? Are boys different from girls in their sex drive? Do boys need different sex education than girls?

The fact that we even ask the questions is intriguing, as it indicates how far we've come from the biological realities in which our children live. While every child is an individual, it would be negligent *not* to realize that adolescent males and females are different in regards to sex, have different quantities of sex impulses (different levels, on average, of drive to reach orgasm), and need some of their education to be "different" from each others'. This does not mean they don't need the same basic education. It means simply that while basic human biology is the same for male and female, the existence of gender in that biology creates a profound difference in how that biology is experienced by the boy and girl. To care for our young, we must deal with the difference.

An adolescent boy gets five to seven surges of testosterone, the sex and aggression hormone, per day. His testosterone level grows during adolescence to twenty times the testosterone level of his female peer. His sense of sex, sex drive, sexual stimulation, sexual impulse, sexual consequence are often very different from a girl's. He needs for us to learn how to educate *him*. Not only because it's good common sense to do so, but because adolescent boys who are undernurtured in the area of sex education are undernurtured to a profound degree that female biology does not allow.

Female biology provides girls with a continual opportunity to understand and "contact" their own sexuality, an opportunity to minister to themselves and get emotional help from others: the menstrual cycle. Adolescent boys aren't reminded *consciously* and for many days every month that they are built to continue the human race. They are reminded of it *unconsciously*, and without support, five to seven times a day when they get their five to seven testosterone surges. A girl can't avoid dealing with her period and how it affects her life. A boy can avoid dealing with his testosterone because it doesn't manifest itself in easily tracked, physical ways.

He gets more aggressive at certain moments of the day, but he doesn't know why.

He feels the tremendous urge to masturbate at certain times of the day, but he doesn't know why.

He starts suddenly fantasizing a girl without clothes on at a certain time of the day, but he doesn't know why.

Our own ancestral cultures, and tribal cultures around the world, create many avenues for sexually educating their boys because they are well aware of how *unconscious* male sexuality is, and how *conscious* a community must make it.

The community must teach the boys about testosterone, their brain activity, fantasy life, sexual urges, respect for the female and the female's world . . . on and on the lessons must go in order for sexuality to become a conscious part of a male's adolescent self-discipline.

While, through the female lens, the adolescent male's cry for sex when he wants it seems immature and aggressive, it is a natural biochemical state for many boys—especially the high-testosterone male—and is often socially essential: For boys who don't get much emotional nurturance at home, in community, or at school, sex becomes a conduit for maturity and manhood. For boys not well raised to be men, promiscuous sex gives them a way of being men. For any boy, living inside a boy's body, it is a huge chunk of manhood the girl can't understand.

This is the reality we live in: Girls and boys do not understand each other. We have taught them so little about each other's nature that they don't know how to nurture each other.

Saying that it is natural for many boys to want lots of sex does not mean we don't protect our girls from sex-aggressive boys. Just the opposite: It means we see the natural reality of a boy's body, and we create a culture that nurtures it to fit the many demands of our society, many of which are driven by female culture. To teach a boy about sex for a few hours when he's eleven, then complain that he wants lots of sex at fifteen, then condemn him for manipulating a girl to have sex at sixteen is to neglect the boy's very life, his very being, and then punish him for being who he is.

Having said all this, what can we do? Here are some suggestions.

1. Sex education needs to be taught differently at different stages. We need to create a teaching module for early adolescents—something like our present fifth- or sixth-grade general sex ed; then an even more powerful,

provocative, and in-depth module for middle adolescents, for freshmen in high school, for instance; then equally strong, equally deep modules for the seniors in high school. Hopefully, collegegoers will take psychology and other courses that will augment their sex education. Currently, other people and I are working to put this kind of curriculum together.

2. Counselors, especially male counselors, need to join teachers in teaching sex ed.

In sex ed classes taught outside the classroom—for instance, Planned Parenthood's male involvement classes—male community members are recruited (in Atlanta, they're college males) to help talk to the boys and young men.

3. Sex education must go hand in hand with emotional education. Teachers and parents need to teach boys as much about their emotional lives as about their sex lives.

4. Parents will have to be educated about the dangers of avoiding emotional and sex education. The dangers of not drastically improving the sexual education of boys are death, disease, teen pregnancy, and emotional neglect. The greatest danger is perhaps that without being educated about sex continuously throughout a boy's stages of brain, hormonal, and physiological advancement, he can't become a man.

5. We need to use a "both/and" approach to abstinence and contraception. We teach abstinence *and* we teach contraception, again staging our teaching to coincide with the maturity of the boy. Especially for early adolescents, we teach abstinence, what I call "The Honorable Journey." We augment already tried-and-true Stage 1 sex ed with in-depth parent and teacher education of boys in the concept of Honor.

As we move into Stage 2, we continue abstinence and honor education but augment it with increased contraception information. Since half our kids are now having sex, we must be realistic about the need to get them using contraceptives. Even if our honor education works well, some kids still will have sex at fifteen.

As we move into Stage 3, we use the full-fledged both/and approach, providing contraception information (and in communities that allow it, contraception packages) while still teaching abstinence.

6. In general, we will have to become less prudish about sex than we are. Our prudishness, our dislike of the words "masturbation," "cunnilingus," "fellatio" will have to go. We will have to become less prudish about the human body and its functions. We are somewhat unique in our prudishness and would gain a lot by looking at how other cultures deal with teen sexual-

ity. In Turkey, for instance, where I spent part of the 1980s, I was amazed to see how generously families talked to children about their bodies and sexual functions. This talk in no way increased sexual activity among teens—that activity is very low. When I spoke with Turkish friends and colleagues about this, they stated the obvious: "If you don't talk to kids about their bodies, they'll go out and use their bodies to find out about their bodies."

Certain religious groups resist this approach. Much of Catholic culture is long on record against masturbation and birth control. Much Protestant culture is on record against masturbation. I respect their points of view, and the "biblical" point of view, which I understand this way: "If you encourage masturbation, it leads away from sexual intercourse. If you encourage oral sex, it leads away from sexual intercourse. Sexual intercourse is the place of divine union and must remain sacred."

Even understanding the idealism of this view, and agreeing that there is a unique divinity in sexual intercourse, I believe that all human choices must be made based on what is best for human survival and adaptation. Now I challenge the traditional religious points of view to realize that since human freedom is the primary secular value of our culture, sexual freedom will only increase. We undernurture our children if we do not provide them adequate sexual training in the face of our present (divinely inspired?) human tendency toward more personal freedom. If we don't adjust our religions, we'll continue to undernurture our kids, and our church has not done its job, which is, at heart, to love our children.

7. We'll have to talk to boys more openly about masturbation, creating less shame around this particular bodily function, one the middle-adolescent boy is often performing once or twice a day.

It is useful perhaps for religious leaders as they gradually adapt mores to new sexual life, to remember that the Bible was written in large part to teach adolescent males and females how to relate to one another in a time when people sought to bring monogamy into the center of human life. The messages about masturbation are directed mainly at a culture that was suffering because of a lack of monogamy.

In large part because of the Bible, monogamy is the center of Western culture. We face different problems now than biblical writers did. Two and three thousand years ago, we needed our adolescents to mate in Stage 1 or 2 (between ages thirteen and sixteen) and we needed these young people to remain loyal to one another. Human survival depended on early mating and lots of copulation so that a couple (and extended family) could have many children, only half of which might survive to productive years.

Life is different now. We *don't* want early mating and lots of copulation. It is crumbling infrastructures in our culture. Religious leaders must now do their part to adapt and to teach sexual education that bolsters later mating. Alternatives to intercourse are now the *essential* subject of any such curriculum, and "Don't touch yourself" and "Masturbation is wrong" are not realistic for most of our Stage 2 and Stage 3 adolescents. God just did not make an adolescent male's sixteen-year-old body in such a way that he can avoid all physiosexual activity without suffering psychosocial problems. The same can be argued easily about the adolescent female's body. Masturbation and mutual masturbation between male and female are fine alternatives to adolescent coitus and ought to be presented as such by religions.

8. One thing that will help all of us make the necessary paradigm shifts is to separate, in our thinking and teaching, the subject of "the human body" from the subject of "sex." Much of our fear of intensive and complete sex education lies in our confusion about our own human bodies. But we need to talk about everything with adolescent boys, in slang, if need be, and in scientific language: "balls," "huevos," "nuts," "testosterone," "ovaries," "dick," "penis," "cum," "AIDS" . . . the list is endless. If I'm scared to talk to a boy about his body in the language that will reach him, then I must get help not to pass that fear onto my child, male or female. To avoid my boy's body is to avoid my boy.

Comprehensive education in male body-life may require me to prepare by reading more about testosterone, biochemistry, the male brain, and fantasy life. This is fascinating material. It changes the way we think not only about our sons but, as you can tell from the book you are reading, about human history.

9. Some sex education ought to be taught to boys and girls together, and some to just boys (and girls) separately. Fetal development, for instance, is something to talk about with boys and girls together. Masturbation might be something for boys and girls to discuss separately (especially in Stage 1 sex ed, when embarrassment levels are distracting).

10. More males need to teach sex education and emotional education, and to be involved in all education in general, from volunteering in classrooms to choosing teaching as a profession.

While we encourage more men to get into teaching, especially into junior high and high school, we can facilitate very easily the inclusion of male parents and community members in "coteaching" certain topics. Teachers can call on male parents to help them teach any field—political science, human growth, literature, business—there are men in communities, often fathers of boys and girls in a specific classroom, who need only to be asked to help. The very presence of the male in the class increases a boy's emotional and psychosocial education.

In the area of sex ed, if men don't participate we can say that the educational system—educators, administrators, and bureaucracy in general—is neglecting the boys. Unless a male stands with the boys to talk to them about masturbation, wet dreams, sexual intercourse, AIDS, pornography, and sexual aggression, the boys' core selves are not learning, with any completeness at all, the lessons we want them to learn about these things. Unless a man or even two or three helps the boys over a few years time to deal with their sexuality, the boys will not have been educated in sexuality.

After-School Programs

Dealing with Latchkey Kids

So many of the problems faced by our educational system are caused by families that are for whatever reasons unable to do their job: provide enough family time, discipline, and attention to children. One of the unfair processes in public education today is the tendency to blame schools for our kids' behavior when, in fact, the rudiments of that behavior began or were not dealt with at home. The school is, after all, only the "third" family, not the first. It does not form our children; it teaches and nurtures relatively formed beings. Though we as parents are overwhelmed, and though in many cases it is difficult to figure out where our obligations as parents end and the schools' begin, there is one area in which clarity is simple: after school. Once a child has left school, he is our responsibility again, and many of us avoid that responsibility. Though we avoid it most often with very good reason, nonetheless, we avoid it, and we put our children at the highest risk of trouble, trouble that ends up involving the school.

Here's what I mean.

Between the end of the school day and the parents' return from work, our boys get in the most trouble, more than late at night, more than while home, more than at school. The bad hours are from about 3:00 P.M. to 6:00 P.M. During this time, kids of all social and economic groups are twice as likely to abuse drugs and alcohol, have sex and get pregnant, join a gang, or become a criminal. We've experienced a 48-percent increase in juvenile violent-crime arrest rates in the last five years. Most of these arrests are males, and much of it takes place in the latchkey hours.

Every one of the problems our kids get into during this time not only affects us at home but increases the school problems—discipline, dropout rates, lower academic achievement, violence. Even if it means we earn less, being there for our kids during this time is crucial.

One of the most frightening things I hear a parent say is: "I don't know who my son's friends are." Parents who are around during the latchkey hours generally know.

Dealing with latchkey issues may seem to be the parents' problem—because the school administrator and the teacher and the coach have finished with the boy—but in fact there's a lot schools can do to help.

Schools can monitor whether every child is involved in after-school activities. Some boys are involved in too many activities for an orderly life, but many are not involved in any. Every boy ought to be involved in at least one athletic, artistic, student government, club, or service activity. Most of our latchkey "troublemakers" are boys who have opted out of activities that girls often dominate—clubs, student government, arts. These boys need to be brought back in. Once schools start to notice the wayward boys—and once parents, too, admit the problems these boys have in making connections with structured, social, group activities—schools, parents, and communities will band together to develop after-school clubs and new passions for already existing school activities.

Violence in the Schools

Our schools are too violent, and our boys and young men are the main perpetrators and the main victims. In Moses Lake, Washington, about an hour and a half's drive from my hometown, a fourteen-year-old male walked into his school and shot staff and students, killing two classmates and a teacher. This was a junior-high male. In Pearl, Mississippi, a group of Stage 2 teens plotted to kill classmates. At this writing, seven teen males are charged. In Jonesboro, Arkansas, a eleven- and a thirteen-year-old male shot and killed four classmates and a teacher. Intimidation, sexual violence, nonlethal physical violence all are daily features of many schools. Teachers in general complain that the classroom has become a place of danger, especially in the inner city. On the playground, fights erupt constantly. As state-sanctioned violence in the school decreases to about nil—corporal punishment is gone in most schools—student violence increases.

The normal cry from the public is, "Why is this happening?" and, logically, "What do we do about it?"

Myriam Miedzian wrote *Boys Will Be Boys*, a book about violence in American male culture. It remains one of the most comprehensive studies of the social factors that create so many violent males. The biological factors are, of course, the increase of testosterone and male cognitive development in adolescence, which are simply not acknowledged enough by parents, mentors, or educators. I hope *A Fine Young Man* presents this material in depth and, in so doing, helps communities better understand males, and thus better understand how to channel male energy away from violence.

Let me highlight some primary areas of difficulty we presently face as we pursue a decrease of male violence.

It is important for us to rethink our approach to violence in our schools, homes, and culture. In order to take discussion and training about violence to the next level, we must start focusing on male-on-male violence as much as we have male-on-female. Most of our violence-prevention programs have been about stopping the sexual violence continuum that girls experience, from sexual harassment to rape. While these programs are essential, we forget in our narrow pursuit that most violence in our culture, including in our schools, is perpetrated on males. With the exception of the home (wherein the most frequent perpetrator of violence on a child is the mother), the most frequent perpetrator of violence anywhere else in the culture is a male, and, more important, in this discussion, his most frequent *victim* is a male.

Male-on-male violence constitutes the majority of our violence school wide (and culture wide), but we do not focus on it enough. To create violence-prevention programs with this focus, we will have to see through a false myth that has been created: that males are consistently trained to take care of other males but oppress and abuse females. In this view, articulated mainly by individuals rightly wishing to call attention to male-on-female violence, the code goes like this: "American males are brought up to be misogynists for whom taking care of the good old boys comes first and perpetrating violence on females is second nature." It is essential we now stand together to counter this belief. The proponents intend to protect our females, but in the end the intention backfires. Male-on-male violence gets little attention, and the true nature of male culture continues to be misunderstood and pathologized, forcing more and more males to abandon the cause of women's rights.

Most American males are not misogynists, and most don't feel "well taken care of" by other men.

And while violence against females has been institutionalized in some parts of our culture, the depth of its institutionalization is hardly comparable to that of male-on-male violence. Males who are taught violence as a way of life are taught to hurt, maim, kill, and slaughter other males first and foremost. Whether in war, in protection of community, in aggressive conquest of land and culture, in street brawls, on sports fields, violence as it has developed is a tool by which men subjugate men and boys subjugate boys first and foremost.

Violence against females is much more rare than violence against males, in statistical terms, and has been since we have collected historical data. This makes it no less palatable. But it does show the obvious and point out that the code that is really taught to males goes more like this: "Protect women and children; if you have to hit, maim, or kill someone, that someone better be a man or you're not a man yourself." This code is not just culturally taught, evolutionary biologists argue. It is a human instinct. It is a male instinct.

Most violence-prevention programming I have seen in schools is based on the false myth that we must break down the "intrinsic" male-on-female violence code. I have heard teachers excoriate adolescent males for "belonging in the culture of men that wants women hurt, subjugated, destroyed, reduced to nothing." This provocative technique, while it gains some good results, leads to cognitive dissonance in most of the adolescent males listening to it. The vast majority of males are not so coded. They are taught that they have a role and that females have a role; they are not taught that hurting women is a norm but rather an anomaly.

Once we understand how our adolescent males are coded we—our families, communities, and schools—will truly be able to teach them about the whole spectrum of violence. Many educators will be shocked to hear males say that they're taught to hurt other males. When we as a culture attack this male-on-male violence training with as much energy as we've attacked male-on-female, we'll be on the road to eradicating violence in our schools.

Structural Solutions in Educational Systems

Having looked at problems our schoolboys face, at brain and biology in the classroom and educational systems, and at three key areas of male trouble where philosophical changes will result in better developmental nurturing, let's now turn to the area of *structural* solutions—ways to change the very physical and pedagogical makeup of the school or classroom. We will not be able to cover every school innovation here—alternative schools, home schooling, new private schools—nor every classroom innovation, so let us cover one classroom innovation and one school innovation. Both are presently very controversial and potentially very rewarding to our adolescent males and females. They involve single-sex education.

As we have delved into everything from learning differences to violence, we have noticed that we have not fully understood or educated males about developmental realities. We have let the two million boys who are learning disabled pile up next to the two million diagnosed ADHD cases; next to the million in and out of juvenile detention; next to the thousands beaten unnecessarily every year; next to the millions who just can't read or write as well as they should, are underachieving, dropping out, neglecting college or professional life because they just can't measure up and don't know why.

Single-sex education is one of those solutions that, while not a panacea, does much to create a well-rounded environment for boys and empower them in everything from channeling aggressive energy to better environments for learning reading.

Single-Sex Classrooms

Paul Fochtman is the principal of Pellston Middle School in northern Michigan. He and his staff were discovering typical problems in their school and decided to try an atypical solution. They found, for instance, that among their sixth-grade students, the males were getting *ten times the amount of Fs as the females, four times the amount of D-minuses, and 2.5 times the amount of Ds.*

Said Fochtman, "I saw that a group of boys needed a different kind of help." He knew well the research that shows that girls in single-sex classrooms often do better in math and science than those in coed classes. To administer to both his boys and girls, he set up single-sex class sections in the morning, including math, science, and language arts, then coed sections in the afternoons. That way, the students were placed in both single-sex and coed environments.

Some of the improvements he is finding: better grades for the students; student posturing curtailed, students freer to ask sensitive questions and questions in general; the classroom environment relatively free from teasing, flirting, and self-conscious behavior that sixth-graders go through normally but that also distracts the learning process and creates discipline problems.

Paul Fochtman has told me how much he values the support of his school board in his pursuit of educational innovation. He and I have discussed other public schools, like a New Jersey school wherein the school board experienced so much pressure from lobbying groups that it had to kill successful single-sex-classroom programs. Schools across the country are experimenting with single-sex classrooms—in California, in Harlem, in small towns, in rural areas.

The single-sex classroom innovation is showing educators that one classroom does not fit all—coeducation is a wonderful way but not the only good way to educate. For boys (and girls) who have academic and discipline difficulties, single-sex classrooms are essential. They are, once we work through the politics, as we'll discuss in a moment, a wave of the future.

If you are on the staff of or a concerned parent in a school district and you want to experiment with single-sex education in a way that avoids legal flak, you might consider suggesting to your schoolteachers or instituting in the schools an activity called "single-sex after-school clubs." Initially, because of national focus on getting more girls interested in math and science, these clubs emerged as after-school science clubs—boys and girls gained separate venues in which to flourish. Girls often found these clubs more conducive to learning science. As one adolescent girl put it, "I don't have to worry about boys interrupting. I can learn what I need to learn."

Now after-school clubs are forming for many other subjects. The areas where there are urgencies for boys are reading and writing. Females dominate those classes so heavily—testing higher, reading better, using more complex verbal skills in both interpretation and expression—that males often need separate-sex help for reading and writing in the same way females do for math and science. Separate-sex clubs can augment all the class subjects as needed.

Results are just coming in on both single-sex classrooms and separate-sex learning clubs. All the data I've seen thus far is positive. Boys and girls are learning well and relieving themselves of distractions. Discipline problems are decreasing. Both adolescent males and females are feeling emotionally safe to develop and grow. As Paul Fochtman put it, "I could not have hoped for better results."

The kinds of results we're seeing in single-sex classrooms apply to single-sex schools as well.

Boys' Schools

Research is coming out frequently now about the advantages of boys' schools. This research does not posit that coeducation is "worse." It simply shows that for many adolescent boys, a boys' school provides a place where developmental and educational disadvantages find positive solutions.

Researcher Diane Hulse did a qualitative study comparing boys' schools and coed schools and found that boys' schools provide boys with better concentration, focus, academic achievement in many areas, personal expression, and self-esteem. Her studies have been presaged and supported by other studies by Cornelius Riordan, William Pollack, Michael Thompson, and numerous others. In chapter 1 we quoted from some of these in respect to the efficacy of male nurturing systems in boys' lives.

When these researchers look statistically at boys who attend boys' schools and those who go to coeducational schools, they find that boys'-school graduates commit less crime, less violence to females, less society- and self-destructive behavior. Some of these statistics depend on class factors—many of the boys going to boys' schools come from families with higher incomes and more opportunities than, for instance, the inner-city male raised in poverty. Despite this accounting, we should not downplay just how much a boys' school teaches a boy respect, honor, compassion, and responsibility.

McCallie School in Chattanooga, Tennessee, commissioned a study to discover why its boys' boarding school was successful and what ought to be changed. The survey results astounded even McCallie administrators. While there were areas of concern to be addressed, on the whole community members and the male students themselves found certain key elements they wanted left intact:

"Let this remain a boys' school."

"Better academic education than we'd get elsewhere."

"Fewer distractions."

"We learn how to live right."

"Respect, morality building, value building."

"Teacher-student ratios are low and helpful."

"Learning how to be a good man."

"We feel safe."

"A sense of brotherhood, of supporting one another."

"Support services for overachievers and underachievers."

"We're given responsible roles in the school."

Robert Byrd, assistant headmaster of McCallie School, has worked over the decades in both the coeducational- and boys'-school worlds. While he sees distinct advantages in both settings, he said about boys' schools:

We find that the boys themselves are major advocates for single-sex education. In both coed and boys' schools, kids answer surveys about what they want most in high school this way: "We want adult responsible roles."

In the educational environment of the boys' school, it's often easier for boys to take on the adult responsible roles. For instance, at McCallie, a team of students helps us select and hire our faculty and staff. This teaches leadership, accountability, responsibility. These boys take this job very seriously. The public, coed environment isn't usually set up for something like this. We just did a community service project in which 400 of our teen males went into community agencies as volunteers. The boys themselves organized the whole thing. Staff were there only as last-resort advisors.

A recently studied phenomenon is that men who have attended boys' schools often have better relationships with women than males who have not. Patti Crane of Crane Associates in Georgia told me she and her research group talked to wives of alumni of boys' schools and wives of alumni of public coed schools. There was much all the wives liked about their husbands, but there was also general agreement that the men who had graduated from boys' schools were better at communicating with wives and better at relating. Patti said she and her associates found this consistently throughout focus groups. This qualitative data gave them some pause, because they had started out some of their research thinking boys who went to boys' schools would be *worse* at relating to females because of their diminished contact with females. But their research bore the conclusion that because males in same-sex schools can relate more clearly and less distractedly with other males, they learn to relate and communicate more effectively in general and thus end up better communicators with wives. Robert Byrd was not surprised by this data. He said, "Our boys at midnight talking to their roommates in our boarding school talk about things with each other they could never talk about anywhere else with anyone else. They learn to be intimate

with each other and so they know how to be intimate with future partners."
Diane Hulse, author of a broad, in-depth study, "Brad and Cory: A Study of
Middle School Boys," discovered results similar to Crane's.

Patti's research indicates not only similar emotional advantages for
many girls who go to girls' schools but also that in educational environments
when girls feel disempowered because of the presence of boys, it is less because boys are inherently disempowering to girls than because there is a
second sex in the educational environment. The presence of that second sex
provides profound distractions to developing communication and relationship skills among the first sex. So it is with boys who are often behind girls
in coeducational environments: It is not because the girls are disempowering; rather it is because they are a second sex that can distract the educational
process. Patti said, "We had not expected to find this, but the conclusion is
now unavoidable for us."

Crane's and Hulse's research is the tip of the iceberg in the data I am
hearing from boys'- and girls'-school communities around the country.
That the "second sex" can be female or male is important for many reasons,
perhaps most of all because it shows us an alternative way of looking at male-
female dynamics. It gets rid of the inflammatory and simplistic "girls are just
victims of boys" idea that dominates so much present cultural thinking. It
connects much better with the vast expanse of human history in which boys
and girls have been separated for certain years of education because the society or tribe did not believe it appropriate or helpful to throw them together
during their times of intense physiological, biochemical, psychological, and
cognitive development. Tribal cultures throughout the world separate girls
and boys during ages ten to fifteen specifically because the pressure of being
together creates a constant tyranny of first sex toward second sex. The girls
tend to tyrannize earlier because they mature more quickly, the boys later,
when they catch up in maturity and can utilize available gender-role tyran-
nies. Separating the sexes makes sure there's less second sex during the adolescent formative years. The males and females come together after the time
of separation and find themselves able to marry, live, and work together.

While this tribal model won't work for our culture on a vast basis, it is
still a useful one to remember. It shows a resonance between what advocates of separate-sex education are finding, what developmental psychologists know about adolescent-development stages, and what tribal and our
own ancestral cultures practiced.

We've gone through a kind of "boys' school—girls' school" cleansing period over the last few decades. Earlier in this century, many girls' schools

were mainly "finishing schools" for girls, keeping them stuck in subservient roles. Many boys' schools included dangerous practices—the crushing of male emotional development and the teaching of gender superiority for males. Girls' and boys' schools are not about that anymore. They provide some of the most state-of-the-art education available to all children seeking any and all opportunities, whether male or female.

There are many kinds of boys' schools. They are private schools, so mainly higher-income families take advantage. Hopefully we will be able to push through the politics and create public boys' schools for whoever needs them in the near future. Some boys—high-testosterone, those with trouble learning, easily distracted, underachievers—desperately need boys' schools. Boys' schools in inner cities, state run, would help us solve a lot of our violence issues. They also would help minority and lower-income males compete better in our culture. The very places where we may need boys' schools most are least likely right now to create them—the politics get in the way.

The Politics Surrounding Single-Sex Education

The politics surrounding single-sex education are in transition and in confusion. At base is the philosophy that if males and females are going to get equal education and opportunity, they must be educated in the same classrooms and schools. While males and females being educated together can be a wonderful thing, the blanket assumption that they *must* be educated together shows a profound neglect of adolescent development.

The idea that we must have complete blending of male and female daily life in order to have equity is one that grew early in feminism as the strategy that fit a Marxist, class-systems approach to gender issues. Women are second-class citizens in the patriarchy, the thinking went. They are barred from the "man's world" and kept in a "woman's world." Thus we must get rid of "the man's world."

This logic, useful for a time, can be seen now as simplistic. It does not take into account other human factors besides gender and class dilemmas. It does not take into account adolescent sexual biology and the tensions it brings to coed environments. It does not take into account different learning styles and the crisis of education that follows for a child who isn't taught well because of gender and because the teacher just doesn't understand how to educate each sex. It does not take into account children's needs for same-sex bonding systems, systems that, in adolescence, often become the most powerful and helpful nurturers of children, in the home and in the school. It doesn't take into account that there is a natural developmental drive in both males and females to delineate themselves by gender and find their own sex/gender groups through which to feel not only whole but safe when they face problems in education, self-development, life in general. *Finally, it doesn't take into account that keeping males and females constantly together creates a psychosocial pressure that coeducational systems often are not built to handle.*

While the separate-but-unequal logic serves the cause of gender equity in the workplace better than any other we've so far discovered, as a blanket strategy for the education of children it can no longer be supported by research as supreme. In fact, coeducation is presently under attack primarily because it hangs on so tightly to the idea that education's mission is to resocialize young people to become equal gender partners in the society and workplace. While that mission is important, the paramount one is to educate kids the best way it can in the basic critical faculties they need to live in the world. When educational systems are obsessed with old gender and class thinking, they cannot do their job.

Title IX

Once we fully study single-sex education, we will see that Title IX, as written, is a flawed law and needs to be reworked. While it must remain an essential part of our culture's move toward gender equity, especially as it applies to sports programs that don't give equity to females, its academic enjoinments will be reevaluated.

Title IX reads:

> *A recipient (an institution that receives government money) shall not provide any course or otherwise carry out any of its education program or activity separately on the basis of sex, or require or refuse participation therein by any of its students on such basis . . .*

It is easy for us to see the early gender-class ideology in the language of Title IX—separate means unequal, so we will outlaw separation.

However, we accept separation as fairness in sports because of obvious male/female physiological differences. I think when we perceive the profundity of male/female developmental and brain difference, we will recognize separation as fair in certain parts of academics, especially reading/writing and math/science. We will see through our hidden assumption—

unproven and ultimately unprovable—that separating girls and boys necessarily harms women.

While Title IX was being written there was a great deal of racial consciousness-awakening in our culture, calling us to remove any kind of segregation. To overturn the parts of Title IX that are nonadaptive, we will have to see that gender issues and race issues are not the same. There are no structural brain differences between an African American and a Caucasian, for instance. There are no structural differences either between the physiologies of the races except the most cosmetic kind. Between males and females, however, there are at least seven structural brain differences. These internal and external differences are too profound for us to say, "Segregation is wrong." By way of compromise, we might publicly emphasize coeducation until adolescence, then in junior high and/or high school, emphasize the availability of single-sex education. Adolescence is, after all, the time of the most pressure on male/female dynamics, pressure that often subverts learning at all levels.

Other Educational Innovations

Family Stories

Let me end this chapter with some wonderful stories. There are many innovations and adjustments being made today by families and schools who are addressing the issues of boys in educational distress.

Fred in Chicago, a man who worked in sales management, provides a strategy for helping his struggling adolescent boy with accountability and motivation.

"I've been in sales all my life. I know about accountability," he told me. "I know about motivation. I know how essential these are in life. They were primary values I taught my kids and ones I tried to put into practice with them."

Fred's son, fifteen, had to go across town to get to the private prep school in which he was enrolled. He had to take two trains and a bus. Over time, the inconvenience became numbing. Simultaneously, his grades were falling, though not because of the commute. They fell because he was having trouble in some of his classes, trouble that kept building up until he lost his motivation to practice good study habits. One day he asked Fred to drive him to school, and Fred saw an opportunity.

A Fine Young Man

"I'll drive you," he said to Steve, "but we have to leave at 6:30 A.M. That's the only way I can get you to school and get to work on time." This wasn't strictly true, Fred told me. He could have gone in later. But he wanted to find a way to get Josh more motivated and get him to be more accountable to the demands of his schooling. He had a plan, which he checked out with Steve's teachers, a plan they helped him put into place.

He drove Steve to school at 6:30, leaving Steve nothing to do at school but study! From 7:45 A.M. to 8:45 A.M., Josh sat in the room of one of his teachers who came in early anyway, and did the work he wasn't doing anywhere else. His grades went up. Father and teacher had developed a plan and executed it in a way that gave Steve the boost he needed.

Fred developed another innovation. When Steve went to college, he had grade trouble again—he partied more than he studied. At twenty, a sophomore, Steve had such poor grades that his potential for expulsion grew. This was not what Steve wanted.

His father said, "If you agree to it, I'm going to call you every weekday morning at 6:30 A.M. and every weekday night at 10:00 P.M. I'm going to call you to listen and to motivate. Short calls, but calls that tell me you're working, and calls that tell you I'm here. What do you say?"

Reluctantly, his son agreed. This went on for five months. Steve got back on track. Steve is now twenty-five and graduating from law school.

Fred had the knack for finding innovations that not only helped Steve in the tasks he needed to do, but also increased bonding time between father and son. The drives in the car, the calls on the phone built that bond. Fred's teacher was also an innovator, seeing the potential for helping a boy and agreeing to take that extra bit of time to be there for him and his family.

Judith was a single mom I met in Omaha. Her innovation took a great deal of her time but, in her words, "The sacrifice was worth it. And I learned a hell of a lot about economics!"

Here's her story. Her son, Tony, an eighteen-year-old freshman in college, lived at home. He had started college with high hopes of transferring to another school as a sophomore, a school difficult to get into. But he was getting too many Cs in his freshman year. He had to get a B at least in economics in order to meet the qualification to transfer to the engineering program he wanted. Nagging didn't seem to help mother and son. Tony would just say, "I can't do it. I want to, but I can't. It's too hard." Judith saw that her son's self-doubt and frustration were a thousand times worse than her irritation with his lack of "get-up-and-go." She had to do something to help him get rid of the self-doubt, but what? She couldn't reach into his head and fix this for him. What if, she thought, she supported him another way?

Her idea was to take his economics class with him! She became his study buddy. He didn't feel comfortable with her in the classroom, so she got him to tape every lecture and she read every chapter he had to read. She listened to the tapes on her way to and from work. She called his professor to explain what she was doing and ask permission to call now and again if she needed a little help understanding a concept. The professor agreed to make his teaching assistant available to her, an arrangement he didn't have to make but one which showed his flexibility and care for his students.

So the plan went into motion. Every night after dinner, Judith and her son studied economics together. He got the B he needed. She said to me, "Now he's a senior, and I don't understand his engineering stuff, not most of it, but I provided support at the moment he needed it. It's one of the things I'm most proud of as a mom."

Innovations like Fred's, Judith's, and their accommodating teachers' show the adaptability any parent, mentor, or educator is capable of when faced with a boy who is having trouble in school.

Our educational system is already overburdened and under-admired. It is my hope that as we try to modify it to help our boys, we will provide it the motivation and funding to truly learn what boys need and, in learning that, to provide an environment for boys so much better than its present one that the schools benefit in better achievement of their mission and fewer discipline problems. I hope, too, we as parents and mentors will never forget that we are the last stand in the troubles our adolescent boys face—we are empowered to come up with innovations and energies of our own when the educational system fails our sons.

CHAPTER EIGHT

Virtual Masculinity

Adolescent Boys and the Media

"Nature's imperative . . . and her overarching developmental rule, which has enormous consequences, is that no intelligence or ability will unfold until or unless given the appropriate model environment."

JOSEPH CHILTON PEARCE,
EVOLUTION'S END

"Those who tell stories hold the power in society. Today television tells most of the stories to most of the people, most of the time."

GEORGE GERBNER, 1992

The poster on the wall shows Michael Jordan holding a basketball. The poster behind the door shows Michael Jordan in *Space Jam*. A poster from the movie *Lost in Space* is rolled up against a wall, ready to be mounted. Against the back wall of the room is a computer. On a table at the foot of the bed is a small television. On the top of the dresser is a boom box. Among the toys are leftovers from childhood, a *Toy Story* Woody, a Power Ranger, and the new "toys" of a young teen, a biking magazine, a sticker on a notebook from a local alternative rock station. On the desk are America Online diskettes, printouts for homework and entertainment.

How much time does this boy spend with the characters and machines of his media, his "virtual" world? How much is he watching that TV? Does it affect him? Does MTV affect his brain development? Is he playing the video games? What effects do these have on him? Is he learning anything substantial from the movies he watches? What's the effect of Internet access on him? When he forms bonds with media and sports figures, how do they affect him?

Probably the world we know least about, and thus are least equipped to help our young navigate, is the virtual world—the world of the media. For an adolescent male, there is hardly a more powerful world in his life than his virtual world.

What Do We Know About Media Use?

There is constant argument regarding what we actually know about media use and its effects. While no one professional can pretend to have the final word on this subject, it is essential that no parent or professional let the sheer volume of available research and argument dissuade common sense. No one can successfully argue that media doesn't have a profound effect on our youth. Debate rages on only the fine points.

I will argue in this chapter that TV and other media *have become family members* in the lives of our youths. The Tim Allens, the Michael Jordans, the Arnold Schwarzeneggers, the Alicia Silverstones have become part of the youths' families. In order to argue that point, I must first present how much time and energy *we* are spending with these people. People don't become family unless we frequently invite them into our lives and the lives of our children. Let's look at some facts about the quantity of media use in our kids' lives. You'll be familiar already with some of these facts.

- The average American household has its television on 6.7 hours a day. The average number of minutes per week that parents spend in meaningful conversation with their children is 3.5.

- By the time the average American kid reaches age eighteen, he will have spent 22,000 hours watching television, double the time he will have spent in classroom instruction and more than any activity other than sleeping.

- 66 percent of American households have a TV set on while they are eating dinner.

- *Advertising Age* reported in 1992 that the average teenager who works part-time generates an income of about $6,000, most of it disposable.

- An average kid in America spends five or more hours a week seeing television commercials. By the time he is twenty-one, he'll have seen one million commercials.

- For every child born in America, a television is made. *Connoisseur* magazine reported in 1990 that 250,000 children were born each day and that same number of TV sets were made each day.

- By the age of sixteen, the average American kid will have seen 200,000 acts of violence on TV. Thirty-three thousand of those will have been acts of murder.

- The number of stories on the nightly news that concern crime, disaster, or war comprise 53.8 percent of the broadcast. The percentage of air time given to public service announcements is .7 percent.

- Americans watch 250 billion hours of TV annually. The number of videos rented daily is 6 million, while the number of public library items checked out daily is 3 million.

- Good statistics on Internet use and adolescent males are not yet available, but we know the use can be counted in the millions, and hours of daily use are increasing among teen males.

The Media Are Family Members

The average immediate adolescent boy spends lots of time at home relating not to his family but to people and stimulants in his virtual reality. He's on the computer an hour or more a day. He watches the television a few hours a day. His eyes wander briefly before bed to Michael Jordan. His heart wanders briefly toward the eyes of a young female teen heartthrob whose picture, cut out from *People* magazine, he has pasted on the side of his desk, at eye level as he sleeps.

This boy loves his mom, his dad, his friends, his family. He enjoys the company of his teachers, his church group, his neighborhood comrades. He bonds with all these people, and the environments—homes, churches, schools, playgrounds—that sustain the bonds. And he also bonds with people he's never met, on the television, on the posters, on the Internet.

Many in his community—including his parents—don't think his bonds with Michael Jordan or Ray Gun in his evening chat room or Alicia Silverstone could be strong bonds; after all, they are bonds formed through machines and on paper.

His community and his parents are wrong. The bonds he forms with these virtual friends are *family* bonds. He invites Michael Jordan to live in his bedroom. He encounters Jerry Seinfeld and numerous other pals in his house, even bedroom. He studies Alicia in his bedroom. He has friends all over the world in his bedroom. He takes cues from them about how it's proper to eat, to deal with challenges, to look. They are some of his moral guideposts. They live in his house. They eat with him, they sit with him, they dream with him. Sometimes, they seem to understand him better than his own parents, even his own friends; certainly better than his teachers and other acquaintances. These people are his "invisible" family—highly visible as images and voices from machines, but invisible as "family" members.

The boy himself doesn't even understand the depth of the bonds he makes with his virtual friends and mentors, role models and provocateurs. It's not really his job to understand. It's his job to play, to search, to learn, to bond. It's his parents' and elders' job to provide him with models, mentors, friends, and provocateurs with whom to bond and through whom to learn life's mysteries. The boy himself doesn't understand that there are elders behind the Jordan posters and the Internet and the TV and the Fantastic Four, elders who control the consumption of the boy's bonds, elders who know very well that their representations live in the bedrooms of the boys but who consider only the profit to be made from the bond, not the upbringing of the boy into healthy manhood.

In *The Wonder of Boys,* I introduced the concept of the three-family system, arguing that a child's nuclear family unit—the one that provides day-to-night care—is the first family; extended family units, including blood kin, like grandparents, and nonblood kin, like day-care providers, godparents, and close family friends, are second family; and community entities, like church, school, and the media, are third family. Sometimes schools, churches, and even the media can become so important to the boy they become *second* family. It takes three families to raise children, I argued, because children are tribal creatures. We've developed that argument further in this book, I hope with success, and now we stand ready to focus on how the media is, for most boys, third family. We will provide frank challenges not only to the media creators but also to ourselves as local elders—parents, mentors, and educators—in our boys' lives.

How Children Bond with Media Figures

Children, certainly until their adolescent cognitive development takes place, tend to see their whole world as family. Think of an eleven- or twelve- or fourteen-year-old boy who still, even after a decade of hounding him to avoid strangers, gets into the car of a stranger and is abused by that stranger. The boy trusts even those with whom he has little bond. For that trust not to exist, he has to develop some sort of instinct against someone, a stranger, for instance, who is jittery and yells obscenities at him. Or he has to be warned off so well that even a predator's manipulations can't sway him.

A boy trusts, and so he learns mathematics and reading. A boy trusts and so he learns how to become a good father himself. A boy trusts, and so he learns from a role model to get drunk and perhaps even assault another boy, or girl.

A boy trusts the world even when the world has bashed him and beat him. He still strives to be loved and will form what bonds he can so that he is loved.

A boy in America trusts Dad and he trusts Shaquille O'Neal. He trusts Mom and he trusts Arnold Schwarzenegger. There is not an either/or mentality in him—e.g., Mom's okay but Shaquille O'Neal's not. He has to be *convinced* O'Neal's not because his first impulse is to trust the elder, the glamorous, successful icon. An early-adolescent boy is starved for relationship, and relationship means family. If we but extend the definition of family to the three families a boy really lives in, we will see that he bonds powerfully with the people he sees on television, meets on the Internet, holds up like icons in his room. He bonds with them in the only way he knows how—by making them part of his interior family. He feels befriended by them, he feels loved by them, he feels rejected by them. Once I watched a twelve-year-old boy pushing his way toward Ken Griffey, Jr., at a Seattle Mariners' game, hoping for an autograph. Griffey missed him, and the boy wept.

Sometimes people resist this three-family view of child psychology. People who make profits off children resist it. Parents who are already overwhelmed resist it. These people insist that the boy's "family" bond with Mom and Dad, "teacher" bond with Mrs. Johnson at school, "peer" bond with friend Jimmy, and "role model" bond with Michael Jordan are substantially different bonds. They insist that Michael Jordan is, after all, just a basketball player; Mrs. Johnson is just a teacher; Jimmy is just a buddy. They're not family.

A Fine Young Man

To the boy they are second and third family, and in adolescence especially, second and third family are nearly as important as first. Unfortunately, the boy often learns from his media third-family members to do things we would put his first family members in jail for teaching him. He learns to get laid as soon and as fast as he can. How did he learn that if he formed no bond with his teacher? (If you've ever tried to teach something to an adolescent male with whom you have no bond, you know the futility of it.) Had his mother taught him to get laid at age fourteen, she would have been accused of abetting statutory rape. The media sends the boy the message constantly. The television commercial cannot be charged with a felony. It is "virtual" in our present thinking, not "real." Yet to a thirteen-year-old, the TV commercial is both real *and* unreal.

Let us make no mistake. A boy's bond with Michael Jordan is not the same as his bond with his mother. However, let us no longer think that because it is quantitatively different (in the amount of love he gives Michael Jordan as compared to his mother) that it is qualitatively so. If we continue with this error, we not only teach the boy violence through the media and promiscuous sex and all sorts of things we fear, but in so doing we continue his emotional neglect and alienation.

He forms close bonds with action figures, chat-room friends, poster boys, and so on, and we don't notice; if we don't notice, we don't help him interpret his experience; if we don't help him interpret his experience, he is all the more alienated, struggling between first-, second- and third-family systems that neglect one another. Stuck in this place, the boy is an imposter in each system, not quite fitting in his home bond because his family doesn't see what he sees in his media world; not quite fitting in his school bonds because his school speaks neither the language of his first nor his third family. Our male youths are alienated in the main because they live in three families that barely talk to one another and barely strive to be accountable to one another.

This circumstance, which I see in threefold terms, is relatively new.

1. It involves the forgetfulness of how bonding really works—forgetfulness of the three families children really live in;

2. It involves the forgetfulness of our responsibilities as members of all three families to put the child's welfare before other concerns, including personal time, educational ideology, or corporate profit; and

3. It involves the hands-off approach parents, mentors, educators, and media take with one another, as if all three family systems do not have to be responsible to one another in a human society.

This threefold problem, which is best studied in our childrens' relationships with the media, needs drastic solutions, many of which we'll suggest here.

But first, let's learn how we got into this spot historically. Let's understand what our great grandparents did with the third-family bond in their time, watch how it became media-centered in our time, and wonder about why the human community would so uncautiously give up the care of its children to machines.

How Storytelling Works

The Media as Storytellers

Joseph Campbell was one of the wisest men of our century. A mythologist, he spent his life discovering how stories all over the world are quite similar. That similarity indicates the depth at which the human psyche lives in the same interior landscape, no matter its cultures, creating stories through which to teach its young how to live, its adults how to thrive, and its elders how to pass on what they have learned before they themselves pass on. Fifty years ago he wrote a book called *The Hero with a Thousand Faces*. It exhibits one of the worldwide patterns: the hero's journey. In this journey, adolescent males, whether in Africa, Native America, Central Europe, Asia, or New York City, travel through their three family systems and then into the "fourth and fifth worlds"—the worlds of the strangers in other kingdoms and of the spirits, the nonliving—initiating themselves and being initiated into manhood. At the end of their journey they find out something amazing: Even the creatures of the fourth and fifth worlds are actually part of their original three worlds, their original family! The demons and giants and snakes and Sirens and rabbits all are actually pieces of the man himself, integrated in his psyche, as if one's stories are one's dreams of one's own life. Enemies he fought in stranger kingdoms turn out to be uncles long lost or provocateurs sent to test him by God, who is the center of the family in all things. No matter where the hero goes, he comes home. No matter where he proves the mettle of his manhood, he finds himself back home. Home looks different, for now he's a man, but it is only when he recognizes that the human family is everywhere, only then does he become a responsible man, a hero, a king, capable of caring for his community.

The masks now worn by the media already were worn by creatures from and tellers of mythic stories in the villages and towns of our foreparents. The stories were about and/or told by the Bible, the brothers Grimm, tribal elders in Africa or Asia, traveling minstrels, town criers, Grandma and Grandpa, Mom and Dad. Until just a few decades ago, *Hercules*, *Anastasia*, *Mortal Kombat*, Schwarzenegger's *Commando*, and "Touched by an Angel"— all the tales now on screens were in the heart and voice of someone a child knew firsthand. But then something occurred in culture that was perhaps as earth-shattering as the destruction of the dinosaurs, or the invention of war, or the discovery that coitus creates a child: Machines became the vessels for first some, then a lot, and more recently *most* of the stories our human children hear, absorb, and tell.

With the advent of image-creating machines, media, rather than people, told stories to our children. Because we were a technological society (we believed in the grace and power of technology), we grouped televisions in with toasters and cars, thinking: "Well, it's just another machine to help me and my family. It really can't do harm. Once it breaks, I'll buy another." Over a period of about thirty years, image-making machines gradually took over the storytelling function, a function we neglected to realize as sacred and profoundly subtle; especially in a child's adolescence, not to be confused with toasting a piece of bread or electrically driving a screw into a hole or adding numbers on a calculator or computer. Image making is storytelling, and storytelling is one of the key ways young human beings gain identity.

Concomitantly, we neglected also the effects of image-making machines on the brain. Already we weren't paying much attention to the brain and biochemistry, so why would we when media became involved?

This neglect allowed people to get away with saying the most amazing things:

"Kids aren't really affected by what they watch."

"There's no proof that watching violence causes violence."

"What's wrong with letting kids watch some sexy images?"

"We mustn't allow censorship of any kind."

With this mindset, adults think nothing of allowing their three- and four-year-old children to watch movies like *Spawn* or *Batman and Robin*— movies so violent that they affect permanently the developing brain of the four-year-old; and they give over much of the caregiving function to the storytelling machine, plopping kids in front of the television for hours and hours each day. Finally, all this neglect has led to what we now know to be permanent attention-span problems in media-addicted adolescents and adults.

Over the last few years, media literacy campaigns, prodded by the general public perception of the influence of the media, have begun to include brain information. Once we actually learn how the brain develops, we realize the implications of not monitoring and controlling our children's media stimulation. Seeing ourselves as neglectful is not a bad thing—as my mother used to say, "A little guilt never hurt anybody." But we can't even get to feeling a little guilty if we don't understand how adolescent brain development and media stimulation are related.

Media Stimulation and the Brain

In earlier chapters we've looked at how the adolescent male's cognitive development occurs. We've matched that with biochemical development. Let's add to it other essential components of the human nature that develop within the brain from birth on through adolescence, and explore how adolescent brain functions are stimulated and affected by media intake.

It's useful for us to think of the brain in three parts—the *reptilian* or survival-oriented brain; the *cerebral cortex*, which controls intellectual functions and creativity; and the *limbic system*, the bridge portion or the emotive center of the brain. (My descriptions of the brain here are necessarily circumspect. For a much more complex picture of the different areas and functions of brain systems, check out books like *Brain Sex, Sex in the Brain,* and *The Runaway Brain.*)

Hormones and the Media

Testosterone is a chemical that affects all three portions of the male brain (estrogen and progesterone affect the female triadic brain).

It stimulates the territorial imperatives of the reptilian brain, imperatives that create defenses and boundaries and that increase territorial aggression: "This is *my* block. Find your own!"

It affects compassion development—for instance, one person could think: "Leave him alone, that's the right thing to do," while another thinks: "How could you have abandoned him at just that moment?"

It affects emotional responses, delaying them, for instance.

Testosterone levels in us are affected by media. For example, after a male watches a hockey game on television, his testosterone level goes up. The hockey game stimulates, among other things, the testosterone level, which stimulates so much else in the brain. If the male's attention to the hockey game was pretty intense—he rooted for the Red Wings with special passion— we might also find his cortisol level rise (cortisol is the stress hormone). Like testosterone, cortisol washes through the brain and affects male behavior even after the game is finished and the TV turned off. The male can appear to us more anxious or irritable. In point of fact, at a hormonal level, he's more agitated.

Imprinting

If a brain is bombarded with certain images over and over, it will *imprint* those images—i.e., make them real. Imprinting is most applicable to children from birth through late adolescence, less applicable to adults, whose brains are already fully formed (though imprinting does still affect adults, as imagery-brainwashing studies have shown). Thus an adult brain tends to need more bombardment for a brainwashing result to occur, a child's or adolescent's less.

The developing brain imprints many times a day—grabs an image from its environment and imprints it as hard-and-fast reality. We can understand this process by studying memory. If you think back to an especially important event in your childhood, you'll recall it with startling internal quality of image, even sound, even smell. That meal at Grandma's house when you were ten imprinted, and you remember it because it imprinted. Similarly, a powerful experience with media imprints. When I was a middle teen I saw the movie *Carrie.* At the end of this movie a hand comes up out of a graveyard and grabs a girl. It was so frightening to me and the movie audience around me that we all collectively screamed. Decades later, I remember it vividly because of the imprinting. Whenever, for instance, I see earthen ground laid out the same way as it was in that scene, I feel a charge of fight-or-flight in my reptilian brain—a kind of internal shiver—even now, in my forties.

Often when I'm in graveyards, I see the hand flash, an internal synaptic experience that colors my last respects of an individual with a visceral, imprinted fear of the *Carrie* grave.

When we look at how our kids take in media imagery, we must recognize bombardment and imprinting. If, during my first decade of life, I imprint random horrifying or sexually explicit imagery from media, and because I watch so much of it and I am bombarded with it, my brain becomes partially consumed by these imprints. If, in adolescence, I just keep getting bombarded during my time of high cognitive development, I am imprinting, superimposing, and forming in my developing abstract intellect a reality that is filled with sex, violence, degradation, and so on. To argue that I'm not affected by this would be to argue that my body would not be affected by repeated knife stabs. The brain is quite fragile, quite tender. It needs care and protection in the same way human flesh does. If we stab it, it will bleed.

One might say, "Well, so maybe imprinting and bombardment might have *some* effect. But if they did, wouldn't the human brain use its survival mechanisms to take away the dangerous imagery? Wouldn't the brain go into self-protective autopilot? Wouldn't the brain, when it's *really* getting hurt, decide to turn off the television or leave the room? Yes, it would, and since it doesn't—since kids and adults keep consuming all the sex, violence, and so on—isn't it logical to say, in fact, that media isn't a danger at all?

It's a good logical try, and it's one used by media advocates, but there's a problem with it. Unfortunately, the brain's self-protective mechanisms don't work when the stimulant is more powerful. Every brain seeks to protect itself, as does every human body, but when the stimulant is more powerful than the mechanism, the mechanism must adapt to the stimulant.

Overriding Natural Neural Protections

Media stimulants are more powerful than the brain's self-protection in three ways.

1. They often move faster than the brain can process them. Thus, the brain works just to *process* rather than analyze and throw out the stimulant.

2. They are addictive. Addiction bypasses the brain's self-protection, whether the addition is to a drug, tobacco, an alcoholic substance, or a medium. All these are external stimulants taken in through the senses or bodily functions and affecting the brain.

3. Most media are visual and rely on "fixated eye movement," a state of visual consciousness that lulls the brain into a state of relaxation, making it

"off guard." While off guard, the brain is more susceptible and gullible to quasi or virtual realities, confusing them with "real life."

Let's look at number three first. Fixated eye movement is what we call the state of consciousness that a student has who is staring out into space while a teacher is talking. His eye movement is fixed, so cortical functioning is limited and not very conscious. If you ask the student what he's seeing, he'll probably say, "Huh? Oh, nothing." There isn't much going on. He's very relaxed. Gloria De Gaetano, one of our most foremost thinkers in the field of media literacy, very rightly compares the fixed eye movement state with being "zoned out."

When we're zoned out, whether as adults or children, we don't do much analyzing or thinking. If something does stimulate us, we take it in without much argument. Now, consider what happens when our kids zone out in front of a television. They zone out during the years of their most powerful brain development, so they take in lots of imagery and information right to the center of brain development while in a very vulnerable state. We must remember that the adolescent brain constantly expands its neurotransmission, neural webs, dendrite production, and so on. What a brain takes in during these formative times are what shape the brain! If that brain is constantly zoned out in front of a screen whose images move too fast to be analyzed for content but are intense enough for it to be imprinted, then neurotransmission and the neural web will develop along the lines of the stimulants—far more than we realize. Self-protection of the brain is bypassed by fixated eye movement and quick imagery.

The issue of quick imagery is number one on our list. It cannot be underestimated. We live in a culture of stimulation that moves faster than our brains are capable of handling. One of the prevailing contemporary theories as to why we in America suffer such high rates of depression, thought disorders (e.g., schizophrenia), and brain disorders (e.g., ADHD) is that our media/technology environment is too stimulating for our brains, whose process of neurotransmission still runs at a "sane" pace, one that is more appropriate to the stimulation of a few hundred years ago. Media imagery runs at an "insane" pace—that is to say, the stimulation of today is too much for the brain.

Quick-moving imagery produces an addiction response in the brain, number two on our list. Watch a child's attention go to a quick-moving image instinctually, like a car suddenly turning a corner or a flicker of light in the room. The reptilian brain attends first to the quick-moving image, whether in the backyard or on the television.

When fast-moving images bombard us over and over and over again, we form an addiction. The brain just keeps getting stimulated instinctually until it figures that this activity is normal and wanted. Gloria De Gaetano describes this process as *stimulus addiction*. She is just one of many researchers who have been trying to teach us for nearly two decades about addiction to television, video games, and computers.

In 1980, researcher Jerome Singer alerted us to "orienting responses" produced by television. In 1986, a number of researchers used EEGs to measure these brain responses. They confirmed what Singer observed:

> *The TV set . . . using constantly changing short sequences, holds our attention by a constant sensory bombardment that maximizes orienting responses . . . We are constantly drawn back to the set and to processing each new sequence of information as it is presented . . . The set trains us to watch it.*

This addiction is created not only in the orienting responses of the cerebral cortex or the reptilian vigilance, but also in the limbic system, where emotive content, both received and expressed, is mainly located.

The limbic system is immensely fragile in a human child. It finds the psychosocial life of humanity difficult to process, which explains why kids and adolescents need so much love and nurturance, so much "refueling" and teaching about emotions—how to process them; how to experience, express, and, when necessary, expel them; how to discipline them; how to identify them in others with accuracy and compassion; how to value them; how to trust them. Watching television can be very addictive simply because it provides an easy approach to complex emotions. A kid, by nature, looks for easy (not necessarily healthy) ways out. Television provides these.

Television provides an adolescent boy with a kind of "media state of altered consciousness," giving him, because the content of the TV shows is generally so facile, a world of "lazy emotion" in which to become emotionally lazy.

While playing a video game, for instance, the boy with the joystick in hand feels like the master of the situation. No matter the troubles he may need to process in his life, he can fixate on the game or television show or movie or computer game for hours of relief and of lazy consciousness. In this state, he need not deal with the unpredictability of real-life social situations and emotional relationships, with reality's challenges, which exist so that he as a boy can become a man; rather, he escapes these challenges,

jumps right to a feeling of control or mastery. A little time spent in this escape is not a bad thing. Too much is.

TV commercials present another area of concern for limbic and emotion
development. An early-adolescent male is beginning a long life journey in
which, according to statistical research, he will spend more than two years of
his life watching advertising on television. During a boy's adolescence, these
ads and the stereotypes propagated through movies, video games, and television shows hit him at exactly the time of great vulnerability. His body is
changing; his brain is changing; he's very insecure. Media stereotypes, like
the joystick in the video game, give him easy access to the illusion of security. For an adolescent boy, strength and social suitability come from material objects and a materially suitable, mechanical body—one that can wear the
best athletic shoes, the right clothes. In the world of the media, strength and
social suitability are not gained by well-rounded internal and interpersonal
development. If the boy had these, the media and advertisers could not target and prey on his weaknesses—what he doesn't have—to get him to buy
something to fill the holes in himself.

When we look at the development of boys in particular, we need to pay
close attention especially to video games and advertisements. Boys' brains
start out emotionally disadvantaged anyway. Their addiction to and stimulation by visual media like TV and video games continue their disadvantage
rather than serve to alleviate it. Their third-family members are not helping
them but hurting them.

Gloria de Gaetano writes clearly on this subject:

*The demographics of video game usage tell us that the heaviest users are
eight- to fifteen-year-old boys—the initial market target of Nintendo.
However, two areas of the brain continue to grow and develop through
childhood and into adolescence: the corpus callosum (which connects the
two hemispheres and allows the integration of left and right brain
processing) and the prefrontal areas (which enable higher level learning
such as reading for meaning, reflecting, planning and problem solving).
What is needed during this time of development are activities that develop
and integrate the functions of the two hemispheres: cognitive activities
which challenge the child to plan, design, create and master skills needed
later in life; physical activities which bring awareness and control of the
motor skills of the whole developing body; awareness of emotions that are
involved in relating to people; and the cognitive connections to these*

emotions that facilitate understanding. Without the mental effort needed to develop these connections a person grows up handicapped . . .

Our boys are addicted to visual stimulants in the media, stimulants that not only do not help them develop limbic and neocortical areas but, in fact, handicap their development.

Watching kids relate on a TV screen is not relating.

Overstimulating sensory functions of the brain with fast-moving images means less ability for other functions to develop.

Addicting oneself to the fast images means constantly returning to a well that provides only a very limited quality of drink.

Playing the same video game over and over again while the corpus callosum and the prefrontal lobes are developing neglects their development, predisposing the child for future setbacks.

The bottom line in all this is clear: The child's brain is not able to bypass media stimulants dangerous to it. An adult brain can, for the most part, but not a child's or an adolescent's. The late-adolescent brain, which resembles an adult brain, is far better off than a young-adolescent brain. No brain, adult, adolescent, or child, should be taking in media stimulants without a very specific plan or discipline in place.

What First Families Can Do

Complaining about the media is one thing. Taking personal responsibility for our children is another. While we're working on the media—our third-family member—to understand its responsibilities, what are things we can do at home?

1. Monitor television-viewing time. Keep weekly journals until we have enough information at home to know how much our boys are watching. Armed with this information, and the information about brain development we now have, talk to our youths about the media and its effects on them. Work out with them schedules whereby they *never* engage in more virtual activity than real activity in a two-day period, e.g., they never spend more time watching television than playing sports, being with friends, and participating in the first family.

Utilize different "per day" TV viewing amounts for different years. For instance, a ten-year-old may watch perhaps an hour a day, a thirteen-year-old two a day. An hour of video games is considered the same as an hour of TV.

2. Take all televisions out of childrens' bedrooms. From early on in children's lives, teach them that television is more an adult thing than a child thing. Restrict it the way we restrict coffee or tobacco intake for our kids. By the time they are ready to forge their own ways (late Stage 2 and Stage 3), they will tend not to watch it as much, not having been habituated to it and addicted to it when young.

3. If the television is on in your house during meals or any other important family activity, turn it off from now on.

4. Use the television as a critical environment. Analyze its programming constantly with kids. The media is nothing to be reverent about. It is a machine producing images. Use it as the subject of dinner-table conversations. Laugh at its stereotypes while discussing them during family time. A favorite line in my house is: "What are they trying to sell us *now?*" Once we answer the question, we then ask: "Do we need it?" Ninety-nine percent of the time, the kids chime in: "No!"

5. Even when your boy is an adolescent, you must restrict TV use. "This is a house that does not value television very much, so here we watch only _____ hours a week." Your son may sneak off to a friend's house to watch what you won't allow, but at least in this sneaking he's relating to someone else, someone else's family, someone else's home and world. In between watching the restricted television, a baseball game starts up, a conversation transpires with his friend's mom or dad, plans are made for an evening's adventure with friends—all better than the boy watching hours of television at home.

6. Our boys model us, so we have to restrict our own television viewing, too. When we do watch, we can have good staging moments for our kids using television. For instance, we can say, "Son, when you turn fourteen, it's appropriate for you to watch _____. The first time you watch it, we're going to watch it together and talk about it and figure out what it's all about."

7. Pick stories and programs that are sexually suggestive and use them to carry on necessary sexual discussions with our boys. Just as ancient storytellers used their stories to teach sexuality, we can use ours. Our boys are exposed to the media no matter what, so let's always use it to teach them what *we* need to teach them.

8. Utilize v-chips and all other channel-blocking technology as needed. It's made to help every first family that has an interest in protecting kids.

9. Monitor Internet use. Deny access to chat rooms until children are of the appropriate ages. Certainly a Stage 1 boy should not have access. Late Stage 2 boys may. The maturity of your fourteen- or fifteen-year-old will determine what kind of access he gets.

Software now exists that can block sites that carry titles or key words inappropriate for children or teens. Check out this software and use it generously.

10. Take back the job of storyteller. Give our kids lots of our own stories and lots of time with Uncle Pete and Aunt Alice and Grandma and Grandpa and others who will tell the kids stories of life lived hard and well, stories filled with heroes and villains, obstacles and initiations, stories that took place at home and far away—the stories of life itself.

A New Vision

I was lecturing in a Midwest city. A father of two boys came, a man who was also an anchor at a local television station. When I brought up media, he said: "Yes, but how can anyone really *prove* the media has a negative effect? Don't all adolescents in any culture absorb whatever images the culture provides? If it isn't Schwarzenegger, it'll be something else. And if you do prove the media's got a big effect, doesn't it just make family life *more* important? Shouldn't Mom and Dad decide what the kids watch? The media has to operate out of free-speech principles. The family has the control."

He summed up in a few paragraphs the obstacles we face regarding media accountability. His point of view still may emanate from spokespeople for a long time, but with constant pressure from us, it will have to accommodate new thinking and a three-family vision. Who would have thought twenty years ago that the tobacco companies would one day be held accountable for the effects they have on our children?

We are seeing greater interest on the part of media and sports figures to act as role models and wise guides through the maze of media. This behavior needs to increase, of course. Sports figures like Charles Barkley ("I'm no one's role model") need to be educated as to how our children's psyches really operate. Sports figures and anyone else who counters our requests for help with "I'm paid to perform, not be a role model" have to be educated about how they have become family members and have to be reminded that every child is every adult's responsibility. People who make movies—stars especially, who exist heroically in the public eye—need to establish and voice media discipline of their own. Bruce Willis, for instance, told *USA Today* that he thought his movie *The Jackal* was so violent he wouldn't let his kids see it till they were eighteen. That kind of strong, child-protective statement—one in which the star himself understands that what's fun for adults is often dangerous for kids—can affect the lives of thousands of families.

"Many of our stories about men here in Anatolia are about boys and young men in the second decade of their lives. Our adolescent males must make a journey toward themselves. In making this journey, they must compel the forces of nature and society to care for their fire, their spirit. Often this fire in our boys will frighten the culture, yet it is the very heat that molds the metal of our civilization. As such, it cries out to be directed, to be refined in our young men every day of their journey."

—AHMET BEY, TURKISH STORYTELLER
(TRANSLATED BY MICHAEL GURIAN)

PART FOUR

The Refining Fire: Caring for the Spirit of Our Young Men

CHAPTER NINE

Nurturing the Core of Manhood

"My country is the world, and my religion is to do good."

THOMAS PAINE

In 1986, my wife and I traveled to Ankara, Turkey, where we would spend two years living in a very old culture that was going through many late-twentieth-century changes. I would teach mainly Turkish and Arab students at Ankara University. I would research male development, the kind of research that has led to this and some of my other books. Gail would become the mental-health therapist for the American embassy, opening a center that specialized in the needs primarily of women and children.

Turkey remains a land where the majority of men walk down the street arm in arm, kiss on both cheeks, and embrace in a style unprecedented in the U.S. It remains a land where tradition rules the lives of men and boys, yet many of the traditions are Western democratic ones. East and West meet in Turkey, with arranged and polygamous marriage existing in the East, but cities like Ankara looking toward Europe and America as if to a new sun.

Turkey, or "Anatolia," as it is known geographically, has hosted twenty-nine civilizations, including Sumerian and Hittite, Greek and Trojan, Roman and early Christian, Ottoman and British, and, of course the Turks themselves, a proud, friendly people whose passion for life and service were inspired, early in this century, by their own Thomas Paine, the orator and leader Kemal Ataturk. As my wife and I worked and studied in Turkey, we were surprised to see just how much we could learn there, not about just Turkey but about the roots of our own American civilization—Byzantium, Mesopotamia, St. Paul's journey—so much of it occupies or borders Anatolia.

A Fine Young Man

For my own study of male development, Turkey was just the right place to land. I had experienced boyhood in India, going to British and Indian schools. I had experienced boyhood also in urban America and rural America, in cities as diverse as New York, Laramie, and Durango. Furthermore, I had experienced boyhood on a Native American reservation. I had experienced it in Hawaii, in the thick of Polynesian and Pacific Rim cultures. I had gone to public schools and private schools, been educated by secular teachers and by Jesuits. I had experienced boyhood through many religious lenses: Jewish (my ethnic origin), Hindu, Bahai, Quaker; then, as a young-adult searcher, Catholic and Buddhist, then Unitarian. My parents' lives had been lives of searching for truth throughout the world's civilizations and religions, thus so had mine. Neither my parents nor I, however, had experienced Islamic culture and religion. In Turkey, I would do so. And there, consolidating much of what I had experienced, I would finally notice that no matter where we travel in the world, the basic message of life is very much the same.

In my life-journey—as a boy and then a man, a teacher and a therapist, a husband and a father—I have found that one social truth transcends all others: that the world is not a fearful place to those who observe gently and clearly how when it comes to caring for our young, all cultures share certain key, or *core*, values, and all seek to implement certain *core* strategies. If I had thought in the back of my mind that in the Muslim world I would find any different, I learned in Turkey to dispel that thought. Even in the Muslim world, so confusing to us in the United States, the *core* of manhood is marked and clear and resembles our own American standards.

New Models of Manhood

The two years in Turkey were two of the best of our lives. They were followed by a return to Spokane, Washington, where my wife and I now raise two children. These last nine years have taken me to hundreds of schools and conferences, into the lives of countless families and communities. Nowhere in my ten years of teaching and seven years as a therapist have I found an exception to the notion that there are certain universal elements of manhood training for refining in a growing boy the full fiery spirit of a man.

It has taken me forty years of life and fifteen years of research to feel comfortable with the masculine models I've discovered. I presented one of them, the husbandry model, in *The Wonder of Boys*. Two others will be presented in Part IV of this book:

The Core of Manhood

The Ten Integrities

Models of manhood must, I believe, include but also transcend national and political boundaries. Without these transcendent models, we limit our masculine models to politically or religiously "correct" ones, which often do not involve vital biological or historical information, do not take fully into consideration how a boy works or how he fits into a long-term historical adaptation, and ultimately do not free the whole spirit of a man.

I hope you will find in the models I provide the kind of common sense that transcends cultural and personal limitations. If you do not, I hope you will find your own models of masculinity that fully free and channel the beautiful spirit of the masculine in our boys.

The Core of Manhood

The core of manhood is a paradigm representing these four elements:

Compassion

(H)onor

Responsibility

Enterprise

In this paradigm, a boy is not considered well refined—not a man—if he has reached the physical and social age of maturity (the end of adolescence, around twenty-one to twenty-five in our culture) without having developed fully in himself the capacity for compassion, a deeply held sense of honor, visions of responsibility, and tools and skills for healthy, life-sustaining enterprise. If he is missing one of these, his core is damaged or underdeveloped.

We will recognize the disability by a clear imbalance in his life, evident in anything from at-risk behaviors (like drug and alcohol abuse) to obsessive behaviors (like work addiction) to psychological flaws (like the inability to follow through on commitments in the long term) to psychological disorders (like depression) to spiritual emptiness (like a wish for meaning that is unfulfilled in daily or community life).

In India, boys develop this core earlier in life than in the U.S. Boys generally are trained to develop the core before they reach Stage 3. Most Indian males do not have the economic luxury of a long adolescence that our boys have. In Turkey, the conscious development of the masculine core is marked, at age seven, by the ritual circumcision. At seven years old, the boy begins to be led, very consciously, in the development over the next decade of the core. Among the Shavante in Brazil, the core development begins in earnest in a boy's fourth year, when he is brought out in front of the community, assigned a "sponsor" for his masculine journey, and commences his instruction in "how a man behaves."

How might the core of manhood work in the lives of the boys you know and love? Its development certainly starts in a boy's infancy and early childhood, but in our culture it generally needs to become a *conscious* effort of parenting, mentoring, and educating by the time the boy meets the first stage of adolescence. Let's break it down into its primary elements and explore each in the everyday lives of our boys.

Compassion

Sogyal Rinpoche, a teacher of Tibetan Buddhism, writes about compassion:

Compassion is a far greater and nobler thing than pity. Pity has its roots in fear.

Steven Levine, who has spent his adult life helping the dying and the bereaved, completes this thought:

When your fear touches someone's pain, it becomes pity; when your love touches someone's pain, it becomes compassion.

At the root of world teachings about compassion is this idea that compassion encompasses all the other shows of love, that compassion is love itself embracing all of us, and that each of us will move through stages of compassion development in which early on we will think of compassion as things like pity but finally will learn that compassion is much more.

Compassion is kindness and understanding. Yet still more.

Compassion is the combination in the self of emotional attunement and universal spiritual love. It is my individual attuned reaction to another's pain, needs, or emotions, united with my higher self's capacity for universal love of all beings, no matter their circumstances.

At the core of manhood is compassion. Every boy, yearning to love and be loved, wants to become a compassionate man. Every adolescent male is confused by what adult compassion is; how to be compassionate; how to balance emotional attunement with the fighting spirit of competition; how to honor his own unique and personal way of being compassionate; how to adapt to the ways others want him to be compassionate, especially the ways girls and women want him to be compassionate. Let us explore briefly now the key principles of compassion development as they apply to boys and men.

Compassion is at the heart of every religion and spiritual tradition, thus we can turn to those traditions to find spiritual mentors and wisdom for our adolescent males' development of compassion.

Sogyal Rinpoche gives the Tibetan Buddhist key to compassion development:

> *To train in compassion is to know that all beings are the same and suffer in similar ways, to honor all those who suffer, and to know that you are neither separate from nor superior to anyone.*

For Rinpoche, compassion begins and ends in the idea that we all are one. If I learn that I am one with you, I will feel your pain when I act, and so I will always act with compassion. I may have to hurt you, but I will do so knowing that I am one with you and will befriend you through it.

This is compassion at its finest, hard to live up to always, but good to live up to most of the time. The key to living up to it seems to be the understanding of the *universality* of each of us: that each of us is one with everyone else. Not only Buddhism, but every religion preaches this.

Christianity tells us: "God hath made of one blood all nations of men."

Judaism tells us: "Behold how good and pleasant it is when brothers dwell in unity."

Islam tells us: "All creatures are the family of God; and he is the most beloved of God who does most good unto His family."

Shintoism tells us: "Do not forget that the world is one great family."

Shamanic cultures tell us: "We are each a leaf on the Great Tree of Life."

A Fine Young Man

Often we try to teach males compassion by teaching them localized responses to actions or events. "You should have more compassion for your sister," we say. This is good, but not enough. Each of us, as we raise our sons, might look again at religions we've forgotten. It's hard to teach a boy the whole way of compassion if he is not grounded in a religion or spirituality that teaches compassion as something larger than a single act of sympathy.

Compassion begins with compassion for oneself. I have yet to meet an adolescent male who truly feels "good enough" about himself. The state of mind concurrent with adolescence is not contentment but turmoil. Sadly, I rarely meet a grown man who feels good enough. To some extent, the ontological insecurity we live in—the state of constantly having to ensure our survival—makes our lack of contentment a physical and social necessity. Simultaneously, men can spend more of their manhood feeling more content if during adolescence they are taught compassion for themselves. If they are instructed in compassion when their bodies and minds are changing, they will become men who "take care of themselves." If they do not learn that, they endanger themselves (and often others) and/or become workaholics, who never can feel free.

We do not, these days, teach much self-care to our young males. To teach it, we must carry on more conversations about sexuality, emotionality, physicality. We must help them develop spiritual and personal rituals of prayer, meditation, self-care, and soul care. We must give them access to our rituals, whether large ones—like hunting and fishing to discover solitude, or churchgoing, or "time off just for myself"—or small ones—like sitting down to dinner with the family, puttering in the garden, washing the car as if it were a meditation. In other words, we must teach them physical, emotional, mental, and spiritual hygiene. We must surround them with many teachers of this self-care, not just one or two parents.

And we must teach them not only to succeed but to fail. We give them permission to fail by apologizing for our own mistakes (without capitulating authority): "Son, I'm sorry I overreacted. I hurt you, and I wish I hadn't. Luckily I have my love for you to always teach me that I am imperfect and need to keep improving myself." We give them permission to fail by laughing off our own failures as well as theirs. When they fail, we help our boys transform that failure into the next stage of success, teaching them that success is not a product but a process, and failure is a doorway in the present toward success in the future.

Compassion is at its highest when it leads to forgiveness. Taoism, the ancient

Chinese religion, teaches us to "recompense injury with kindness." Christianity tells us the story of Peter, who came up to Jesus and said, "How often shall my brother sin against me, and I forgive him? As many as seven times?" to which Jesus responded, "I do not say to you seven times, but seventy times seven." Judaism tells us: "The most beautiful thing a man can do is to forgive wrong." Parents who cannot forgive their own parents cannot teach their children to forgive. People of races who cannot forgive other races cannot teach their sons compassion. Men and women who cannot forgive each other risk the core development of their children. Forgiveness training lies to a great extent with parents. By the time their sons are adolescents, parents are challenged to forgive all those who have hurt them. We do well to involve our sons in conversations about why forgiveness of another creed, culture, race, religion, or person or persons is hard for us. We let our sons ask questions of us.

Modeling forgiveness and compassion in general is certainly the best way to teach it. Talking about it is essential. Providing boys with teachings of the old masters is essential. Turning to our own root religions can help. Inviting boys to practice forgiveness of bullies, girls who have hurt them; siblings; parents; and even God, who has taken a brother or parent or friend—each of these helps a boy develop into a man who is in constant conversation with himself about the forms forgiveness takes throughout a long life.

Compassion is not something just females are good at. Our culture tends these days to emphasize empathy and sensitivity development in our young men through female models of what these are. Most sensitivity training is performed by women. Much of it stresses how to be sensitive to girls and women. It is useful, but so insufficient that much of it is resisted by many of our males. In the main, I believe males resist this kind of sensitivity training because it does not begin by honoring our males' own natural ways of showing compassion, some of which appear to run counter to what is taught in the female model.

Men, for instance, show immense compassion by leaving home for weeks and months on end to go to work and provide the resources by which their wives and children can survive. This kind of compassion is no longer very respected, much to the confusion of adolescent boys and men. When we begin our sensitivity training of high school boys by saying, "One of the great things about guys is the way they show care and concern, the way they sacrifice their bodies and sometimes their very souls to take care of others. Let's look at some of that. Let's honor it," we have the undivided attention of the males, and their spongelike hearts are primed to absorb other messages about compassion.

Males show immense compassion by problem-solving. This male mode of operation is built on the premise that sad and painful feelings are to be gotten control of and their sources either averted or negated as soon as possible, so that the emotional flow of a group situation remains manageable. Males are driven by a sense that they must protect the larger group from the emotional distress of a particular person within the group. Males problem-solve, hoping to relieve stress from the female, the family, and the small community. Males often are condemned for it.

Problem solving is certainly not the best response in all cases. The female model of enunciating and processing sad and painful feelings rather than quickly releasing or resolving those feelings is essential for both males and females. But to negate the male mode of compassion is to push males away from learning sensitivity.

Males show compassion by leaving others alone. At the core of a man is the sense that others don't want to be penetrated, impinged upon, or emotionally invaded. If unclear whether to embrace, reach toward, or "solve" someone else's emotional pain, males often stand by, wordlessly waiting. This action can seem uncompassionate or insensitive, especially from the point of view of the female model. However, it is a way of showing compassion and needs to be honored. Often boys and men are good at giving the gift of space.

These three "male" ways of being sensitive are the tip of the iceberg. Let us urge all sensitivity and empathy trainers, including all parents, to learn the male modes of feeling and to have a deep respect for the male mode of compassion itself.

Compassion often develops in silence. Frequently I can measure the quantity and quality of a man's compassion by his capacity to be silent. A young man capable of solitude is a man who has learned to love himself. We have taught him and provided structures in which he can learn the internal conversation, carried on in outward silence, that every man needs if he is to feel loved by his God and thus love others as he is loved.

I find that an adolescent male who is always filling up his silences with CDs and video games and television is generally not developing a great deal of compassion. As much as possible, we need to point this out to him. Brain stimulation and brain numbing take away the realm of solitude that seems to frighten some of our boys. But that solitude, once discovered, leads boys deep into themselves.

The Art of Compassionate Conversation

To become compassionate men, boys must be taught the arts of emotional and spiritual conversation. We and all our support systems must provide ways of talking to and with them, constantly. We must not overwhelm them with words. We must unite them with concrete details of compassionate behavior. We must tell them more stories than we do. We must give them opportunities to talk to us, thus we must build relationships of trust with them.

Practically speaking, I find the following conversational strategy especially useful with adolescent males, many of whom are not "good talkers."

Step 1. Make a point in one or two sentences, not much more.

Step 2. Tell a story or anecdote to illustrate the point.

Step 3. Ask for a response. If none is forthcoming, try asking for a story. "Is there a time you did something like that?"

Step 4. Listen for the key word or words in the response. These words usually will involve primary feelings either in direct language or by reference—"afraid," "hurt," "Wow!" They may also be hidden behind filler words like "kind of," "maybe," "sort of."

Step 5. Use those key words as your entrée to the continuing conversation. "Kind of what?" "What was he afraid of?" Even here, in the middle of emotive conversation, it is often useful to talk with the male about "someone else"—perhaps yourself, one of his friends, or a teacher. Sometimes we have to circle back to the boy by first getting him directed to feelings in others, where he feels safer to talk, then bringing him to self.

Step 6. Don't be afraid to allow silences in the conversation. Sometimes he (and you) need time to think or process. But help the young man to see that a silence is not permission to get up and leave for good.

Step 7. Especially now as conversation deepens, it's often useful to be doing something together, not just sitting across a table, trying for eye-to-eye emotive intensity.

Step 8. As much as possible, taper and end conversations with an invitation for him to have the last word. "How are you doing with this now that we've talked, son?" "I'm okay." Let him end the conversation.

Step 9. Bring it up again in some other way as needed. So often, our boys don't "get it" just one time around.

Honor

Sammy was a boy of twelve or thirteen, just starting puberty, whom I observed at a movie theater. Accompanied by his mother and father and in a very bad mood, he occupied a seat just to the left of my family as we all watched *Air Bud*, a coming-of-age film about a dog that ends up playing basketball with a team of boys, bringing new spirit into all the boys' difficult early adolescences. The main protagonist in the film, a boy of ten or eleven, was a little younger than Sammy. As I watched the movie and observed Sammy's crabby asides to his mother and father, I wondered if he was bored by the film or thought himself above it. About halfway through the film, his talking got to be so annoying that I leaned over to ask him and his parents to do something about it. His father, clearly perturbed with his son, told him firmly to follow him out of the theater. I lost track of them and returned to the film.

My daughter, however, needed to use the restroom, so I walked out with her. As she entered the ladies' room, I went to the men's room. Standing at the urinal, I could hear Sammy and his father in the back of the restroom.

"I didn't mean to," Sammy cried. "I felt bad about it all week."

"You lost control of yourself, didn't you?" his father observed.

"Yes," Sammy whispered through tears.

"You have to apologize to him," his father said.

"Yes," Sammy whispered.

As I stood at the sink, Sammy's tears subsided.

"It feels really bad, doesn't it," his father said, "to lose control of yourself that way?"

"Yes," Sammy said. "I don't like it at all."

The father and I made eye contact now. Apologetically, I said to the man, "I'm sorry if I caused a problem for your family." "No problem," the father said, and I learned the story.

Sammy had been at his grandparents' house earlier that week. He had gotten "riled up" (his fathers' words), something that happens "more and more these days" (he was going through puberty and finding his own energy too much to handle sometimes). He got mad at his grandfather, a very old man in a wheelchair, and called him a "stupid idiot." Sammy was basically a good kid whose conscience immediately reprimanded him for what he had done, but he hadn't really been able to talk about it until now, at the movie theater, when all the pent-up tension and shame at his disrespect had flooded out. The boy felt not only bad for hurting a man he loves, but also the shame and confusion that come in adolescence when males who strive for personal honor do things that are dishonorable. Sammy's father, Nick, helped his son notice not only the bad deed but also the search for honor itself. It happened very subtly, in the center of life, with the word "honor" never mentioned between father and son, and during *Air Bud*, a movie in which the father has died, triggering unseen emotional responses in both his celluloid son and Sammy.

Honor and honor codes are essential to boys and men. Because males are both hardwired and soft wired for performance, they are very conscious of how they perform. Boys develop personal codes of honor, and they are spongelike in their absorption of codes of honor suggested to them by their nurturing systems. They watch their parents' honor codes like hawks, remembering every detail. They are vulnerable to the honor codes provided them by mentors. If parents, mentors, and educators don't provide them with honor training, they will learn honor codes from peers, who sometimes promote codes that are dangerous. Simultaneously, if a boy's first family does not take on the burden of honor training, the boy will learn it from third-family media.

The word "honor" must be revitalized in our human conversation if we are to fully develop our boys into men. A boy who does not feel honorable cannot feel whole as a man.

The exact honor code a family teaches is its own. No outside agent can tell a family five or ten principles of honor that *must* be taught. When I travel in the South, in states like Georgia and Alabama, I notice the subtle honor coding by which males often still open doors for females. In those families, that particular element of "respect" is taught. In other families—for instance, in the Pacific Northwest—it is not taught so much. The particular action that a boy encodes through the honor training differs between cultures, but the concept that honor requires respectful behavior is universal.

According to my research, all males are taught these key concepts in their honor training:

1. Loyalty

2. Duty

3. Fairness

4. Virtue (Values)

5. Decency

6. Dignity

7. Character

8. Discipline

If we develop in our males these traits, we will build their sense of honor.

An administrator at a boys' school once told me, "We teach honor by extending trust and responsibility to the boys. Our job is to answer questions when asked, and be nearby. We don't look over their shoulder too much. We don't push ourselves in. The boys learn honor by having men trust them to act honorably."

This administrator's words echoed my own experience. When I was a junior in high school, I got a terrible case of the chicken pox. I was out of school for a very important test. My teacher let me take the test in one hour at home. I was aware during that experience not only of having to fulfill the academic obligations of the test, but also of the core obligations of my own adulthood. A boy might cheat on this test. I didn't want to be a boy. I wanted to be a man. That meant acting honorably.

I did not know then but I know now that honor is what we provide boys as a structure in the self by which the boy can act wisely and well when his compassion is not enough to help him do so. Honor and compassion are, in this way, married in the psyche. When my sense of compassion is confused by a circumstance, I can nonetheless act honorably. If a person sends me mixed signals, for instance, about what she wants from me, I am unclear on how best to be compassionate to her. But even so, I act honorably, according to my codes of honor, until she and I clarify our communication. If I do not have a well-developed sense of honor, I will become undisciplined and probably somewhat dangerous in my relationships when they confuse me. Without a clear sense of honor, I have little firm ground to stand on, and I often become overwhelmed by the wants of another person, carrying on a new course of providing for those wants until my resentment builds enough for me to abandon that person. In my work with married couples I notice a great deal of this behavior. Adult males and females who have been trained in compassion and sensitivity but not honor end up destroying their marriages. They do not have the inner strength to pull back into the self and hold on while the partner goes through immense, confusing inner changes of his or her own.

How are you doing at teaching honor to your son? In order to focus your energies on this question, take a moment to answer these questions:

How have I modeled loyalty this week? How have I gone further and talked with my boy about the loyalty I was modeling?

How have I modeled duty this week? How have I gone further and talked with my boy about my, and his, duties?

How have I modeled fairness this week? How have I gone further and talked with my boy about why I made those decisions about fairness?

You might ask and answer these kinds of questions about all the items we've listed as elemental to the teaching of honor, and make improvements (and give yourself congratulations) as warranted. It is always useful for us to remember that to teach honor, we must not only model it but also help our adolescent boys become conscious of their own processes of developing honor. We talk and listen, providing an ongoing conversation with our boys that engages the heart and soul.

Responsibility

Recently I spoke at a Planned Parenthood conference about ways to get adolescent males to develop more responsibility for their sexuality. Planned Parenthood workers and agencies are in the trenches every day, often working heroically to create programs that help our young people. At this particular conference, we were working to address the lack of "male involvement" programs that help males become more responsible. Planned Parenthood is aware of how important these programs are. The organization knows that blaming adolescent males or excoriating them doesn't really help things. Teaching them responsibility requires funding, more male involvement in program coordination, and so on.

At this conference, in the thick of discussions, a program coordinator said, "But what do we mean by 'responsibility'? I mean, really, what do we mean? Because when I use the word with boys it just turns them off, and these are good guys. Is it the way we're using it? Is it that we don't get what boys think about it?"

Indeed, the word "responsibility" is tossed around these days, usually without clarity on our parts about how boys apprehend it, what they think about it, how they perceive themselves in relation to it. Responsibility sits at the core of masculinity. Our males appear to us to be either irresponsible (abandoning teenage moms during adolescence and then adult moms during midlife) or hyperresponsible (spending all their time working or taking care of others' emotional needs with no clarity as to their own). Our males exist across this responsibility spectrum, receiving our ire at either end and, so often, our indifference when they're in the middle. Let us prepare ourselves to nurture responsibility in adolescent males first by understanding what we actually mean by the word.

Responsibility is generally defined as "the ability to respond." It includes accountability. A person is motivated to be responsible by compassion or by honor: because his compassion is activated by circumstance and/or because he has encoded well his honor as a male. A man who lacks *compassion* will generally not be consistently *responsible.* A man who lacks *honor* will generally not be consistently able to *respond to the needs* of those placed in or near his care. Certainly, a male who has not been taught a clear, important male role will not measure up to general standards of adult responsibility.

Adult responsibility exists in adults, not in children. Adolescent males who impregnate females (usually males in Stage 2 and Stage 3, ages fifteen to twenty-five) and abandon them are being irresponsible, to be sure. They are also being age-appropriate. They are not yet adults. They have not been initiated by their parents and communities into a clear adult male honor code, have not fully developed the capacity for compassion, and certainly have no clear sense of their social roles as males. Saying this does not excuse their actions, but it explains them. It is painful to admit, but from the pain will come more male-involvement programs, more healthy male development, and *then* more responsibility from adolescent males.

A key to teaching responsibility to adolescent males is to match it with privileges. There is little an adolescent male wants more than increased privileges. He wants to be able to drive the car, stay out late, date, read what he wants. Our job is to hinge, during the time of responsibility development, his new privileges on the performance of an equal responsibility. "Okay, son, this is a new privilege. Enjoy it. Its price is this other, new responsibility."

Among the Australian aborigines, masculine responsibility is tied not solely to the material or family world, but also to the spiritual. One of the primary objects of the male's responsibility for his community is to create balance between natural creative forces and the metaphysical plane of existence. Closer to home, we might think about the ways in which Orthodox Jewish males have been responsible for a lion's share of the family's conversation with God. We might think of Protestant males coming to this country hundreds of years ago, Bible in hand, insisting on an important place for that Bible and a father's prayers in God's world. This kind of responsibility is spiritual responsibility. My work with adolescent males has shown me that they want a lot more of that than they're getting. By not giving your son your own family's version of it, you rob him not only of a way that his core can unite with the very cosmos from which it sprang, but also of much teaching about the ins and outs of responsibility that religions and spiritualities provide young men.

A mom told me a story that illustrates some of the practical elements of responsibility development. She lost her husband, a religious man, and in his wake, her sixteen-year-old son became like a father to his learning-disabled younger brother. She said:

> My husband was irreplaceable, and I don't try to make Mark into his father. But Mark himself moved closer to his brother. He took him to church, he tutored him, he protected him. While I was preoccupied with daily survival, emotional and financial, Mark became his brother's keeper. He has developed into someone he wouldn't have been if his father were alive. His sense of responsibility now is kind of awesome.

This mom came to see me because she was worried that her son was becoming hyperresponsible, that he was traumatized and denying or hiding the death trauma through that hyperresponsibility. While that analysis defined some of his situation, it by no means explained all. What was rising in him now, in adolescence, was the core of manhood.

Don't our adolescent males need more family responsibility with each new year of life? They need us to give them not only the car keys but also the responsibility for driving younger siblings around, or grocery shopping, or trips to grandparents—balancing that freedom with responsibility. They need us to point out that as the family gives them more, they give it more, even if this means saving money for college rather than spending it on teenage treats and expecting parents to foot the whole college bill in a couple of years. If we provide family responsibility to adolescent boys, they flourish, because they really want more responsibility than we think. We just have to learn new strategies now—more negotiation than authoritarianism, higher expectations but then higher rewards, more honesty about what the family really faces in order to make it in the world.

Our adolescent males need something by which to measure their success at social responsibility. In *The Wonder of Boys*, I suggested "husbandry" as the new male role. The word itself is a combination of the old English *husbonda* and the old Norse word *bua*, which means to dwell. In ancient cultures it signified a man who measured his life by his success at maintaining his bond with home, community, and land. Husbandry includes ten elements of self-discipline, compassion, and good work:

- Seeking communities and helpmates that afford the man a balance of personal spiritual development, family devotion, and life-sustaining work

- Providing for, protecting, and nurturing those a man loves

- Actively participating in not just one but three families

- Living in concert, not antagonism, with the natural world

- Seeking equal partnerships with women and female culture

- Relying on a male kinship system for support and love

- Working for social change, as it is necessary for the continued adaptation of the species

- Coming to know one's own personal story

- Learning to enjoy the fruits of one's labors

- Remaining flexible and open to change

These are the foundational principles of the male role of husbandry. Husbandry provides, I hope, a new model to our culture by which our boys can grow into fulfilled, socially responsible adult males.

The prime time to teach husbandry is during adolescence, when the boy's body and mind are developing to sustain the lessons.

A male who reaches adulthood without learning a sacred role in life is not fully a man. He will wander through society without an internal compass by which to measure his worth in the society. One day he will be told that providing and protecting are good roles for him, and he'll agree. The next day he'll be told hands-on child care is the most important aspect of his role, and he'll agree. The next day he'll be told that meeting his wife's emotional needs is his most important job, and he'll agree. The next day he'll be told he's supposed to work himself to death, and he'll agree—until he wakes up one day and disagrees, confused and resentful.

Spiritual responsibility, family responsibility, and social responsibility are fragile in a male who does not develop, along with them, *personal* responsibility. For a male, personal responsibility is the ability to respond to situations affecting himself and others with a clear sense of how *he* created or participated in the events. A person with very little sense of personal responsibility will blame others for circumstances and events, not just initially—a normal human defense mechanism—but continually. Men will be to blame, or women will be to blame. Children will be to blame. Coworkers will be to blame. Husbands or wives will be to blame.

A male with a clear sense of personal responsibility is a self-confident male. He has moved through adolescence with attention paid, by his caregivers, to his core development. He knows who he is in the world. He knows where his niche is. He knows himself as a spiritual creature. He knows himself as intrinsic to the social fabric. He knows his role in life. He knows what a man is, and that he is one. He won't spend much time blaming others.

We can easily detect a male who has moved through adolescence without enough instruction in personal responsibility. He will have passed through his twenties and thirties attending as best he could to people's needs, generally hyperfocusing his life on a few processes, like work; and at midlife, when his own personal mortality creeps up on him, he will enter a second adolescence and once again seek a clear sense of who he is and what his responsibilities are. Often, he will abandon his family in order to find these things out.

Personal responsibility, social responsibility, family responsibility, and spiritual responsibility are four areas of focus for those of us who care for young men. When we see around us young men who "are not very responsible," we are called on to look carefully at the responsibility training we've given them. We will, generally, find flaws in one of the four areas of responsibility training. As always, solutions will present themselves:

- Be clear and concrete in the teaching, giving specific negotiating points and providing specific incentives and rewards.

- Ask the boys and young men to participate in their own punishments and rewards.

- Give the males sacred tasks, and remark on their sacredness.

- Involve more people rather than fewer in teaching responsibility.

- Present the learning of roles and responsibilities in test formats, with checklists and choice lists, so boys can gauge their own successes.

- Use books, tapes, CDs, TV shows, movies, and other cultural material, in required curricula and courses, by which male social roles and responsibilities are explained, assessed, honored, and critiqued.

- Criticize in the male's presence those responsibility lessons that run counter to our own sense of what true responsibility is, utilizing careful analysis rather than harping or accusation.

- Be constantly involved in teaching boys responsibility, even boys we have never met.

Donna Britt, a *Washington Post* columnist, tells a wonderful story of her friend Avis, who passed by some adolescent males dressed in disrespectful T-shirts. One boy's said: SHUT UP, BITCH. In a friendly and mature way, Avis approached him about his shirt. In her words, "He blushed as humbly as a kid in Sunday school who hadn't read the lesson. He was polite but couldn't explain why he'd wear a shirt insulting to every woman. He promised he'd never wear it again." When Donna asked Avis about whether she was afraid of the teen boys, Avis responded, "I'm a crime reporter, and the reason some of these kids are walking around with Uzis is because adults are afraid to say anything. Part of adults' *function* is to say, 'You shouldn't do this.' "

Bravo! Without insulting the boys or overreacting to them, Avis did the job of one who cares maturely for our young men. She gave those boys a clear, concrete lesson, meeting them right where they were, unflinching in the face of them. She knew that a combination of strength and personal serenity works best with adolescent boys.

Enterprise

When I was seventeen I worked in a restaurant called The Pasta Factory in Honolulu. The restaurant prepared meals for lunch and dinner customers, and also for airlines. This busboy job was one of many I held during adolescence, mainly in restaurants. I made friends on the job, gained mentors in the world of enterprise, and was valued by others because I could sustain good work. This form of enterprise fed my core. It was pretty normal during my upbringing for kids, especially boys, to get jobs during adolescence. It gave us spending money. It gave us self-esteem. It gave us community. It gave us a new structure to add to the second and third families we may or may not have had in place already. It gave us a sense of responsibility. It taught us compassion and conscience, for there were always tests of these in the workplace. It required diligence, duty, and honor from us.

Once when I was complaining to my grandfather about working, he said: "You can complain all you want, but remember that a man who doesn't make something with his hands, his head, and his heart is not much of a man." My grandfather had come over from Italy during his adolescence without speaking English. He had made a success of himself. In his Italian accent, from his elder mouth, the cliche carried weight. I had to twist being a busboy into "making something with my hands, head, and heart," but I could do it. There's little doubt in my mind that working as a busboy (and before that a janitor's assistant at a bus station) developed in me a good amount of humility. This experience can't hurt any adolescent male.

What I didn't realize when I was a middle adolescent and listening to my grandfather's words was the biological wisdom in them. Indeed, an adolescent male, surging with testosterone and all the social ambition that comes with it; perceiving the world now in many spheres of social and cognitive activity; seeking to find in the world his own particular, unique place where his passions can find voice; and looking for structure, discipline, and challenge by which to become a man, gravitates naturally toward environments where his core will develop. He knows, if unconsciously, that he needs works of *hand, head, and heart* in order to develop his core self; that he must find environments of *enterprise* in which to learn who he is, what his talents are, what he can reasonably expect from the society of work, and what trades will help him in his future. The call toward enterprise is primal in the male. It existed millions of years ago, when he hunted; thousands of years ago, when he farmed; a hundred years ago, when he worked in the steel mill; and it continues now as he joins the economy as a lifeguard, busboy, shelf stocker, or fast-food cook. Every male wants to see the energy of the world move through his hands. Every male wants the mental challenges of work. Every male seeks through all the "menial" jobs to come to the beloved enterprise that will finally spark his passions.

Throughout the world the primacy of the male call to enterprise is nurtured. Laziness is rarely respected. Deeds and work are what matter. Many of our religious traditions strive to give it voice. The Bible tells us that "God will render to every man according to his deeds." In India they say, "God will not ask a man of what race he is. God will ask what he has done." Adolescent males who have little opportunity for enterprise in mainstream society find opportunities that often run counter to the values of that society. Our drug culture follows this model. Young men of enterprise, choosing not to follow mainstream paths or having little or no opportunity to access them, have created a monolithic substructure of enterprise that ultimately embattles and harms the larger culture: crime. Yet, to their core-self-development it is enterprise.

A Fine Young Man

Adolescent males seek the stimulation of enterprise throughout their everyday lives, and unless directed toward actual enterprise will easily find themselves stimulated by virtual enterprise. A fifteen-year-old playing a video game for an hour is stimulating his hands and head enough to fool his heart that he's doing something worth his call to enterprise. One of the reasons why we take televisions out of our sons' rooms, stop buying them every available Super Nintendo, and help them cease overdependency on media is to delete as much as possible the "virtual" stimulations of enterprise and direct them toward actual "doing" itself.

My mother and father, brought up during the Depression, held to the notion that a Stage 2 adolescent should work. They set age fourteen as the time in my life when I would begin work. I rebelled a little, but basically I was glad. With our boys maturing, physically and hormonally, earlier than we baby boomers did, we might pull that year back to thirteen. Certainly, every family will find benefits in setting a time for initiating the boy into adolescent work and helping him remain focused there. If work takes him away from sports, music, social life, then the boy probably will be a workaholic. Work addiction is not what we mean by enterprise. A balance of work with family, church, school, arts, hobbies, and athletic life is the ideal.

For some families, paying a boy to work in the home is enough, especially when he is deeply involved in a number of sports. For others, sports, academics, or arts is enterprise. Each does contain the work of hands, head, and heart, and so each can fulfill the needs of the boy's core development. Simultaneously, work outside the home is sometimes needed more than we realize. A boy who has trouble learning responsibility can learn it well in the workplace because there he is challenged to be accountable to people other than parents. A boy who has trouble finding outlets for his energy finds the workplace an exhilarating and pleasantly exhausting environment. Adolescents with ADHD often benefit from working, especially from physical labor. Aimless, listless, withdrawn boys often flourish at work.

One of the primary jobs of our ancestors' parents was to direct males toward a number of opportunities by which to accomplish what anthropologists call "honorable usefulness." It has always been recognized that a male must feel useful in a meaningful way. One of our primary jobs as elders caring for our adolescent young is give them avenues for honorable usefulness. Much of that usefulness must fit their testosterone levels and their male brains—it may need to involve space, the use of space, work within certain space; some quick tension release, channeled aggression, hierarchical social systems. It needs to provide our boys with leaders, even if these leaders instruct the boys merely in the best way to bus a table. Nowadays especially it may need to involve copartnership with female workers. It needs to make available an environment in which the searches for identity, autonomy, morality, and intimacy can take place. The male's primal call toward enterprise is both an end in itself—to perform and accomplish through work—and a means toward another end—to grow up. Boys grow up by working. Sports, arts, and other activities do instill values and stimulate head and heart, but there's still nothing like working.

Will every male follow the call to enterprise that is part of his core? In our late-twentieth-century society, not every male does. How do we get our males directed toward the enterprise they seek? Many communities offer avenues. In Houston, Texas, 32,000 students participate in a School-to-Work program, part of a national program of the same name that covers some 500,000 students in fifty states. Julia, whose son, Timon, has been in the program, had this to say: "There's a tremendous difference [in Timon]. Every day he has a story to tell about work." In Lincoln, Nebraska, the city zoo hires Stage 1 and Stage 2 teens (some as young as twelve) as "volunteers" during the summer. Corporations have made this program possible by donating the funds. In my own city, a Summer Jobs Fair is an annual event, attracting teens to summer work. Most of the jobs advertised pay about five dollars an hour. So what? the teens say. It's work, it's good to have the money and the experience. One teen, voicing the core call to enterprise wonderfully, said: "We're looking for anything we can get our hands on."

Individual families can provide boys with work. Every working parent will want to at least consider taking sons to work whenever possible.

To fully invigorate our young men's needs for enterprise, we will have to make some cultural adjustments. Each of us will have to devote some time to these.

1. Our boys will have to spend less time with media and more time with work.

2. Our extended families will have to help us find jobs for our children. Optimally, every first family will have assigned a mentor to their child (whether male or female) by the time the child enters adolescence. This grandparent, godparent, good friend will be, among other things, a mentor to the child's enterprise, vocational, and trade activities. Boys love to work while relating to people anyway. Working alongside someone makes it easier (less emotionally threatening) for them to relate to someone. Matching an elder's vocational or avocational interests with a youth's is as natural to many males as breathing.

3. To connect enterprise with core development, we will have to nurture our young to see their work not merely as the means to acquire enough money to become consumers but as a sacred part of life.

4. In some cases of mental or emotional distress among our kids, including brain disorders like ADHD, we may want to turn toward enterprise for a solution. It is harder to be depressed when one is working. Working can also provide focus for the unfocused brain.

5. We will have to convince corporations that corporate health and community health are directly related. Each corporation will have to devote time and money to programs that benefit youths. Incentives affect crime and delinquency rates. Every delinquent male takes its toll on corporate America. We have documented already that a corporation's gains in profits are concomitant with its provision of day care, and now we will have to document how corporate gains in profits affect and are affected by its mentoring programs for young men.

6. "Behavioral competencies" essential to success in enterprise will have to be recognized and taught to young boys, beginning in early adolescence. "Behavioral competencies," a term used by Zwell International, a very forward-looking company based in Chicago, include initiative, influencing others, and analytical thinking. Zwell assesses adult performance using these competencies. Zwell's philosophy is that unless we have a common language about which behavioral competencies a workplace requires, we cannot expect individuals to perform well in the realm of enterprise. These competencies can be taught to adolescents, and indeed Zwell is experimenting with such an idea. Throughout our training of adolescent males, we will have to identify specific competencies for them, and focus on each of them at the appropriate time. The "loose" approach to parenting adolescents is somewhat dangerous now as our workplaces and economies become more competitive.

Wherever your adolescent male fits on the spectrum of enterprise, you benefit by making a plan for the development of his sense of enterprise, a plan which, as he grows, you can share with him and develop more and more as *his* plan, not yours.

The Score Model

We have explored the core of manhood. In this core model are four pillars, as it were, standing at the center of masculinity. If a boy moves through adolescence in the care of parents and community who focus on these four elements, he will lead a better life. In fact, if experience and research from around the world are correct, he can barely lead a good life without this core self.

In addition, every culture, including our own, values service. It is with the addition of that word to our core model that we get the SCORE model. I present it as a way of transforming other uses of "score" among boys—"Last night I scored, man!" or, "Did you catch the score of Saturday's game?"—into something with a "higher" purpose. When we really keep *score* of boys, let us keep our focus not only on compassion, honor, responsibility, and enterprise, but on the activity and process that is the culmination of all four. It is in service and in being guided toward a life of service that a man's compassion, honor, responsibility, and enterprise are actively tested, and actively rewarded.

Service is central to all the world traditions, to the ways in which all religions and cultures raise young people. Jesus said, "It is more blessed to give than to receive." In Judaic literature we find: "Blessed is he that considereth the poor: the Lord will deliver him in time of trouble." The Koran says: "The poor, the orphan, the captive—feed them for the love of God alone, desiring no reward, nor even thanks." The essence of service is in this: raising young people to learn to give without need for reward. If a boy reaches his age of maturity knowing how to do this, he can do nearly anything. He can befriend a cranky, irascible old man who might one day, because of the youth's patience, become his great teacher. He can navigate nearly any workplace dilemma with serenity because he can always see in his actions the way in which he is serving and can, through hard times, be proud of that service, no matter the complications along the way.

In India the Sikhs say: "In the minds of the generous, contentment is produced." Learning a life of service is good not only because religions tell us so, but because a man cannot experience psychological contentment unless he has learned the many ways of generosity. In Connecticut there is a blind musician, Stuart Hemingway, who has recorded famous songs, collaborated on Grammy-nominated albums, and yet performs, unpaid, in middle schools, and finds these "unpaid gigs" some of his most satisfying. His performances and talks inspire young people with more than musical inspiration—the youths are inspired by his presence, his perseverance, and his gift to them. Some want to be musicians because of him. Many want to emulate his grace, generosity, and passion to serve.

More and more communities, churches, and schools are directing adolescent males toward service activities. Colin Powell's call for more teenage (and adult) volunteers is an example of this movement. Jesuit Volunteer Corps, Volunteers of America, Boy Scout volunteers—all are examples of males in service. A Chicago-based program, B.E.D.S. (Building Ecumenical Discipleship Through Sheltering), attracts young people from all over the country in its service program. One Saturday every month, individual families take food to local churches and help serve the homeless. Throughout the country, schools are adding "service" curricula to their junior- and senior-level "human growth" classes. Service is being required by many juvenile detention boards as part of a juvenile's term of rehabilitation. In Tulsa, Oklahoma, juvenile delinquents plant trees.

Training in service begins early, of course. We ought not wait until adolescence. However, adolescence is the time for *intensive* service training because that is when a boy's testosterone-based energy level is rising and needs channels, and his cognitive abilities are expanding exponentially and need direction.

Holidays are good occasions for connecting our youths with people in nursing homes. After-school hours are good for service activities, even if for only one day a week. If sports activities dominate after school, then service activities should dominate part of the weekend. If a boy is so involved in sports that he has no space in his schedule for service, even on weekends, he is overinvolved in sports. Likewise if a boy is involved in any activity to the detriment of time spent in service.

If we belong to no church, synagogue, mosque, or temple we have fewer structured opportunities for service, so we must work harder to find them. Likewise, if we belong to a church that provides no service programs for its youths, we must advocate for them. And if we belong to a church that provides only service programs based in proselytizing, we need to remind the church that true service wants no reward, not even the reward of conversion.

If you are parenting, mentoring, or educating an adolescent male at this time and are not focused on service programs or activities, I hope you'll attack this dearth with vigor. You will most likely find a glow on the face of a boy who serves. He will come to the dinner table full of stories to tell. His heart will have been warmed, and even at times frightened by the feebleness of the people he has served. He will wear on his sleeve a greater respect for all people, including his parents and teachers, because he has seen himself in service.

If we want our boys to learn to serve, we must ourselves serve, and we must converse with our boys about our service. A father who has fought a war but does not discuss the sacrifices he made does his son no service. Unless he suffers posttraumatic stress, in which case such a conversation might do more harm than good, the father needs to use himself and his service as models for the boy. A mother who does not point out her way of serving in the workplace and family robs the boy of service modeling. Any parent or grandparent or other caregiver who has emphasized particular service activities might use Stage 1 of adolescence as a time to induct the boy into that service group or activity. Adolescence is not just a time for free play, academic learning, and free socializing. Whether they say it or not, adolescent males want desperately to serve, because by serving others, their own core principles—compassion, honor, responsibility, and enterprise—and the other principles associated with these—duty, passion, wisdom-learning, modeling, loyalty, expanding personal experience—all are well served.

When a man keeps *score*, he is a man of self-discipline. We know an adolescent male has become a man, with a *core* intact, because we notice that while he may at times blame and find fault with others, he does not base his passion on that blaming. He knows that he himself is responsible for his own life. While he will become dependent on others as survival, reproduction, and romance require, he will always have his own internal center, or core, to return to when his dependencies do not fully meet his emotional needs. As his culture's perceptions of personal psychology move through their rapid and contradictory changes, he will be capable of weathering it all with self-discipline. Through self-reflection, his own unique, and particular, masculine emotional fiber will be clear to him and will be revealed in the world as need be, whether through emotional conversation or action, service or sacrifice, stoic perseverance, or hands-on nurturance of others and himself. If every home, school, church, and caregiver took stock of his or her own perceptions of compassion, honor, responsibility, enterprise, and service and, having taken stock, resolved to consciously teach these to the next generation of boys, our adolescent males would be happier, healthier men. The very core of their being will have been loved in boyhood and adolescence, and from that love they will serve the world.

CHAPTER TEN

The Ten Integrities

"What is a man, if he has not integrity?"

CHINESE PROVERB

Jacob, of the Old Testament, the son of Isaac and Rebecca and the younger brother of Esau, was born in a time of relative stability among his people. He grew through boyhood toward his adolescence. According to traditions, the first son, in this case, Esau, could claim the family birthright (which included rights of leadership) from his father. But Rebecca's intuition told her that Jacob should be the leader of the people. So she orchestrated a trick by which Isaac, who had become old and somewhat blind, would mistake Jacob for Esau and thus grant Jacob the birthright. Isaac himself may not have been as blind as people think, because really the trick wasn't so tricky, and yet he fell for it. Perhaps, some people have wondered, Isaac wanted to be tricked. Perhaps he wanted to reach out and feel Jacob's hands and face and pretend they were Esau's, and in this pretense convey the birthright of his lineage onto his second son instead of his first. Perhaps, even, Rebecca and he were in on it together. We don't know.

We do know, however, that by trickery, Jacob, the younger adolescent son, received the father's blessing; he became the son on whom the birthright was bestowed, which led to the beginning of his long journey toward manhood. And so it is that brothers compete for birthrights, sometimes to the detriment of their love for each other. Jacob and Esau were enemies for a time. Their journeys away and toward each other present to the world a wonderful lesson in ten integrities.

A Fine Young Man

. . .

Over the last fifteen years, I have studied cultures worldwide in various ways, including through their sacred texts, their myths, and their stories, in order to discover bedrock, foundational lessons of childhood. I have found ten integrities that are taught to children around the world, both boys and girls. We will focus here on how they are important to boys. What cultures from African villages to European civilizations to our own American culture teach us is that if a boy does not learn and habituate these ten integrities, he will falter during adolescence and later in life, suffer greatly, and bring suffering to his community. In developmental terms, he is not an adult unless he learns these. In mythological metaphors, he cannot become a king, a full-fledged man in his community, unless he learns these. Ideally, we can teach these to our youths by the time they leave Stage 3. In this chapter, I hope to help parents, mentors, and educators focus their energies on these integrities in homes, schools, and churches. The ten integrities are:

Lineal (or ancestral) integrity

Psychological integrity

Social integrity

Spiritual integrity

Moral integrity

Emotional integrity

Sexual integrity

Marital (or gender) integrity

Physical integrity

Intellectual integrity

Though we begin to teach a boy these integrities very early in his life, it is during adolescence that a boy's body and brain develop the capacities to fully understand, experience, and utilize the integrities.

We notice that when we tell stories to our little boys, generally we do so without much quizzing about application—maybe one or two questions. But the stories we tell to adolescents—for instance, in a literature class—involve massive efforts of critique and personal/communal integration. Fairy tales, folktales, biblical tales all were told similarly centuries ago—to little kids as engaging entertainment, but to adolescents as maps of destiny.

We would do much for our adolescent males if we revived this kind of energy in our storytelling. The Jacob tale—a story about an adolescent male becoming a man—has much to teach. When its plot hinges on the importance of obtaining a family heritage, blessing, and birthright, it teaches the first integrity: lineal integrity.

Lineal Integrity

Every child has the urge to become the product of the energies of his family's past. Everyone in the family line who has come before the boy hums a song of self in his blood and cells. The boy wants to hear this song clearly throughout his journey to manhood. He wants to be a person of his own race, creed, and culture—a person who *belongs* in the world because he has a *birthright*.

One of the reasons open adoption—the practice of allowing adopted children to know their biological parents—is so important to so many adopted kids has to do with this idea of lineal integrity. At some point, every adopted child I've spoken with has had the urge to discover something more than he knows about his parents and lineage. It is like an instinct. The child must respect and protect his environmental upbringing, but he must also be able to enter realms of time and culture that predate it, learn of his birth mother and biological father, and hear the long song of his bloodline and ethnic origin.

Boys without lineal integrity do not hear the voices of their ancestors helping to guide them into manhood. They are less able to develop self-discipline and all the other integrities because their ancestors—even if from the grave—are not spiritually active in teaching them these integrities.

As we discovered in the chapters regarding rites of passage, asking a boy to stand and say his lineage as far back as he knows it is a wonderful experience. So often, boys don't know the names of even their own grandparents. If they do know the names, they know little about these people who gave their lives so that this child could live. A strange kind of aloneness descends on boys when they are confronted with the magnitude of what they don't know about themselves, about their families. They resolve to learn more. This is the urge of lineal integrity, displayed so powerfully in the Jacob story, working its way through the minds and hearts of today's sons.

A Fine Young Man

Here are some practical tools and themes for teaching lineal integrity:

- Genealogies, family heirlooms, and antiques. Get boys interested in these, and teach them how to prepare and refine them. Set boys to work keeping the antiques in good shape or making phone calls to relatives about genealogies.

- Tell lots of stories about ancestors so the boy develops a multigenerational sense of personal ancestry.

- Take many pilgrimages to death places and birth places.

- Cherish and discuss family letters, journals, and Bibles.

- Institute and maintain a sense of family tradition in present life—at the dinner table, during holidays.

- Protect religious traditions and rituals as much as possible.

- Teach respect for all elders, not just ones that are relatives.

You'll notice that in this list there is no mention of ethnic hatred or racism. Lineal integrity is not about hating another group; rather, it is about loving oneself.

Let's return to Jacob's story. You may remember that this young man, having successfully received the lineal blessing from his father, incurs his brother's wrath. His brother, Esau, goes to his father and angrily insists on himself being blessed. In Isaac's response is some fodder for our suspicion that Isaac has known all along what is happening and, in his brilliance as a father, is guiding his two sons. He seems to believe Esau needs some key psychological lessons, perhaps in humility. When Esau asks for a blessing, his father responds with this prediction of destiny:

> Behold, thy dwelling shall be away from the fatness of the earth, and away from the dew of heaven from above: And by thy sword shalt thou live, and shalt serve thy brother: and it shall come to pass when thou shalt have the dominion, and thou shalt break his yoke from off thy neck.

Esau vows internally that he'll take revenge against Jacob. Rebecca and Isaac make sure to send Jacob away. They send him to Haran, where Rebecca's brother, Laban, lives.

If we interpret Isaac's words and his and Rebecca's parental actions from the point of view of the adolescent male's developmental journey, we find that the father is preparing the son for the next step—psychological integrity.

Psychological Integrity

Psychological integrity is a person's capacity to be a separate, honest self, who *chooses* his psychological dependencies rather than having them chosen for him. When we are children, our dependencies are chosen for us. We are born or adopted into a first family and become dependent on its care-givers. Adolescence is the time for the development of independence and individuation. If we don't develop independence during adolescence, we grow up, get married, but remain boys. We end up making our wives our mothers. Somewhere in midlife we reinvigorate the pursuit of psychological integrity that we should have accomplished in adolescence, revisiting adolescence often like a ghost revisiting the scene of death. Psychological integrity and all its aspects—individuation (becoming a unique, individual self), the ability to give care to others, nurture others, make good choices, keep self-esteem high, know one's own intrinsic self-worth—depend in large part on one's ability to psychologically separate from childhood caregivers and become one's own caregiver in adolescence.

In the Jacob tale, Isaac and Rebecca seem to know that Esau is not psychologically capable of accepting, with integrity, the birthright he wants. He simply is not ready. Jacob himself is not ready for the whole kingship and must make a long journey. But the parents seem to have more confidence in Jacob's psychological maturity.

Often in myths, biblical tales, and folktales, a male's psychological integrity is discovered in his relationship with his brothers. In a Grimm fairy tale, "The Gnome," two elder brothers deceive the youngest about a dwarf, who ends up blessing the youngest with treasured information about where the core self hides. In the Turkish tale of Keloglan and the Giant, four elder brothers fall asleep in the face of adversity, and in shame try to convince the youngest brother, Keloglan, that he's too weak to face the giant. In the end it is Keloglan who succeeds. In the stories of male development, whether it is a giant, a dwarf, or a disguise that tricks a father, the core self emerges in the context of brother helping, shaming, tricking, or even trying to kill brother.

Is the core theme in literature that a boy becomes a man, in psychological terms, by competing with his brothers? Perhaps there is some of that: We do seek our independence in concert with and competition with others. But even more than that, in primal tales of a culture, brothers generally represent the developmental male as a whole, divided by the story into parts. Esau and Jacob are the developing male as a whole. Esau is the part that must overcome hatred and shame and find humility and then a self. Jacob is the part of an adolescent male that must journey far away, suffer many deceits and hardships, and finally persevere in finding a self. We are complex creatures who seek psychological integrity in many ways throughout adolescence. We must learn to be humble toward our fellows while simultaneously learning to become men of great success. Early in this story, Esau holds the candle of humility, Jacob the candle of social success.

Here are some practical themes and tools for teaching psychological integrity.

Pain is normal. Helping a boy become an individuated man hurts. It hurts him and it hurts us. We let go of him and send him toward mentors, activities, girlfriends, male friends, colleges, trades, and we ache for him and his childlike dependency on us. He lets us go, aching for his dependency on us. Much of middle-adolescent anger in our children is actually anguish at the loss of that comfortable dependency.

Talk about psychological integrity with your children. We must talk to our boys about what independence is. They must feel, by our attention to its details in their lives, that we are like Isaac and Rebecca, carefully navigating it with them.

Bless the boy with psychological integrity. We need to make the boy conscious of integrity: "Here are some specific ways I think (we think) you will need to develop core self." Or: "Look at how you feel when you make a mistake in school or sports. It throws you for days. Part of your destiny, son, will be to heal your need for absolute perfection in yourself." Or: "Look at how you feed on laziness. Your destiny, son, lies in finding a work or art to love enough to get you off your butt. Don't be like me, a workaholic who hates his work. I know your laziness is partially rooted in not wanting to be like me. So don't be. Find something to love in your work."

Allow the individuation and psychological separation process to occur. Moms and dads have to let kids go. Jacob had to leave his comfortable home. This is psychological separation in the heart of a biblical tale. It is essential in the life of every child. Leaving home doesn't necessarily mean kicking a kid out when he's eighteen. It means letting him make his own choices, without fear of our intervention or authoritarianism.

Separation does not mean abandonment. When Rebecca sends Jacob off to Laban, she directs him to her brother. She does not sever Jacob, an adolescent, from his caregiving family. Similarly, we brutalize and damage the process of psychological integrity when we abandon our youths, either physically or emotionally, to their adolescence. This abandonment most often occurs when we let our boys go so much that we no longer help them monitor their after-school hours, their TV watching, the time with girlfriends. Stage 2 is when we are most likely to confuse separation with abandonment. Our boys might become so troublesome that we say, "Oh, well, let him go. We're all sick of each other anyway." Stage 2 is the very time when our boys need us both to let go and to maintain a strong family focus on those things that are essential for development:

Family rituals

Family holidays

Contact with elders

Family and around-the-house responsibilities

Respect for parents

Motivation to do well in school and/or trade

More and more the adolescent male must and will learn psychological integrity on his own, but the initial lessons, especially the necessary psychological separations from Mom and Dad, are blessings given by parents to sons in their everyday interactions with those boys.

Jacob's tale continues, and he prepares for his journey away from his mother and his father. His mother releases him. His father gives him some final words, telling him that he is allowed to marry the women in the house of Bethuel but not the daughters of Canaan. Esau hears of his father's interdiction and goes off to do exactly what his father has forbade. Jacob goes off to do as his father has told him.

One night as Jacob sleeps, using a stone for a pillow, he has a vision. He sees a ladder extending from earth to heaven, with the angels of God ascending and descending. He hears God speak to him, telling him of his relevance in the world. He hears God express love and care for him: God says, " 'I am with thee and will keep thee in all places whither thou goest, and will bring thee again into this land; for I will not leave thee.' "

When Jacob awakens he is a changed soul. He experiences immense fear and awe. He sees himself differently. To symbolize the sacredness of the night's communion, he takes the stone he used as a pillow, makes it a pillar, and pours oil on it. He calls the place Bethel. Standing there, he vows that he will one day return to his land of origin and make peace and, further, that he will give back to the world and God ten times what he himself will be given in life.

In this section of the story, three of the ten integrities are revealed. We'll look at each one separately: Social integrity, spiritual integrity, and moral integrity.

Social Integrity

In Jacob's tale, as in so many others around the world, things happen in order of importance to a people. Often, lineal integrity begins an adolescent's journey because the people believe that a man's life is first and foremost a continuation of the lives of his ancestors. Following lineal integrity comes psychological integrity—the idea that once a boy has concentrated on his lineal and thus ancestral/communal destiny, it is okay for him to focus on himself as an individual. Having built some sturdiness in his individuality, these ancient cultures reasoned, he is capable of understanding and following some of the social rules—e.g., rules regarding intertribal relationship— not just by rote or because we force him to as a child, but because now he is ready to become one of the champions or masters of the society. Thus Isaac and Rebecca give Jacob lessons in lineal and psychological integrity before social. Those done, Isaac lays down for his son essential social rules regarding the house of Bethuel.

The ancient wisdom of Jacob's story still holds true today: Before a boy can fully understand and accept social rules that may be hard for him to put into effect in his life, he needs to feel strong as a member of his own group, family, or tribe, and as an individual. If he does not, he's likely to become antisocial, in other words, to be more like Esau: likely to break the rules one by one, using that as a way to call attention to the fact that he does not feel whole in the society and thus will not adhere to its rules.

Social integrity is a person's sense of belonging in society, a person's sense of realness in that society, a person's sense of wanting to be an honest, helpful member of that society. There is more social integrity for us to learn about as Jacob's story continues, but for now, it is useful for us to note that Jacob's parents don't send him off without first telling him what is expected of him in his society, specifically regarding marriage. Each of us today is required, if we believe this ancient wisdom to be worthwhile, to tell our young people what is expected of them—not just the little household rules to follow, but substantial ones as well. While we don't usually tell our sons whom to marry, we set other rules.

Whom to include in one's social sphere. If we don't teach inclusiveness of all peoples, the human territorial (testosterone-driven) urge toward excluding often will win out. If we don't model inclusiveness and forgiveness of other groups and go with our youths to places where the disadvantaged or marginalized need our help in finding equality, we are not teaching our children modern social integrity.

How to respect and care even for those people we dislike. Our charge, generally, as late-twentieth-century Americans, is to teach our young people the social integrity of: "I don't like what you say, but I'll fight to uphold your right to say it." That social rule is as powerful in our day as Isaac's prohibition of marriage to a social enemy.

How to treat women and be treated by them. These rules also are as forceful as Isaac's interdiction. We are challenged to talk to our boys about, lead them in, and model the appropriate treatment of females. We teach no harassment, no sexual assumptions, and more talk between the sexes. Simultaneously, we do our males (and ultimately our females) no good if we don't teach them how to recognize when they are being manipulated and abused and villainized by females.

These are just some of the aspects of social integrity, some of the practicalities we pursue during a boy's adolescence. More will emerge as we continue exploring integrity in Jacob's story.

Spiritual Integrity

Jacob, an adolescent male, probably in late Stage 2, receives social rules from his father, starts the powerful passage away from his parents toward psychological integrity, carries with him the power of his lineal and parental blessing, all while walking from one town to another, from one family group to another. He knows how to adapt to and survive discomfort, transforming the hard stone into a pillow for sleep.

In his sleep, after a long day of walking, he has a vision. In that vision are revealed some of the key themes of spiritual integrity.

When we speak of spiritual integrity, we do not necessarily mean religion. Religion may be a large part of a boy's spiritual life, but for many people, religion seems to mitigate spiritual life. We live in a time when religions are in transition, and people's attitudes toward them are in flux. This does not mean spirituality should wither.

Using Jacob's story as our model, we can measure spiritual integrity by:

- An adolescent male's ability to search for and find meaning in his existence

- An adolescent male's sense of fear (awe) in the presence of spirit

- An adolescent male's ability to make personal rituals, tributes, and worship

- An adolescent male's call to peace, forgiveness, and resolution of social and moral dilemmas through spiritual activity such as prayer and service

- An adolescent male's faith that he is loved by God (or Higher Self or the Universe) and is, therefore, an incarnation of love itself in this world

In these areas, our sons may be private, may have their own rituals, prayers, and other personal ways of seeking and worship that we mustn't invade. Nonetheless, they still need and want contact and teaching, if not from us, then from second- and third-family members.

Surveys tell us that the majority of us, at some point in life, will have a vision similar to Jacob's, a vision in which we become one with God. For those of us who do not experience a particular instance of revelation, vision means something broader: a lifelong faith. Surveys tell us also that nearly 90 percent of Americans answer the sentence "Do you believe in God?" in the affirmative. So it is safe to assume that most of us have felt or are ready to feel the spiritual integrity that Jacob felt.

No matter our religion, no matter if we are scientific humanists to the core, if we look closely at our adolescent males, we will find that each boy is like Jacob—each senses mystery in the cosmos and needs relationship with that mystery. A literal religious interpretation will ultimately suppress that sense of mystery, as will literal scientific humanism. An adolescent boy seeks *his own* relationship with the divine, *his own* vision of Jacob's ladder, whether in stories, church, synagogue, mosque, temple, conversations about the workings of life and the universe, camping trips in which he "sleeps on stones" in the great cathedral of nature.

Spirituality is actually a hardwired instinct. We can track spiritual-integrity development to the very first hominid who saw spirit in a rock or tree. We are hardwired to *belong* in the universe in which we live.

We should note the wise timing of Jacob's contact with God. That contact happens when Jacob is in mid-adolescence, even moving toward late adolescence, and in transition between dependency on his parents and adult life away from them. He has been given social rules and lineal power, but he needs a larger, cosmic frame for them in order to move fully into the next stages of manhood development. In other words, that vision of spiritual integrity takes place at the center of the journey to manhood.

Moral Integrity

After Jacob's vision, after Jacob becomes one with God, he makes some vows about rightness of action: to forge peace with his brother one day, and to live a life of service. Thus moral integrity is introduced in this story.

When we speak of moral integrity, we mean, certainly, "doing what's right." But we all know that as boys become men, "what's right" becomes cloudy. So moral integrity in the lives of adolescent males is not just about learning certain rules and sticking to them. Only in the first few years of life is morality mainly about following rules by rote.

An adolescent's cognitive, psychosocial, and physiological developments are dependent on the boy's moral development evolving beyond simple rule-following into realms of moral intuition. The young adult must be led by his families, and must discover in his own social, psychological, spiritual, and moral life the ability to *intuit* what is right and pursue that path of rightness to its end.

Four important questions face us as we develop our sons' moral characters in middle and late adolescence:

1. Has he experienced abuse, trauma, or neglect that makes normal moral development more difficult? So often we try to teach moral integrity to boys and young men who haven't received enough love, individuation, attention, sense of clan, or social skills to fully develop morally. Often these

unloved boys grow into adolescent males who actually despise themselves and don't realize it. Every social policy we create to protect moral integrity in our society will work better, and we will be better able to build the foundation for morality training, once we recognize that the boy's core self must be attended to first.

2. Have we adjusted our morality teaching to adapt to his new cognitive skills and social life? We adjust by acknowledging the stages of moral development (something I covered in depth in *The Wonder of Boys*) and changing our approach to morality to fit those stages. We adjust also by bringing the boy continually into the dialogue about his moral education. He starts suggesting punishments, for instance, by the time he's about eleven or twelve.

3. Are we carrying on enough conscious morality training, in all three families, to build moral integrity in a boy? One thing Jewish families tend to be good at are "pilpuls"—little arguments, often at the dinner table of an Orthodox home, about passages from the Torah or Talmud, arguments in which small and large moral issues get debated. We all might try something like this, utilizing our own sacred texts or forming moral conversation spontaneously by talking within our family about current events. One family I worked with had four children, each of whom was required on a given evening to bring to the table a moral issue to be debated.

4. Are there moral or immoral agents and stimulants in any of the three families that crush or hurt moral-integrity development? If there are—for instance, in peer groups or the media—we make it a primary concern of our family and clan to negotiate and, if need be, force a change in this area. We intervene, utilizing extended family members, teachers, and wise peers. As we force the end of one kind of dangerous stimulant—e.g., drug or media addiction—we make sure the boy has some other activity or work or way of receiving love to substitute for the relinquished substance, practice, or relationship.

Having explored the first five integrities, let us return to Jacob's story and see the development of four more. As Jacob continues on his journey toward Haran, he comes to a bucolic place where sheep graze and there is a well. The stone over the well needs to be lifted so that the animals can have water. Jacob asks the people near the well if they know of Laban, Rachel, and his other kin. The people point out a beautiful young woman walking, with her sheep, toward the well. "That is Rachel," they say. As Rachel approaches,

Jacob lifts the stone off the well and introduces himself to his cousin. Jacob is portrayed as wonderfully emotional: "Jacob watered the flock and embraced Rachel and lifted up his voice, and wept." They proceed toward Laban's house, where there is again rejoicing. Jacob finds a second home almost immediately among his kin in Haran.

After he has stayed a month, his affections for Laban's family grow, including affections for Rachel. He works with Rachel, who is a shepherdess, and for Laban. Laban determines that Jacob should not work uncompensated; rather, because he is a responsible young man, he deserves wages. Jacob suggests that he work seven years for Laban, at the end of which he would gain permission to marry Rachel. Laban agrees. "Jacob served seven years for Rachel," the story says, "and they seemed unto him but a few days, for the love he had of her."

Laban, however, chooses to deceive Jacob; after watching him work for seven years, Laban substitutes Leah, Rachel's elder sister, for Rachel. After the marriage, a shocked Jacob confronts him. Laban says that because Leah's the oldest, she has to be married first. Jacob works seven *more* years, winning the right to marry Rachel as well, and also couples with a handmaid. Leah and the handmaid bear children. Rachel, Jacob's true love, does not bear any at first. Later she does. Jacob works for all the family, building the family's wealth and reputation.

Emotional Integrity

There are a number of places in this story where Jacob shows emotional integrity. It is perhaps most clear as a theme when he weeps for joy at seeing Rachel.

Emotional integrity is a person's emotional self-discipline. It includes appropriate emotional responses to external stimulants and enough range of emotional expression to ensure self-awareness and good communication with others. Jacob appears to have emotional range, to be able to express himself, and to be able to communicate joy and love to a future spouse. His emotional integrity does not develop in a vacuum but clarifies itself after some of the other integrities have been established.

Jacob does not define himself only by stoic denial of emotion, nor is he the kind of young man who is emotionally out of control. He knows that emotionality is an important part of his family line. He has, after all, some wonderfully emotional relatives—Isaac, Rebecca, Abraham, and Sarah. He has modeled emotional life from his kin and kind.

Jacob has psychological integrity—individuation and independence—which makes emotional integrity not only easier but essential. A man who is well on the path of individuation is not always worried about personal weakness. He is not worried about earlier dependencies—especially dependencies on early caregivers—devouring his adult self. He can show more *range* of feeling because feeling does not weaken him or make him regress to boyhood. Much of the middle-adolescent male's tendency to be either ultra-repressed or emotionally out of control stems from his trouble with individuation.

Jacob knows a lot of the social rules and so can feel emotional within the container of human society.

He is a young man of deep spiritual connection. Spirituality is emotional life experienced in cosmic proportion and relationship.

He has a sturdy sense of moral character. A moral base makes emotionality easier. It helps teach a person what self-control of feelings and behavior ought to look like.

When Jacob weeps and embraces his cousin, his tears are to be celebrated as exemplary of his emotional range as a male. It is also hard won in a Stage 3 adolescent male who probably has worked painstakingly during Stages 1 and 2 to develop this range.

Parents and close caregivers build emotional integrity by modeling emotionality, talking to boys, and helping them feel and name feelings, as well as by challenging adolescent males to be emotional whenever powerful events can trigger emotion. Jacob's emotions are triggered by the major event of meeting his other family. We too can help our boys by involving them in events of this kind—family reunions, graduations, drama activities in school, sports activities (sports are deeply emotion-filled). Our boys may not express as much feeling as our girls do in sending notes, Hallmark cards, or talking a lot about relationships. So we have to direct them as much as possible to activities that powerfully *force* emotive range.

Having said this, let us reiterate that a Stage 1 and Stage 2 adolescent male is a heavily transitional creature who *may not have ideal emotional range.* We may have to keep trying to get him to talk, to breathe, to participate in activities that stimulate healthy emotional responses. We may have to help him notice the particular ways he is and is not emotional. We most certainly will have to see him for who he is. In other words, we can't assume that he's unemotional just because he doesn't talk much about feelings *we* want him to talk about.

Our great balancing act as people who care for young men goes something like this: At times, we have to help our males across the tightwire toward feeling, and at times we have to detach and just watch them succeed or fail. Often a boy is on track emotionally even when we worry. If he's not on track, if he's only showing anger and nothing else, or only being stoic with no range, we may need to get help from other mentors, extended family members, or professionals. In my experience, the quickest route to emotional range and integrity is to bring in more caregivers, mentors, and clan members: more teachers of emotion.

Sexual Integrity

If Jacob's delight at seeing Rachel is an indication of some of his range of emotion, his ongoing romantic desire for her is an indication of emotional and sexual ranges uniting. Jacob has developed enough in the other integrities to be ready now to take on sexual integrity, one of the most difficult, important, and elusive for the young male.

Because we have focused on adolescent-male sexuality in a number of places elsewhere in this book, we will not add to our list of practical tools and theoretical approaches here. We'll pay attention to only some telling details of this story, as there is wisdom in it for all our youths' journeys.

Notice the wonderful imagery of stone and well. Sleeping with his head on the stone led to his spiritual vision. The stone is thus associated with Jacob's own spiritual development. Now a stone lies over the well of water. Jacob lifts the stone off the water. In ancient stories, water is very often the source of life. It is also just as often a symbol of the feminine. Jacob's spiritual journey is directly linked to Rachel's feminine energies.

Let us notice also when Jacob's sexual awakening transpires. It transpires only *after* a number of the other integrities have been established in his psyche. Unlike that of many of our adolescent males, Jacob's sexual and romantic desires do not function as substitutes for other integrities, or as *the* major life teacher, but as one teacher among many. Jacob attends to his sexual integrity as a young man who is mature enough to handle it.

He does not require of Rachel the blessings he should get from Mom and Dad. He has those.

He does not require of Rachel the social rule-giving he should learn from elders. He knows the rules.

He does not require of Rachel the development of his emotional core. He has an emotional self established.

He does not require Rachel to teach him how to be a moral male. He knows how.

None of this means he and Rachel won't teach each other things about all the integrities. It means, simply, that Jacob is not misusing his romantic interest to propel him into manhood.

Our adolescent males are often undernourished by us and end up forming obsessive bonds with females. Not only are these bonds psychologically damaging if they break abruptly, but they carry too-high expectations. In my book *Love's Journey*, I tracked some of the development of romantic obsession, through the last few hundred years. I argued that our adult males and females rely much too heavily on each other for the kind of teaching and developmental experience that extended families are supposed to give. This idea is even more true for adolescents. Many of our adolescent males and females get too close to each other too quickly, and try to get the other to "raise" them into adulthood.

Marital Integrity

Jacob's story has much to teach also about marital integrity—a male's conscious commitment to his mate and her kin. Jacob's culture allowed simultaneous marriage with more than one partner, and our culture tends more toward serial marriages and monogamy; Jacob's culture had clearer patriarchal-survival, or male-dominant, gender roles, while our culture seeks partnerships in those areas. Often, because of these differences, people will throw out biblical wisdom about gender relationships. Let's not do that. We'd be missing some important lessons for our boys.

Though the *content* of our marital-integrity teaching could differ from that of the old patriarchs'—e.g., gender equity and monogamy—we would gain a great deal by retaining some of the *form* they taught. In particular, they stressed loyalty to spouse, hard work in order to earn love (in other words, love is linked not only to romance but to responsibility), and caregiving not only to spouse and children but to extended family.

Loyalty to spouse is an area of great concern now for our adolescent males. We instruct males about loyalty by teaching them a code of conduct toward females very early in life. Part of that code is gender equality. Part of that code is male responsibility. We have neglected hard-core marital-integrity teaching because, in reality, our marriages have very little integrity to them. After going through a phase of attempted monogamy, we have continued the illusion of monogamy while in fact becoming quite polygamous (our divorce and remarriage rates are nearly one in two marriages). We have neglected marital integrity because it is very hard work and we're busy doing other things. We have neglected it because teaching it begins with sexual integrity, and we spend so little time teaching sexual integrity that we end up barely getting to marital integrity.

The days when a daughter's father held a shotgun on a wooing adolescent male are over. What do we do instead? This is the great question that faces every family, including the media. I have no simple solution, for there is none. The lack of marital integrity sits, along with economic deprivation, at the heart of our welfare debate. It sits with us in nearly every therapist's office. Most people who seek therapy are children of parents who had difficulty with marital/sexual integrity and/or are adults themselves who wrestle with their own sexual and marital integrity.

The Jacob tale gives us good thematic focus, even if its polygamy and patriarchy are not the solutions we seek.

It inspires us to teach loyalty to adolescent males, to teach them to value above all else their responsibilities to those people whom they touch with their lips, their penises, their hearts.

It propels us to teach them to *earn* love by working for it, even if working for it means working hard for seven years to develop emotional integrity, good communication skills, good conflict skills.

It provokes us to teach them loyalty to the extended family. A male who learns responsibility to extended family in his own bloodline is more likely to form emotional bonds with his spouse's. A boy who is loyal to Mom, Dad, Grandma, Grandpa, and family friends is more likely to be loyal to his wife and her kin. It will be second nature to him. He is more likely to take on the kingship of being not only a husband to his wife and father to his child, but a model in the center of the group.

To these lessons from Jacob's story we must certainly add gender integrity. Males who are locked in old misogynistic behavior—ass-pinching, sexual harassment—have not learned what is required of a mature male in the twentieth century. They let their testosterone run them. They do not bring the ten integrities to their testosterone.

Physical Integrity

Throughout his journey, Jacob develops his physical integrity. Physical integrity is a person's self-discipline of physical body. Elements of sexual integrity are linked to it, but mainly it involves the helpful use of body to self and world.

In order to use one's body helpfully and healthily, one must:

- Know one's body

- Respect and care for one's body

- Learn to focus one's body

- Enjoy one's body

- Find freedom in one's body

Jacob shows these things in his ability to physically survive during his journey, his removal of the stone from the well, his hard work for fourteen years. Earlier in his life he was taught enough of the warrior arts to be able, later, to prepare for combat with his own brother. He utilizes his physical integrity—his labor—to earn the right to find freedom in sexual and marital integrity. Freedom here means the freedom to be himself, not "the freedom to do whatever he pleases." A boy's or man's ability to be a free spirit is directly related to his discipline of his body.

We teach our youths lots of physical integrity through sports. More than 20 million boys are involved in sports, and sports activities help them find focus, enjoyment of body, respect of physical life. Other boys put their physical integrity to work through music, art, or hobbies. Most parents of adolescent males find that testosterone makes the male so physically active he needs hard, physical labor to keep him in sync with himself. Some boys put their bodies to work only by playing video games, watching television, or wandering aimlessly on the streets, which does little to develop physical integrity in an adolescent male.

Physical integrity is more important for males than we may realize because often males don't verbally confess how awkward they feel as physical beings. Every adolescent male I've known has worried about his body image. We should not think this only a female problem. With as many males taking steroids now as ingesting crack cocaine, the dangerous medical solution to body image problems is clear to us. For many males, physical and sexual integrity are often directly connected and need care as an associated anguish. Males who don't feel physical integrity won't feel sexual integrity.

When we don't attend to the physical integrity of our adolescent males, we risk problems later: obesity, smoking, lack of exercise, inability to phys-ically process stress. The learning of physical integrity in boyhood and ado-lescence teaches the male how to care for his body as a man.

If there is any single activity available to our males that could come close to satisfying nearly any adolescent male's need for physical-integrity build-ing, it would probably be martial arts. Martial arts, when taught by a person of integrity, teaches not only many of the aspects of physical integrity—re-spect of body, focus, enjoyment—but many of the other integrities as well. In my own private practice, I often "prescribe" martial arts for many of the problems adolescent males face. Good martial arts training is as much about teaching delicacy, fragility, and protection of brittleness as it is about raw muscular power. The martial arts star Jean Claude Van Damme studied bal-let *and* martial arts. The male body is most beautiful when it knows that physical integrity is a dance.

Let us return to Jacob's story. It ends with the exposition of the last of the ten integrities—intellectual integrity—and then the resolution of a number of personal and plot elements. Finally the time comes for Laban to pay Jacob fully for his years of service. Because Jacob has by now earned his own right to his own family, his wives and sons are no longer "payment," and Laban must offer him cattle and other animals.

Jacob shows great intellectual prowess in selecting the cattle he'll take from Laban. He learns what kind of food helps breed the healthiest cattle, and he gives them these "rods of green poplar." Both cattle and goats con-ceive strongly when tended by his techniques, and so Jacob ends up with the stronger breeds, leaving Laban the weaker.

Jacob is ready now to leave Laban's house. He is no longer an adolescent but a man with a large family, including a son borne by Rachel—Joseph, the famous fourth patriarch. He has shown himself a person of all ten integrities.

Intellectual Integrity

Intellectual integrity is the male's understanding of his own intellectual talents and ability to bring those talents to fruition in the world. A boy who becomes an illiterate man lacks intellectual integrity. An adolescent male who can barely write lacks intellectual integrity. A male who doesn't get enough trade or on-the-job training in his youth to compete in a tough marketplace lacks intellectual integrity. A male who can't think critically about what appears in the media lacks intellectual integrity. A man who can't discuss what's happening in his world and family lacks intellectual integrity.

Intellectual integrity is becoming more and more important in our technological world. When some adolescent-development specialists argue that our males and females don't become adults (leave Stage 3) until age thirty-five, they are referring very much to the fact that the intellectual demands on our young people make it difficult for them to "keep up."

If every one of us can hone in our boys their natural, legalistic, Stage 2 minds—through debates on current events, relationships, media, neighborhood life—we will get them to talk more in general and develop their intellects in particular.

As Jacob continues his journey to adulthood, he is taught all the integrities again, but now he receives a man's version of the lessons. He wrestles with an angel, deepening his knowledge of spiritual integrity. This is a supreme rite of passage (some would argue the most famous rite of passage in all of Western literature). In it he learns humility and how to focus on the world around him once and for all above his own self-interest. He comes away scarred—a little lame—but irreversibly matured.

He also makes psychological and social peace with his brother. He becomes the patriarch of his lineage. He learns and teaches social rules to new peoples. While we won't pursue it here, you might want to read the Jacob story on your own. Find the ten integrities, and follow Jacob's development to the end of his story, when he builds the altar and becomes—is renamed— "Israel," one of the forefathers of what we now call Western civilization.

The ten integrities are taught to males and females both, though often in different ways. We have explored how we can teach them to our male youths. Just as most other world cultures have much to learn from us about technology and material development, we have much to learn from our own ancestors and other cultures about the holistic development of young men. I hope the Jacob story has inspired you to seek the integrities in other stories, and to use other stories to illustrate these integrities for young men. The most important lesson from the world's stories about adolescent males in development toward manhood is this one:

We cannot say a boy is a man unless he has *appropriately mastered* the *ten integrities*.

Lineal. He must know himself as the product of his ancestry.

Psychological. He must have accomplished individuation and gained adult personal identity.

Social. He must understand society's most important social rules.

Spiritual. He must have a refined spiritual life, spiritual practice, and vision.

Moral. He must have accomplished the development of moral character.

Emotional. He must have developed emotional range and self-discipline.

Sexual. He must have learned to honor his own and others' sexuality.

Marital. He must understand the sanctity of romantic, marital, and gender-equal bonds.

Physical. He must know and respect his own body, and use it for service.

Intellectual. He must have accomplished the necessary development of his cognitive and intellectual faculties in order to live in the world of adults.

In the end, much of what ancient wisdom directs boys toward is husbanding a family and community. All integrity, in the end, becomes the art of husbandry and fulfills acts of service. As we raise our adolescent males and seek a standard for manhood, we might ask ourselves this question: Is he capable of caring for a child? If the answer is No, we will find that the reason lies in his lack of one of the ten integrities. When the answer is Yes, we will find that the boy we once held in our arms has moved through the stages of adolescence beloved by us and protected in our world, and has become the man we always dreamed of nurturing. The best of adult life awaits him.

Epilogue

One of the great tasks of the new millennium is certainly the invigoration of a healthy, robust, compassionate, and successful masculinity for our adolescent males. I hope that this book has helped to inspire you to see the wonder and beauty in those boys. I hope it has inspired you to embrace those boys, direct them, unite them with their own souls as only we who love them can do. They are such vulnerable, fragile creatures. Yet they are also potentially so loving, so wise, so wonderfully powerful.

Often when I travel and teach male development, I am asked if I'm pessimistic or optimistic about the state of our adolescent males, and indeed about the state of masculinity in general. Moms, dads, and everyone who spends his or her life looking into the eyes and hearts of boys have reason to wonder about how the culture will ultimately care for and judge its young men. The culture as we know it is harsh on these young men, looks down on them, overreacts to them in fear, overreacts to masculinity in general, or neglects any particulars in masculinity that seem to take some hard work. All in all, we don't live in a very male-friendly time.

But when people ask me about pessimism, I respond with hope, and some questions:

How can we help our males grow in all ways, not just in the ways that make them money or points?

How can we honor again the biology, the deep hidden nature, of the male?

How can we create a culture that allows three or more families to care for our high-energy, risk-taking, fun-loving, self-sacrificing, angry, jubilant, stir-crazy, task-focused, passionately loving adolescent males?

How can we open our hearts to masculinity again, congratulating it for cocreating the very civilization we live in, while tempering its excesses with discipline, structure, and clarity of attention?

How can we bring spirituality back into the core of manhood, so that boys can become men who live and breathe life itself?

Epilogue

We live in a wonderful time, a time when masculinity can come alive again and be one of the most vital forces on earth.

I am hopeful. I hope that this book has helped you create fine young men in your life. I hope I'll meet some of those men during my lifetime. I hope I'll shake their hands, look them in the eyes, and listen to them tell me stories of you, and all your efforts, and all your love for them.

Notes and References

A number of statistical databases and contemporary studies have made it possible for me to present adolescent-male development as I do in this book. I will refer to them specifically and bibliographically in these notes. When I have completed the reference in the text of a particular chapter, I will not repeat that reference here.

Introduction

See the October 27, 1997, *Newsweek* cover.

If you have not read *The Wonder of Boys*, you might enjoy it. It explores why boys are the way they are, what they need, and how to provide boys of all ages with direction, discipline, structure, and love, especially boys from birth to ten years old.

Chapter 1: Jason and His Brothers: What It's *Really* Like for Adolescent Boys in America

The State of Male Adolescence Today

I hope this chapter shows enough of what adolescent males face so that you will become inspired to explore their suffering from all personal and policy standpoints. You can become more involved in this exploration than you ever could before, and you can continue it for the group that speaks most deeply to your own life experience, because of the Internet.

Nearly everything I present to you in this chapter appears somewhere on the World Wide Web, especially on Websites for various governmental agencies.

Fifteen years ago, when I first started studying adolescent males in earnest, I could barely find a statistic that showed the nature and circumstances of adolescent males. Now, however, you and I can access data of genuine quality and immense volume in a short period of time. As I write this chapter, I am surrounded by perhaps twenty times the amount of data, on tables, chairs, the floor, in files all around me, than I can use in this book.

Here, then, are the sources of the statistics I've presented:

For statistics on crime, violence, and at-risk behavior:

Bureau of Justice Statistics
Federal Bureau of Investigation

Notes and References

Youth Risk Behavior Surveillance System (YRBBS)
Centers for Disease Control and Prevention

The latter two sites have been very valuable to me in my research. Most of the statistics presented in the chapter about suicide, violence, teen death, drug use, weapons, and alcohol use come from them.

Court Appointed Special Advocates (CASA)
The National Center on Addiction and Substance Abuse at Columbia University
FBI Uniform Crime Reports
See also *Body Count*, by William Bennett, John J. DiIulio, Jr., and John Walters (New York: Simon & Schuster, 1996).

For child abuse statistics:
National Child Abuse and Neglect Data System (NCANDS) and the National Incidence Study (NIS)
The National Clearinghouse on Child Abuse and Neglect Information

See also these books and articles:
Reaching Up for Manhood, by Geoffrey Canada (Boston: Beacon, 1997). This book is both social and personal, about growing up as a boy in the inner city.

Fire with Fire, by Naomi Wolf (New York: Bantam, 1994). It acknowledges the higher incidence of abuse of male children than female.

The Myth of Male Power, by Warren Farrell (New York: Simon & Schuster, 1994). This book is a must-read for anyone who wants to understand, from a statistical and analytic perspective, what men and boys suffer internationally in all the human-health indicators.

Knights Without Armor, by Aaron Kipnis (Los Angeles: Tarcher, 1991) and *Gender War/Gender Peace*, by Aaron Kipnis and Elizabeth Herron (New York: William Morrow, 1994). These two include both theory and statistics about male mental and physical health.

Jon Pielemeier of *The Seattle Times* has one of the best journalistic collections of data in his article "Man Is the Fellow Victim, Not the Enemy," reprinted in *Seattle M.E.N.* magazine, February 1992.

Fatherless America, by David Blankenhorn (New York: Basic Books, 1995), is another generous source of statistics regarding the state of our children.

For ADHD statistics, see the International Narcotics Control Board. They report that 10 to 12 percent of boys ages six to fourteen are using Ritalin.

A recent *Counseling Today* article (February 1998) by Peter Guerra reported that between two and three million American boys are on Ritalin.

See also *Why Johnny Can't Concentrate*, by Robert Moss and Helen Huff Dunlap (New York: Bantam, 1992), and *The Wildest Colts Make the Best Horses*, by John Breeding (Austin, TX: Bright Books), which focuses on how to help "very active" children without resorting to drugs.

There are two sides to the Ritalin story, and like so much else in the analysis of ado-

lescent boys, both sides have their merit. As a boy of eleven, I was diagnosed as hyper-
active and put on Ritalin. It helped me and my parents. Simultaneously, a lot of what I
needed was a different kind of school and family environment—a better structured,
more attentive one. After six months of my being on Ritalin, my teacher, Mrs. Kono,
called my parents and asked them to take me off the drug. "He's just not himself," she
said. "I'd rather have crazy Mike than this lump." My parents, recalling this time in our
lives, point out that luckily "you grew out of your hyperkinesis."

I may have been lucky indeed.

Having worked with other adolescent males who take Ritalin, and having now the
benefit of hindsight, I can see that in my case, Ritalin was a useful tool, for a time. Nowadays, however, we have around two million "crazy Mikes" on Ritalin, and many do not
need it. Many of these adolescent males are being betrayed by a social system and family system that, quite simply, undernurtures them: gives them too little structure, over-
stimulates them with media, and provides them too little hands-on love and attention.

If you are in contact with an adolescent boy who does clearly need help with his
ADHD, experimenting with alternative medicines sometimes can be helpful. While traditional psychiatric or medical care is the most acceptable place to start, homeopathic
remedies like *Medorrhinum* also have helped many ADHD patients.

Perhaps the best critical resource on ADHD, especially on our misdiagnosis of it, is
a John Merrow PBS report entitled "A.D.D.: A Dubious Diagnosis?" This state-of-the-
art document is a great support to all parents who have seen their children misdiagnosed or overdiagnosed, and to anyone who works for less reliance on the short-term
effects of drugs and more reliance on increased involvement in boys' lives. Contact
Learning Matters, the PBS production group in New York, to get a copy.

For statistics on the emotionally disturbed and mentally ill, see:

National Institute of Mental Health
Children's Defense Fund

For statistics on male sexual abuse:

Protect Your Child from Sexual Abuse: A Parents' Guide, by Janie Hart-Rossi, available
    through Parenting Press of Seattle

See also Mic Hunter's many fine books on male sexual abuse.

For education statistics:

Educational Testing Service Gender Study (May 1997), by Nancy Cole
U.S. Department of Education, National Center for Education Statistics, National
    Assessment of Educational Progress (Youth Indicators, 1996)
Digest of Education Statistics
Diane Ravitch is quoted from *Congressional Quarterly*, 1994
Education Resources Information Center (ERIC)

Aspiration survey results (at eighth and twelfth grades) by the DOE are quoted from
The National Men's Resource (Winter 1995)

Notes and References

For National Education Assessment, see U.S. Department of Education, National Assessment of Educational Progress
See also these books and articles:

Who Stole Feminism, by Christina Hoff Sommers (New York: Simon & Schuster, 1994), especially pages 160–165
Girls and Boys in School, by Cornelius Riordan (New York: Teacher's College Press, 1990)
Thirteenth Generation, by Neil Howe and Bill Strauss (New York: Vintage, 1993), for statistics on suicide, illegal drug use, and weapons in and around schools

For statistics on the learning disabled, see the Center for Research on the Education of Disadvantaged Students (CDS)
As I prepare these footnotes, I notice that few of the statistics I've used have not appeared in at least two or more of the Websites and/or books/articles I've noted here. Once one starts to research, these statistics about male physical, mental, emotional and physical health are readily available. Oliver Wendell Holmes once said, "Every society rests on the death of its males." Must it always be this way? Is there an alternative? If the twentieth century has been the century of the woman in our cultural consciousness, I suspect the twenty-first century is going to be the century in which the male's place in the world is much better understood.

The Fragile Self

"The Fragile Sex," by Michael D'Antonio, in *Los Angeles Times Magazine,* December 4, 1994, a very detailed article that lays out many of these points of fragility
Sex on the Brain, by Deborah Blum (New York: Viking, 1997), especially chapter 3, for the NICHD, Belsky, and numerous other studies of male fragility
"The Relation Between Masculine Role Conflict and Psychological Distress," by Glenn Good, John Robertson, Louise Fitzgerald, Mark Stevens, and Kim Bartels, in *Journal of Counseling and Develoment,* September/October 1996

Judith Wallenstein has studied the effects of divorce for almost three decades. See, for instance, her book *Second Chances,* with Sandra Blakeslee (New York: Ticknor and Fields, 1988).

Adolescent Male Self-Esteem

Reviving Ophelia, by Mary Pipher (New York: Ballantine, 1995)
Failing at Fairness by David and Myra Sadker (New York: Scribners, 1994)

Christina Hoff Sommers, author of *Who Stole Feminism,* is a gentle and perceptive advocate for fairness in self-esteem research. Her work has informed me greatly and inspired some of my thinking.
Valuable resources for exploring the plight of black adolescent males in particular—a demographic group that carries many of the biggest burdens in our culture—are *The*

Scapegoat Generation, by Mike Males (Monroe, ME: Common Courage Press, 1996), which examines poverty conditions and their effects on all young people; *A Man's World,* by Ellis Cose (New York: HarperCollins, 1995); *Nurturing Young Black Males,* edited by Ronald B. Mincy (Washington, DC: Urban Institute Press, 1994); and *Reaching Up for Manhood,* by Geoffrey Canada (Boston: Beacon Press, 1997).

Adolescent Male Posttraumatic Stress

In brief, what we are seeing is a testosterone-driven biochemical system that creates increased instinctual aggression in the male brain. When stress hormones like cortisol are released in the male biochemical system, males are more likely to show aggression than females, who are driven by estrogen and progesterone in their systems. When a testosterone-driven system faces increased external stress and/or decreased internal security, its likelihood of responding aggressively is higher than that of a nontestosterone-based system. This is true not only for humans but for other animals as well. It is unlikely we will ever see anywhere near as many females as males in prison, or as many who are antisocial, physically violent, or who reject common morality, for very biological reasons. This biology is just the beginning of what we are discovering about the affects of trauma and neglect on males.

Chapter 2: Protecting the Emotional Lives of Adolescent Boys

My understanding of the way testosterone and the male brain work is gained from a number of medical sources. Until the book *Brain Sex,* by Anne Moir and David Jessel (New York: Laurel, 1989), there was no single resource for all the different fragments of research from endocrinology and neurology journals. *Brain Sex* collected them in a superb way. Then a three-part series appearing on The Learning Channel and based on the book brought some of the research into the visual world. I hope everyone interested in the interior worlds of male and female development will read *Brain Sex* and watch the videos. What I share with you in this book is very much the tip of the iceberg. More books have come out since *Brain Sex,* including *The Runaway Brain,* by Christopher Wills (New York: Basic Books, 1993), and the very detailed *Sex on the Brain,* by Deborah Blum (New York: Viking, 1997).

Research on crying, tear glands, and prolactin has been spearheaded by William Frey, a biochemist at Regions Hospital in St. Paul, Minnesota.

A beautiful anthology that often touches on the emotional life of our boys is *Boyhood, Growing Up Male: A Multicultural Anthology,* edited by Franklin Abbott (Freedom, CA: The Crossing Press, 1993).

Chapter 3: The Crucial Passage: Nurturing the Second Decade of a Boy's Life

Childhood and Society, by Erik Erikson (New York: Norton, 1950)

Manhood in the Making, by David Gilmore (New Haven: Yale University Press, 1990)

Notes and References

The Forest of Symbols, by Victor Turner (Ithaca: Cornell University Press, 1967)

Voices of the First Day, by Robert Lawlor (Rochester, VT: Inner Traditions, 1991)

A Brief History of Male Adolescence

There are a number of valuable sources for understanding the history of human adaptation and development from hunter-gatherer times to the present day. Here are just a few of them.

Sexual Strategies, by Mary Batten (Los Angeles: Tarcher/Putnam, 1992)

Brain Sex, by Anne Moir and David Jessel (New York: Laurel, 1989)

Shadows of Forgotten Ancestors, by Carl Sagan and Ann Druyan (New York: Random House, 1992)

Mystery Dance, by Lyn Margulis and Dorion Sagan (New York: Summit Books, 1991)

The Moral Animal, by Robert Wright (New York: Vintage, 1994)

Chapter 1 of my book *The Wonder of Boys* also is helpful.

The Masculine Nurturing System

The Big Brothers and Big Sisters study was accomplished by Public/Private Ventures of Philadelphia. The national BBBS office in Philadelphia has copies of the study.

The Boy Scouts of America make available, through any local chapter, brochures documenting their studies.

Quotes and studies regarding boys' schools were given to me by the International Boys' School Coalition, and appear in their catalog. The International Boys School Coalition is based out of University School, 20701 Brantley Road, Shaker Heights, Ohio 44122. Its president is Brewster Ely, of Town School for Boys in San Francisco (415-921-3747).

Girls and Boys in School, by Cornelius Riordan (New York: Teachers College Press, 1990)

The story about "puttering" comes from *Spokesman-Review* columnist Jim Kershner.

A Three-Stage Program for Raising Boys into Men

Jim States, M.D., is a psychiatrist associated with Adolescent and Young Adult Medicine in Spokane, Washington.

One of the best presenters on staging both male and female adolescence is the adolescent-development trainer Wayne Pawlowski of Planned Parenthood Federation of America, working out of the Federation's Washington, D.C., office. My I AM I format (identity, autonomy, morality, intimacy), featured in chapters 4, 5, and 6, was structurally inspired by Wayne's identity, independence, integrity, intimacy format.

Chapter 4: Stage 1: The Age of Transformation

The Formative Years

You and Your Adolescent, by Laurence Steinberg and Ann Levine (New York: Harper-Perennial, 1997)

Adolescent Development, by Richard M. Lerner and Graham B. Spanier (New York: McGraw-Hill, 1980)

The Developing Person Through Childhood and Adolescence, by Kathleen Berger, with Ross Thompson (New York: Worth Publishers, 1991)

Parenting Teens with Love and Logic, by Foster Cline and Jim Fay (Colorado Springs, Pinion Press, 1992)

What to Expect from a Prepubescent Adolescent Male

The "What to Expect" books are published by Workman Publishing.

For boys who want to read something about their own development, I will be publishing a book with Grosset & Dunlap, entitled *A Boy's Manual*. It will help them understand, in their own language, a great deal of what both *The Wonder of Boys* and *A Fine Young Man* contain in regards to hormonal changes, brain development, physical changes, and emotional life. It will be illustrated. Girls interested in understanding boys will enjoy a second book I'm doing with Grosset: *What Makes Boys Tick: A Guidebook for Girls.*

Other resources include:

"Coming of Age," a booklet published by Dial Plus Health and Beauty Awareness Council, 800-258-3425

The Portable Pediatrician's Guide to Kids, by Laura Walther Nathanson (New York: HarperPerennial, 1996)

The Search for Morality

The Wonder of Boys, chapter 7.

Bringing Up a Moral Child, by Michael Schulman and Eva Mekler (New York: Doubleday, 1994).

The Search for Intimacy

While the vast majority of what is covered in *A Fine Young Man* applies to both heterosexual and homosexual adolescent males, nonetheless homosexual readers or readers concerned about the specific needs of gay adolescent males may feel shortchanged. I apologize to those readers and call their attention to chapter 5. I cannot in this book cover specific needs of homosexual males in the depth needed, and I hope someone else better versed in that field will write a book specifically utilizing the biological, cultural, and developmental material for homosexual adolescent males.

Notes and References

The Stage 1 Rite of Passage

Stan Crow can be reached through the Woodenville Unitarian Church in Woodenville, Washington, a Seattle suburb, or through ICA Journeys, at 1504 Twenty-fifth Avenue, Seattle, Washington 98122.

Peter Wallis can be reached through The Passages Center, 206-782-3341, or at 9040 Evanston Avenue North, Seattle, WA 98103.

St. Luke's Community Methodist Church in Dallas, Texas, a mainly African-American Church, has a wonderful rite-of-passage program.

Chapter 5: Stage 2: The Age of Determination

The Teen Male Who Seems to Be Suffering and We Just Don't Know Why

As I have noted before, let me call attention again to *You and Your Adolescent*, which is a wonderful resource for more help than I can give in these pages in regards to specific troubled teens.

The Search for Intimacy

This fear of the feminine is something I've covered in depth in *Mothers, Sons and Lovers: How a Man's Relationship with His Mother Affects the Rest of His Life* (Boston: Shambhala, 1993).

The Emergence of the Homosexual Adolescent Male

A Place at the Table, by Bruce Bawer (New York: Touchstone, 1993)
See *The Wonder of Boys* for biological research on homosexuality. See also *Brain Sex*.

The Vision Quest Model

For more insight into the vision quest, I encourage you to make community connections with individuals in your area who practice this method, whether they are Native American or other people trained in and/or responsibly experimenting with the vision quest. An interesting article on the European roots of vision questing is "A Cauldron-Born Quest," by James M. Wright, in *Shaman's Drum: 46* (1997). For those of us who use the vision quest in our own way—e.g., not imitating directly a particular Native American tribe's way of doing it—it is essential that we create our own methods *after* we've come to understand how the vision-quest tradition is indigenous to our own racial or ethnic groups. Wright's article and much of Joseph Campbell's work in mythology can help Caucasians understand the vision quest as a world phenomenon and one that our own ancestors practiced.

In my work as a vision-quest leader, I have met a number of people around the country who are adapting vision-quest models for use with non-Native American adolescents. Stan Crow and Peter Wallis were mentioned above. Let me also mention Gary Plep and Sue Amende-Plep of the Family Therapy Institute in Los Gatos, California, 408-379-4212.

Bernard Weiner, a father in the Bay area, put into book form a weekend quest he and his friends led their sons on. His book, *Boy into Man: A Father's Guide to Initiation of Teenage Sons,* is available from Transformation Press, San Francisco.

Native American Hyemeyohsts Storm's book, *Seven Arrows* (New York: Ballantine, 1972), remains a classic resource on Native American vision quests.

Chapter 6: Stage 3: The Age of Consolidation

The model of the king in *The Prince and the King* could not have been developed without the earlier scholarly work of Douglas Gillette and Robert Moore in their book *King, Warrior, Magician, Lover* (New York: HarperCollins, 1992).

My book *Love's Journey* (Boston: Shambhala, 1994) is a resource for teaching intimacy. It presents twelve stages of intimate partnership.

Chapter 7: Schoolboys: Adolescent Boys and the Educational System

The resources referred to in this chapter were explicitly quoted and reviewed in chapter 1. Endnotes for them appear in the notes and references for chapter 1.

Ronald E. Koetzsch has written a wonderful book called *The Parents' Guide to Alternatives in Education* (Boston: Shambhala, 1997). For anyone seeking an alternative-education environment, this is a must-read.

The dialogue in which *A Fine Young Man* participates began in earnest, by my observation, in the fall of 1996. Many of us had been writing and talking about boys' issues for some time, but not until Karen Peterson's cover story on the subject in *USA Today* (November 14, 1996) did the issue hit the national press. *The Boston Globe, The Wall Street Journal,* then radio and TV media from Rush Limbaugh to "The Today Show" focused on the issue, and hopefully will now increase their focus. The issues surrounding our boys and the "boys' movement" that is evolving in our culture have found a large audience in local and regional media—local newspapers, radio programs, television shows. Let me point out two that specifically deal with males in the educational system:

> "Test Scores Indicating Marked Gender Gap," by Mike Norton, in the *Traverse City Record-Eagle,* October 12, 1997, a very fine article on learning differences and boys' learning difficulties
> "Single Sex School Idea Stirs Feminist Ire," by Frank Zepezauer, in *INSIGHT* magazine, October 20, 1997

These represent hundreds of similar articles that are adding up to an expanded national consciousness in regards to how our boys are doing in and around school. I apologize to their writers that I cannot call attention to all of them.

Notes and References

For learning style differences, see the new, corroborative research out of Australia, which was provided to me by Principal Paul Fochtman of Pellston Middle School in Pellston, Michigan, who is writing his dissertation on this and related subjects. Educational psychologists and other researchers in the U.S. and Europe have been watching these learning differences develop for more than thirty years (see, for instance, research collected in *Brain Sex*, by Anne Moir and David Jessel). More recently, other cultures, including Japan and Australia, have been confirming the differences. With so many different cultures reporting similar male-female learning differences, the argument that culture, not nature, controls learning-style differences is becoming weaker.

Better might be to acknowledge that the differences are primarily natural—brain related—and are enhanced by a culture's attempts to help children feel comfortable with their learning styles. That classrooms will unconsciously divide along gender lines because of the styles stands to reason as well—males falling behind in reading and writing, where their brains are less capable, and females in math and science. The task for educators now is not to argue the "culturalism" of the differences but to notice the culturalism of our neglect of both boys and girls where they are naturally weak; to address our educational errors as soon as possible by enhancing math and science for girls and reading and writing for boys.

See also "Where Have All the Men Gone?" by Ben Gose, in *The Chronicle of Higher Education*, June 6, 1997.

Improving Sex Education

Beyond the Birds and the Bees, by Beverly Engel (New York: Pocket, 1997)

After-School Programs

The statistics on latchkey adolescents come from a report submitted to Janet Reno by Fight Crime: Invest in Kids, the national crime prevention alliance. The study was done by a number of individuals, including James Alan Fox, dean of Northeastern University's College of Criminal Justice, who noted that we should expect at least a 17 percent increase in these problems within the next decade. The study asserted that the primary reasons for the problems are lack of adult supervision and decreased availability of constructive activities (see the September 11, 1997, syndicated article by Muriel Dobbin, Scripps-McClatchy).

Violence in the Schools

See Myriam Miedzian's study *Boys Will Be Boys* (New York: Anchor Books, 1988). She links basic qualities of masculinity (what she calls "the masculine mystique") to violence. We know now about elements of brain chemistry (see, for instance, Ruben Gur's work and *Brain Sex*), which make her link biologically clear. We can also watch cultural factors change normally aggressive males into violent ones. Male aggression, given the right stimulants, crosses the line into violence more easily than we like to think. A male's natural protectiveness of his body or psyche often becomes violent. With more and more adolescent males feeling lost, frightened, neglected, and traumatized, we will see only an increase in male violence overall. Knowing this gives us our greatest incentive neither to deny male aggression nor to excoriate it, but to *understand* it, and then to channel it into physical activities, emotional development, expanded spiritual consciousness, moral focus, social opportunity, and a sense of service.

See also:

Helping Teens Stop Violence, by Allan Creighton and Paul Kivel (Emeryville, CA: Hunter House, 1992)

The Eight Essential Steps to Conflict Resolution, by Dudley Weeks (New York: Tarcher/Putnam, 1992)

Boys' Schools

For a comprehensive catalog of articles and studies on single-sex education from a boy's perspective, contact the International Boys School Coalition at University School in Cleveland, Ohio, or Town School in San Francisco, California. Cornelius Riordan, William Pollack, Michael Thompson, Diane Hulse, Brewster Ely, John Farber, Richard Hawley, and their associates all have done innovative work in assessing single-sex education from a boy's perspective.

Brad and Cory: A Study of Middle School Boys, by Diane J. Hulse (Hunting Valley, OH: University School Press), is one of the most comprehensive studies available about boys, education, and boys' schools.

Patti Crane is founder and president of Crane, 9020 Laurel Way, Alpharetta, Georgia 30202-5900.

McCallie School is located in Chattanooga, Tennessee.

Chapter 8: Virtual Masculinity: Adolescent Boys and the Media

I am indebted to Gloria DeGaetano for most of the statistics regarding television use. See her recent book, *Screen Smarts,* and her workbook, *Television and the Lives of Our Children* (Redmond, WA: Train of Thought Publishing, 1993).

See also "The Power and Limitations of Television: A Cognitive-Affective Analysis," by Jerome Singer, in *The Entertainment Functions of Television* (Hillsdale, NJ: Lawrence Erlbaum Associates, 1980).

The National Institute of Mental Health is a valuable resource for statistics and information regarding media use among teens.

Anyone interested in this topic will enjoy the work of Neil Postman and the classic by Jerry Mander, *Four Arguments for the Elimination of Television* (New York: Quill, 1978).

Chapter 9: Nurturing the Core of Manhood

Many of the quotes from religious texts and traditions are part of our common knowledge. Many of the others, however, are not, and I'm indebted to Jeffrey Moses for

Notes and References

his wonderful collection *Oneness: Great Principles Shared by All Religions* (New York: Fawcett Columbine, 1989).

Compassion

Glimpse After Glimpse, by Sogyal Rinpoche (New York: HarperCollins, 1995)
Levine's statement appears in Rinpoche's discussion of compassion.

Enterprise

The School-to-Work program was reported by Michael Ryan in *Parade* magazine, March 9, 1997, p. 16. The number for the School-to-Work Learning Center is 800-251-7236.

Chapter 10: The Ten Integrities

The Jacob story appears in Genesis 25–35.
A wonderful book about helping develop spirituality in family life is *Raising Spiritual Children in a Material World*, by Phil Catalfo (New York: Berkley, 1997).

Index

Index

Index

Index

Index

About the Author

Michael Gurian is a therapist, educator, and author of seven previous books, including the national bestseller *The Wonder of Boys.* He has served as a consultant to families, therapists, school districts, community agencies, youth organizations, churches, criminal justice professionals, the judiciary, the media, and policy makers. His training videos for parents and volunteers are used by the Big Brothers and Big Sisters Agency throughout the United States and Canada.

Gurian's work reflects the diverse cultures (European, East Indian, Middle Eastern, and American) in which he has lived, worked, and studied. Before becoming a lecturer and consultant, he taught at Ankara University and Gonzaga University.

Michael Gurian shares a private therapy practice with his wife, Gail. They live in Spokane, Washington, with their two children.

Michael Gurian
P.O. Box 8714
Spokane, WA 99203
http://www.Michael-Gurian.com

ALSO BY MICHAEL GURIAN

*The Wonder of Boys: What Parents, Mentors and Educators
Can Do to Shape Boys into Exceptional Men*

THE NATIONAL BESTSELLER

"A provocative book that may electrify the debate over how this
nation raises its sons."   —*USA Today*

"Full of good insights and advice."
—*Los Angeles Times*

"*The Wonder of Boys* will help future generations open the lines of
communication between men and women by giving us what we
need to raise strong, responsible, and sensitive men."
—JOHN GRAY, author of *Men Are from Mars,
Women Are from Venus*

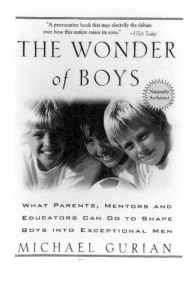